An
ANTHOLOGY
of
CONTEMPORARY
BRITISH & AMERICAN VERSE

Edited by

V.R. Badiger
Renuka Janbow

ISBN
Hardcase 979-8-89610-852-8
Paperback 979-8-89610-263-2

CONTENTS

Contents

Contents

Contents

ABOUT THE EDITORS

Prof.V.R. Badiger is, now, the retired professor of English Dept. of English, Gulbarga University Kalaburagi. He has 39 years of teaching experience in graduate and post-graduate levels. He has guided 18 Ph.D., candidates and 30 M. Phils, successfully and written 15 reference books in English and 2 in Kannada. His *Collected Stories* was published in 2019. He has edited *Journal of English Literatures* for a period of 10 years from 2008 to 2018.

Dr. Renuka Janbow, being an Associate Professor in English, has been serving in Government First Grade College, K.R.Puram, Bangalore-560036. Having sixteen years service, her area of specialization is also Anglo-Indian Literature and British Literature. She has attended several seminars and presented research papers and published two books.

FOREWORD

I have gone through several previously published anthologies of English poetry. They have covered the poems from Chaucer to Hopkins and Seamus Heaney, those published by Macmillan India Limited. No doubt, there are good text books with references, meanings of difficult words and short biographical sketches for the under-graduate students. Now, it is necessary to revise and expand an anthology beyond 1920. In those earlier anthologies, there are no poems published after 1950. Prof V.R. Badiger, having nearly forty years of teaching of English and American poetry, has come out with this new anthology that included some poets who came after Seamus Heaney and included their poems. He has also included the new American poets who were born after 1950. Nearly there are two hundred poems.

Of course, there are no references but only biographical sketches to help the students and teachers to know about the life of the poets also. Personally I wish him best of luck in this literary endeavor. It is genuinely hoped that the teachers and students of English and American literatures shall be benefitted by this comprehensive anthology which covers the poets of the modern, the post-modern and the contemporary period.

Prof Kannan P.
Professor & Chairman, Dept of English
Karnataka State Akkamahadevi Women University,
Vijayapura, Karnataka

PREFACE & INTRODUCTION

When I edited published previously *An Anthology of Post Colonial Poetry*, my friend Prof Shreekeerthy B.N. suggested that it should have an introduction. I did not think that it was necessary; but I am compelled to write it.

For this *Anthology of the Anglo-American Poetry*, I took his suggestion and attempted this short introduction. The contemporary also means 'modern'. Modernism and realism are two main stylistic development within the period. David Lodge makes a distinction between modernism and realism: "Modernism turned its back on the traditional idea of art as imitation and substituted the idea of art as an autonomous activity."(Poplawski, 557). Modern poetry and contemporary poetry do not make much different except the period of time. It is directly against the Victorian poetry. Modern poetry was begun by W.B.Yeats who invested his poetry with private and universal symbolism. He is followed by T.S.Eliot, under the influence of the great French symbolist poets – Mallarme, Verlaine, Laforgue and Baudelaire, continued with the use of symbolism but in free verse. Compared to him, the poetry of W.B.Yeats appears to be in traditional of stanza forms.

There was a period war poetry what was realistic and describing the terror and horror of the war and significance of the bravery and heroic death. Wilfred Owen, Siegfried Sassoon, Isaac Rosenberg, Edmund Blunden-the war poets of the thirties such as C.Day-Lewis, Louis Mac Niece and Stephen Spender, Auden tend to be seen in categories of their own largely defined by the traumatic experience of war on the one hand and the politically charged climate of the thirties on the other...in Lodge's terms, they aspire to the condition of history rather than of music – and they can thus be counter-posed, at least, to some extent, against modernism." (Poplawski, 558) Ezra Pound, the founder of imagism, wrote poetry of his own style and themes and style.

The modernist poets like Yeats, Eliot and Pound produced a "poetry that distinguishes itself from ordinary referential discourse by violently dislocated syntax and bewildering shifts of register ... in which there are no narrative or logical climaxes but instead vibrant, suggestive, ambiguous images and symbols."(Poplawski, 557)

The imagistic poetry was followed by the free verse introduced by the great American poet Walt Whitman in his magnum opus *Leaves of Grass*. Later some poets who attempted to write surrealistic poetry using images of surrealism, under influence of the James and Joyce. Some American and Afro-American women poets have written feminist poetry. E.E.Cummings and Marian Moore wrote poetry in their own skid and with their own themes.

Thus the modern poetry is a kaleidoscope nature – a variety of poetry came out with a variety of themes and styles. The contemporary poetry is the Anglo-American poetry of the 60s and 70s. Some new poets after Seamus Heaney are included . This Anthology is a dire need of the present times as the old anthologies of British poetry became old and outdated; there is need for expanding its limitations and revise and re-edite not only British but also American poetry. It is hoped that it his highly useful for the graduate and post-graduate students of autonomous post-graduate colleges and departments of the Universities.

Previously published anthologies of the contemporary English verse have covered the poems from Chaucer to T.S.Eliot. There are no published poems after 1960, included. I have included some more poets who came after Seamus Heaney and included their poems. The word 'contemporary' also means' modern'. This anthology begins from W.B.Yeats (b.1865), the Nobel Prize winner Irish poet and first of the modern poets; I have included the new American poets who were born after 1950.

There are two hundred-eighty-three poems of ninety-nine poets. Of course, there are no references but biographical sketches help the students and teachers to know more about the life of the poets. The black and white photos of the poets are added to enrich the understanding the gender of the poets so that there is no confusion.

I hope that the teachers and students of English and American literatures shall be benefitted by this highly innovative anthology which covers the poets of the modern, the post-modern and the contemporary period. Sincerely I acknowledge the writers, editors and publishers of previous anthologies. My hearty greetings to my wife Dr.Akkamahavei P. (Ph.D) and my children Mrs Swetha (B.E.,) Sujatha (MBBS, MS) and Santhosh Kumar V.B. (MBA) and my friends. Personally I thank the Notion Press for bringing out this second anthology of mine, with and grace and beauty.

– V.R. Badiger & Renuka Janbow

01

W.B. YEATS (1865-1939)

Born on 13 June, 1865 in Sandy mount, Ireland in 1865 in Ireland, he grew and attended schools in Ireland and later migrated to England. He was educated in Dublin and London and joined the field of journalism. Later, he involved in the Irish freedom movement, having friendship with Maud Gonne, a beautiful political activist. His poetical works are – *The Second Coming* (1920), *Sailing to Byzantium* (1921) and *The Wild Swans at Coole* (1921) *A Vision* (1925). He wrote poetry, making use of Irish, myths, legends and history. He was given the Nobel Prize for Literature, being in the great tradition of the symbolist movement, began by Arthur Symons. He died on 28th January, 1939 in Roquebrune in France in 1939 and buried in Drumcliff, Cemetery, Ireland.

SAILING TO BYZANTIUM

I

That is no country for old men. The young
In one another's arms, birds in the trees,
—Those dying generations—at their song,
The salmon-falls, the mackerel-crowded seas,
Fish, flesh, or fowl, commend all summer long
Whatever is begotten, born, and dies.
Caught in that sensual music all neglect
Monuments of unageing intellect.

An aged man is but a paltry thing,
A tattered coat upon a stick, unless
Soul clap its hands and sing, and louder sing
For every tatter in its mortal dress,
Nor is there singing school but studying
Monuments of its own magnificence;
And therefore I have sailed the seas and come
To the holy city of Byzantium.

III

O sages standing in God's holy fire
As in the gold mosaic of a wall,
Come from the holy fire, perne in a gyre,
And be the singing-masters of my soul.
Consume my heart away; sick with desire
And fastened to a dying animal
It knows not what it is; and gather me
Into the artifice of eternity.

IV

Once out of nature I shall never take
My bodily form from any natural thing,
But such a form as Grecian goldsmiths make
Of hammered gold and gold enamelling
To keep a drowsy Emperor awake;
Or set upon a golden bough to sing
To lords and ladies of Byzantium
Of what is past, or passing, or to come.

THE WILD SWANS AT COOLE

The trees are in their autumn beauty,
The woodland paths are dry,
Under the October twilight the water
Mirrors a still sky;
Upon the brimming water among the stones
Are nine-and-fifty swans.

The nineteenth autumn has come upon me
Since I first made my count;
I saw, before I had well finished,
All suddenly mount
And scatter wheeling in great broken rings
Upon their clamorous wings.
I have looked upon those brilliant creatures,
And now my heart is sore.
All's changed since I, hearing at twilight,
The first time on this shore,
The bell-beat of their wings above my head,
Trod with a lighter tread.

Unwearied still, lover by lover,
They paddle in the cold
Companionable streams or climb the air;
Their hearts have not grown old;
Passion or conquest, wander where they will,
Attend upon them still.

But now they drift on the still water,
Mysterious, beautiful;
Among what rushes will they build,
By what lake's edge or pool
Delight men's eyes when I awake some day
To find they have flown away?

EASTER 1916

I have met them at close of day
Coming with vivid faces
From counter or desk among grey
Eighteenth-century houses.
I have passed with a nod of the head
Or polite meaningless words,
Or have lingered awhile and said
Polite meaningless words,
And thought before I had done
Of a mocking tale or a gibe
To please a companion
Around the fire at the club,
Being certain that they and I
But lived where motley is worn:
All changed, changed utterly:
A terrible beauty is born.

That woman's days were spent
In ignorant good-will,

Her nights in argument
Until her voice grew shrill.
What voice more sweet than hers
When, young and beautiful,
She rode to harriers?
This man had kept a school
And rode our wingèd horse;
This other his helper and friend
Was coming into his force;
He might have won fame in the end,
So sensitive his nature seemed,
So daring and sweet his thought.
This other man I had dreamed
A drunken, vainglorious lout.
He had done most bitter wrong
To some who are near my heart,
Yet I number him in the song;
He, too, has resigned his part
In the casual comedy;
He, too, has been changed in his turn,
Transformed utterly:
A terrible beauty is born.

Hearts with one purpose alone
Through summer and winter seem
Enchanted to a stone
To trouble the living stream.
The horse that comes from the road,
The rider, the birds that range
From cloud to tumbling cloud,
Minute by minute they change;
A shadow of cloud on the stream
Changes minute by minute;
A horse-hoof slides on the brim,
And a horse plashes within it;
The long-legged moor-hens dive,

And hens to moor-cocks call;
Minute by minute they live:
The stone's in the midst of all.

Too long a sacrifice
Can make a stone of the heart.
O when may it suffice?
That is Heaven's part, our part
To murmur name upon name,
As a mother names her child
When sleep at last has come
On limbs that had run wild.
What is it but nightfall?
No, no, not night but death;
Was it needless death after all?
For England may keep faith
For all that is done and said.
We know their dream; enough
To know they dreamed and are dead;
And what if excess of love
Bewildered them till they died?
I write it out in a verse —
MacDonagh and MacBride
And Connolly and Pearse
Now and in time to be,
Wherever green is worn,
Are changed, changed utterly:
A terrible beauty is born.

THE SECOND COMING

Turning and turning in the widening gyre
The falcon cannot hear the falconer;
Things fall apart; the centre cannot hold;
Mere anarchy is loosed upon the world,

The blood-dimmed tide is loosed, and everywhere
The ceremony of innocence is drowned;
The best lack all conviction, while the worst
Are full of passionate intensity.`

Surely some revelation is at hand;
Surely the Second Coming is at hand.
The Second Coming! Hardly are those words out
When a vast image out of *Spiritus Mundi*
Troubles my sight: somewhere in sands of the desert
A shape with lion body and the head of a man,
A gaze blank and pitiless as the sun,
Is moving its slow thighs, while all about it
Reel shadows of the indignant desert birds.
The darkness drops again; but now I know
That twenty centuries of stony sleep
Were vexed to nightmare by a rocking cradle,
And what rough beast, its hour come round at last,
Slouches towards Bethlehem to be born?

02

EARNEST DOWSON (1967-1900)

Earnest Dowson (1967-1900) was born on 2nd August, 1967 in Lee, in Kent, United Kingdom. In 1889, he was infatuated with an 11 years old girl Adelaide "Missie" Foltnowicz, the daughter of a Polish restaurant owner. His great uncle was the Prime Minster of New Zealand. He studied in the Queen's College, Oxford but left in March 1888 without taking his B.A., degree. In 1899, Robert Sherard gave him shelter as he became penniless. His main collections are- *Verses* (1896), *Decorations in Verse and Prose* (1899) and *The Poems and Prose of Earnest Dowson, with Memoir by Arthur Symons* (1919). He died on 23 February, 1900 at the age f 32 and was buried in the Roman Catholic Church.

A LOST LOVE

I seek no more to bridge the gulf that lies
Betwixt our separate ways;
For vanity my heart prays,
Hope droops her head and dies;
I see the sad, tired answer in your eyes.

I did not heed, and yet the stars were clear;
Dreaming that love could mate
Lives grown so separate:-
But at the best, my dear,
I see we should not have been very near.

I knew the end before the end was nigh;
The stars have grown so plain;
Vainly I sigh, in vain
For things that come to some,
But unto you and me will never come.

BEYOND

Love's aftermath! I think the time is now
that we must gather to, alone, apart
The saddest crop of all the crops that grow,
Love's aftermath.

Ah, sweet–sweet yesterday, the tears that start
Can not put back the dial; this is, I trow,
Our harvesting! Thy kisses chill my heart,
Our lips are cold; averted eyes avow
the twilight of poor love; we can but part,
Dumbly and sadly, reaping as we sow,
Love's aftermath.

GROWTH

I watched the glory of her childhood change,
Half-sorrowful to find the child I knew,
(Loved long, ago in Lily – time)
become a maid, mysterious and strange,
with fair, pure yes – dear eyes, but not the eyes I knew
or old, in the olden time!
till on my doubting soul the ancient good
Or her dear childhood in the new disguise
Dawned, and I hastened to adore
The glory of her waking maidenhood,
But kinder than before.

A LAST WORD

Lets us go hence the night is now at hand;
The day is over worn, the birds all flown;
And we have reaped the crops the god shave sown;
Despair and death, deep darkness o'er the land,
Broods like an owl, we cannot understand
Laughter or tears, for we have only known
Surpassing vanity vain things alone
Have driven our perverse and aimless band.

Let us go hence, somewhere strange and cold,
To Hollow lands where just men and unjust
Find end of labour, where is the nest for the old,
Freedom to all from lover and fear and lust
Twine our torn hands! o pray to the earth enfold
Our life-sick hearts and turn them into dust.

03

WALTER DE LA MARE (1873-1956)

Walter de la Mare was born on 25th April, 1873 in Charlton, London, United Kingdom. He was an English poet, story-writer and novelist. He is probably remembered of his children books although he wrote poetry and horror fiction, like Edgar Allan Poe. He studied in St Paul Cathedral School, and worked from 1789 to 1908 in the Statistical Department. In 1892, he joined Amateur Dramatic Club. He married Elfrida Ingpen. His poetical works are – *Songs of Childhood,* (1902), *Poems* (1906) and *The Listeners* (1912). He *Selected Poems* came out in 1931. He died on 22nd June, 1956 in Twickenham, United Kingdom.

SOMEONE

Someone came knocking
 At my wee, small door;
Someone came knocking,
 I'm sure-sure-sure;
I listened, I opened,
 I looked o left and right,
But naught there was a – stirring
 In the still dark night;
Only the busy beetle
 Tap-tapping in the wall,
Only from the forest
 The screech-owl's call,
Only the cricket whistling
 While the dew drops fall,
So I know not who came knocking,
 At all, at all, at all.

ALL THAT 'S PAST

Very old are the woods
And the buds that break
Out of the brier's boughs,
When March winds wake,
So old with their beauty are–
Oh, no man knows
Through what wild centuries
Roves back the rose,
Very old are the brooks';
And the rills that rise
Where snow sleeps cold beneath
The azure skies
Sing such a history
Of come and gone,

Their every drop is as wise
as Solomon.

Very old are the men;
Our dreams are tales
Told in dim Eden
By Eve's nightingales;
We wake and whisper awhile,
But, the day gone by,
Silence and sleep like fields
Of amaranth lie.

THE LISTENERS

'Is there anybody there?' said the Traveller,
Knocking on the moonlit door;
And his horse in the silence champed the grasses
Of the forest's ferny floor:
And a bird flew up out of the turret,
Above the Traveller's head
And he smote upon the door again a second time;
'Is there anybody there?' he said.
But no one descended to the Traveller;
No head from the leaf – fringed sill
Leaned over and looked into his grey eyes,
Where he stood perplexed and still.
But only a host of phantom listeners
That dwelt in the lone house then
Stood listening in the quiet of the moonlight
To the voice of the world of men:
Stood thronging the faint moonbeams on the dark stair
That goes down to the empty hall,
Hearing in an air stirred and shaken
By the lonely Traveller's call.
And he felt in his heart their strangeness,

Their stillness answering his cry,
While his horse moved, cropping the dark turf,
'Neath the starred and leafy sky;
For he suddenly smote on the door, even
Louder, and lifted his head:-
'Tell them I came, and no one answered,
That I kept my word,' he said.
Never the least stir made the listeners,
Tough every word he spoke
Fell echoing through the shadowiness of the still house.
From the one man left awake:
Ay, they heard his foot upon the stirrup,
And the sound of iron on stone,
And how the silence surged softly backward,
When the plunging hoofs were gone.

04

ROBERT FROST (1874-1963)

Born on 26 March, 1874, in San Francisco, California, USA. His family moved from San Francisco to Lawrence. His father was William Prescott Frost and mother, Isabelle Moodie. He studied in Lawrence High School, Dartmouth College, and later in Harvard University (1887-1899). He married Elinor Frost. As a nature poet, he is often compared with William Wordsworth of England. *A Boy's Will* (1913) and *North of Boston* (1914) are his main collections of poems. He died on 29th January, 1963 in Boston, Massachusetts.

THE ROAD NOT TAKEN

Two roads diverged in a yellow wood,
And sorry I could not travel both
And be one traveler, long I stood
And looked down one as far as I could
To where it bent in the undergrowth;

Then took the other, as just as fair,
And having perhaps the better claim,
Because it was grassy and wanted wear;
Though as for that the passing there
Had worn them really about the same,

And both that morning equally lay
In leaves no step had trodden black.
Oh, I kept the first for another day!
Yet knowing how way leads on to way,
I doubted if I should ever come back.

I shall be telling this with a sigh
Somewhere ages and ages hence:
Two roads diverged in a wood, and I—
I took the one less traveled by,
And that has made all the difference.

RELUCTANCE

Out through the fields and the woods
And over the walls I have wended;
I have climbed the hills of view
And looked at the world, and descended;
I have come by the highway home,
And lo, it is ended.

The leaves are all dead on the ground,
Save those that the oak is keeping
To ravel them one by one
And let them go scraping and creeping
Out over the crusted snow,
When others are sleeping.

And the dead leaves lie huddled and still,
No longer blown hither and thither;
The last lone aster is gone;
The flowers of the witch hazel wither;
The heart is still aching to seek,
But the feet question 'Whither?'

Ah, when to the heart of man
Was it ever less than a treason
To go with the drift of things,
To yield with a grace to reason,
And bow and accept the end
Of a love or a season?

MENDING WALL

Something there is that doesn't love a wall,
That sends the frozen-ground-swell under it,
And spills the upper boulders in the sun;
And makes gaps even two can pass abreast.
The work of hunters is another thing:
I have come after them and made repair
Where they have left not one stone on a stone,
But they would have the rabbit out of hiding,
To please the yelping dogs. The gaps I mean,
No one has seen them made or heard them made,
But at spring mending-time we find them there.
I let my neighbor know beyond the hill;

And on a day we meet to walk the line
And set the wall between us once again.
We keep the wall between us as we go.
To each the boulders that have fallen to each.
And some are loaves and some so nearly balls
We have to use a spell to make them balance:
'Stay where you are until our backs are turned!'
We wear our fingers rough with handling them.
Oh, just another kind of out-door game,
One on a side. It comes to little more:
There where it is we do not need the wall:
He is all pine and I am apple orchard.
My apple trees will never get across
And eat the cones under his pines, I tell him.
He only says, 'Good fences make good neighbors.'
Spring is the mischief in me, and I wonder
If I could put a notion in his head:
'*Why* do they make good neighbors? Isn't it
Where there are cows? But here there are no cows.
Before I built a wall I'd ask to know
What I was walling in or walling out,
And to whom I was like to give offense.
Something there is that doesn't love a wall,
That wants it down.' I could say 'Elves' to him,
But it's not elves exactly, and I'd rather
He said it for himself. I see him there
Bringing a stone grasped firmly by the top
In each hand, like an old-stone savage armed.
He moves in darkness as it seems to me,
Not of woods only and the shade of trees.
He will not go behind his father's saying,
And he likes having thought of it so well
He says again, 'Good fences make good neighbors.'
Once by the Pacific
The shattered water made a misty din.
Great waves looked over others coming in,

And thought of doing something to the shore
That water never did to land before.
The clouds were low and hairy in the skies,
Like locks blown forward in the gleam of eyes.
You could not tell, and yet it looked as if
The shore was lucky in being backed by cliff,
The cliff in being backed by continent;
It looked as if a night of dark intent
Was coming, and not only a night, an age.
Someone had better be prepared for rage.
There would be more than ocean-water broken
Before God's last *Put out the light* was spoken.

THE GIFT OUTRIGHT

The land was ours before we were the land's.
She was our land more than a hundred years
Before we were her people. She was ours
In Massachusetts, in Virginia,
But we were England's, still colonials,
Possessing what we still were unpossessed by,
Possessed by what we now no more possessed.
Something we were withholding made us weak
Until we found out that it was ourselves
We were withholding from our land of living,
And forthwith found salvation in surrender.
Such as we were we gave ourselves outright
(The deed of gift was many deeds of war)
To the land vaguely realizing westward,
But still unstoried, artless, unenhanced,
Such as she was, such as she would become.

05

GERTRUDE STEIN (1874-1946)

Gertrude Stein, an American poet, novelist, playwright, and art-collector, was born on 3 February, 1874 in Allegheny. Her parents were – Daniel Stein and Amelia Stein. Her collections of poems are – *Tender Buttons* (1914), *Three Lives* (1909), *The World is Round* (1939), *The Making of Americans* (1925), and *Patriarchal Poetry* (1953). She was the good friend of Marianne Moore. She was influenced by Hemingway, Sherwood Anderson, E.E. Cummings, Ralph Ellison, and Richard Wright. Leo Stein and Michael Stein were his children. She died on 27 July, 1946, in American Hospital, Neuilly-Sur-Seine, France.

PRECIOSILLA

Cousin to Clare washing.
In the win all the band beagles which have cousin lime
sign and arrange a weeding match to presume a certain
point to exstate to exstate a certain pass lint to exstate a
lean sap prime lo and shut shut is life.

Bait, bait, tore, tore her clothes, toward it, toward a bit,
toward a sit, sit down in, in vacant surely lots, a single
mingle, bait and wet, wet a single establishment that
has a lily lily grow. Come to pen come in the stem, come
in the grass grown water.

Lily wet lily while. This is so pink so pink in stammer,
a long bean which shows bows is collected by a single
curly shady, shady get, get set wet bet.

It is a snuff a snuff to be told and have can wither, can is
it and sleep sleep knot, is a lily scarf the pink and blue
yellow, not blue nor odour sun, nobles are bleeding
bleeding two seats two seats on end. Why is grief. Grief
is strange black. Sugar is melting. We will swim.

PRECIOSILLA

Please be please be get, please get wet, wet naturally,
naturally in weather. Could it be fire more firier. Could
it be so in ate struck. Could it be gold up, gold up
stringing, in it while while which is hanging, hanging in
dingling, dingling in pinning, not so. Not so dots large
dressed dots, big sizes, less laced, less laced diamonds,
diamonds white, diamonds bright, diamonds in the
in the light, diamonds light diamonds door diamonds
hanging to be four, two four, all before, this bean, lessly,

all most, a best, willow, vest, a green guest, guest, go go
go go go go, go. Go go. Not guessed. Go go.

Toasted susie is my ice-cream.

IF I TOLD HIM: A COMPLETED PORTRAIT OF PICASSO"

(FIRST PUBLISHED IN VANITY FAIR IN 1924)

If I told him would he like it. Would he like it if I told
him.
Would he like it would Napoleon would Napoleon
would would he
like it.
If Napoleon if I told him if I told him if Napoleon.
Would he like it if I
told him if I told him if Napoleon. Would he like it
if Napoleon if Napoleon if I told him. If I told him if
Napoleon if Napoleon if I told
him. If I told him would he like it would he like it if I
told him.

Now.
Not now.
And now.
Now.
Exactly as as kings.
Feeling full for it.
Exactitude as kings.
So to beseech you as full as for it.
Exactly or as kings.

Shutters shut and open so do queens. Shutters shut and
shutters and

so shutters shut and shutters and so and so shutters and
so shutters
shut and so shutters shut and shutters and so. And so
shutters shut
and so and also.

And also and so and so and also.
Exact resemblance. To exact resemblance the exact
resemblance as
exact as a resemblance, exactly as resembling, exactly
resembling,
exactly in resemblance exactly a resemblance, exactly
and resemblance. For this is so.

Because.
Now actively repeat at all, now actively repeat at all,
now actively
repeat at all.
Have hold and hear, actively repeat at all.
I judge judge.
As a resemblance to him.
Who comes first. Napoleon the first.

Who comes too coming coming too, who goes there, as
they go they
share, who
shares all, all is as all as a yet or as yet.
Now to date now to date. Now and now and date and
the date.
Who came first. Napoleon at first. Who came first
Napoleon the first.
Who came first, Napoleon first.
Presently.
Exactly do they do.
First exactly.
Exactly do they do too.

First exactly.
And first exactly.
Exactly do they do.
And first exactly and exactly.
And do they do.
At first exactly and first exactly and do they do.
The first exactly.
And do they do.
The first exactly.
At first exactly.
First as exactly.
As first as exactly.

Presently
As presently.
As as presently.
He he he he and he and he and and he and he and he
and and as and
as he
and as he and he. He is and as he is, and as he is and he
is, he is and
as he
and he and as he is and he and he and and he and he.
Can curls rob can curls quote, quotable.

As presently.
As exactitude.
As trains
Has trains.
Has trains.
As trains.
As trains.
Presently.
Proportions.
Presently.
As proportions as presently.

Father and farther.
Was the king or room.
Farther and whether.

Was there was there was there what was there was
there what was
there
was there there was there.
Whether and in there.
As even say so.
One.
I land.
Two.
I land.
Three.
The land.
Three
The land.
Three
The land.
Two
I land.
Two
I land.
One
I land.
Two
I land.
As a so.
They cannot.
A note.
They cannot.
A float.
They cannot.
They dote.
They cannot.

They as denote.
Miracles play.
Play fairly.
Play fairly well.
A well.
As well.
As or as presently.
Let me recite what history teaches. History teaches.

06

JAMES MASEFIELD (1878-1967)

James Edward Masefield, OM, was born on 1st January, 1878 in Ledbury, United Kingdom. He was an English poet and writer who was the Poet Laureate of England from 1930 to 1967. He married Constance Masefield, a teacher. His collections of poems are – *Sea Fever: Selected Poems* (19002), *The Box of Delights* (1935), *Cargoes* (1930), *The Midnight Folk* (1927) and *Poems of John Masefield* (1916). He also wrote the plays like, *The Tragedy of Pompey the Great*. For literary excellence, he got the Shakespeare Prize. He died on 12th May, 1967 in Abingdon, United Kingdom. eHhh

CARGOES

Quinquireme of Nineveh from distant Ophir,
Rowing home to haven in sunny Palestine,
With a cargo of ivory,
And apes and peacocks,
Sandalwood, cedarwood, and sweet white wine.

Stately Spanish galleon coming from the Isthmus,
Dipping through the Tropics by the palm-green shores,
With a cargo of diamonds,
Emeralds, amethysts,
Topazes, and cinnamon, and gold moidores.

Dirty British coaster with a salt-caked smoke stack,
Butting through the Channel in the mad March days,
With a cargo of Tyne coal,
Road-rails, pig-lead,
Firewood, iron-ware, and cheap tin trays.

SEA-FEVER

I must down to the seas again, to the lonely sea and the
sky,
And all I ask is a tall ship and a star to steer her by,
And the wheel's kick and the wind's song and the white
sail's shaking, And a grey mist on the sea's face and a
grey dawn breaking.

I must down to the seas again, for the call of the running
tide
Is a wild call and a clear call that may not be denied;
And all I ask is a windy day with the white clouds
flying,

And the flung spray and the blown spume, and the sea-
gulls crying.

I must down to the seas again, to the vagrant gypsy life,
To the gull's way and the whale's way where the wind's
like a whetted knife;
And all I ask is a merry yarn from a laughing fellow-
rover,
And quiet sleep and a sweet dream when the long trick
's over.

A WANDERER'S SONG

A WIND's in the heart of me, a fire's in my heels,
I am tired of brick and stone and rumbling wagon-
wheels;
I hunger for the sea's edge, the limit of the land,
Where the wild old Atlantic is shouting on the sand.

Oh! I'll be going, leaving the noises of the street,
To where a lifting foresail-foot is yanking at the sheet;
Toa windy, tossing anchorage where yawls and ketches
ride,
Oh, I'll be going, going, until I meet the tide.

And first I'll hear the sea-wind, the mewing of the gulls,
The clucking, sucking of the sea about the rusty hulls,
The songs at the capstan at the hooker warping out,
And then the heart of me'll know I'm there or thereabout.

Oh I am sick of brick and stone, the heart of me is sick,
For windy green, unquiet sea, the realm of Moby Dick;
And I'll be going, going, from the roaring of the wheels,
For a wind's in the heart of me, a fire's in my heels.

THE LEMMINGS

Once in a hundred years the Lemmings come
Westward in search of food, over the snow;
Westward until the salt sea drowns them dumb;
Westward, till all are drowned, those Lemmings go.
Once, it is thought, there was a westward land
Now drowned where there was food for those starved
things,
And memory of the place has burnt its brand
In the little brains of all the Lemming Kings
Perhaps, long since, there was a land beyond
Westward from death, some city, some calm place
Where one could taste God's quiet and be fond
With the little beauty of a human face.
But now the land is drowned. Yet we still press
Westward, in search, to death, to nothingness.

07

CARL SANDBURG (1878-1967)

Carl Sandburg was born on 6th June, 1878 in Galesburg, Illinois, USA. He was a poet, biographer, journalist and editor. He studied in Lombard College but he was a non-graduate. His parents were August Sandburg and Clara Mathilda. His main collections of poems are – *Chicago* (1914), *Chicago Poems* (1916), *Corn Huskers* (1918) *Fog* (1926), *The People, Yes* (1936), and *Complete Poems* (1950). For three times, he got the Pulitzer Prize for lyrical poetry. He died on 22nd July, 1967 in Flat Rock, North Carolina, United States of America.

CHICAGO

Hog Butcher for the World,
Tool Maker, Stacker of Wheat,
Player with Railroads and the Nationís Freight Handler;
Stormy, husky, brawling,
City of the Big Shoulders:

They tell me you are wicked and I believe them, for I have seen your
painted women under the gas lamps luring the farm boys.
And they tell me you are crooked and I answer: Yes, it is true I have
seen the gunman kill and go free to kill again.

And they tell me you are brutal and my reply is: On the faces of women and children I have seen the marks of wanton hunger.
And having answered so I turn once more to those who sneer at this
my city, and I give them back the sneer and say to them:

Come and show me another city with lifted head singing so proud to
be alive and coarse and strong and cunning.
Flinging magnetic curses amid the toil of piling job on job, here is a
tall bold slugger set vivid against the little soft cities;

Fierce as a dog with tongue lapping for action, cunning as a savage
pitted against the wilderness,
Bareheaded,
Shoveling,
Wrecking,
Planning,

Building, breaking, rebuilding,
Under the smoke, dust all over his mouth, laughing
with white teeth,
Under the terrible burden of destiny laughing as a
young man laughs,
Laughing even as an ignorant fighter laughs who has
never lost a battle,
Bragging and laughing that under his wrist is the pulse,
and under his ribs the heart of the people,
Laughing!

CRIPPLE ONCE

When I saw a cripple
Gasping slowly his last days with the white plague,
Looking from hollow eyes, calling for air,
Desperately gesturing with wasted hands
In the dark and dust of a house down in a slum,
I said to myself I would rather have been a tall sunflower
Living in a country garden
Lifting a golden-brown face to the summer,
Rain-washed and dew-misted,
Mixed with the poppies and ranking hollyhocks,
And wonderingly watching night after night
The clear silent processionals of stars.

FOG

The fog
on little cat feet
It sits looking
over harbor and city
on silent haunches
and then moves on.

GRASS

Pile the bodies high at Austerlitz and Waterloo.
Shovel them under and let me work–
I am the g rass ; I cover all.

And pile them high at Gettysburg
And pile then high at Ypres and Verdun.
Shovel them under and let me work.
Two years,, ten years, and passengers ask the conductor:
What place is this?
Where are we now?

I am the grass
Let me work.

COOL TOMBS

When Abraham Lincoln was shoveled into the tombs,
he forgot the copperheads and the assassin...in
the dust, in the cool tombs.
And Ulysses Grant lost all thoughts of con men and
Wall street, cash and collateral turned ashes...in
the dust, in the cool tombs.
Pocahontas's body lovely as a poplar, sweet as a red
haw in November or a pawpaw in May, did she
wonder? does she remember?...in the dust, in the
cool tombs.
Take any streetful of people buying cloths and
grocers, cheering a hero or throwing confetti
and blowing tin horns...tell me if the lover are
losers....tell me of any get more than the lovers...in
the dust...in the cool tombs.

A FENCE

Now the stone house on the lake front is finished and
the
workmen are beginning the fence.
The palings are made of iron bars with steel points that
can stab the life out of any man who falls on them.
As a fence, it is a masterpiece, and will shut off the
rabble
and all vagabonds and hungry men and all wandering
children looking for a place to play.
Passing through the bars and over the steel points will
go
nothing except Death and the Rain and To-morrow.

AT A WINDOW

Give me hunger,
O you gods that sit and give
The world its orders.
Give me hunger, pain and want,
Shut me out with shame and failure
From your doors of gold and fame,
Give me your shabbiest, weariest hunger!
But leave me a little love,
A voice to speak to me in the day end,
A hand to touch me in the dark room
Breaking the long loneliness.
In the dusk of day-shapes
Blurring the sunset,
One little wandering, western star
Thrust out from the changing shores of shadow.
Let me go to the window,
Watch there the day-shapes of dusk
And wait and know the coming Of a little love.

08

WALLACE STEVENS (1879-1955)

Wallace Stevens was born on 2nd October, 1879 in a Lutheran family of Dutch and German descent in Reading, Pennsylvania, United States of America. He was a modernist poet. First, he studied in New York Law School and then Harvard, and worked in an Insurance Company. His collections of poems are – *Harmonium* (1923), *Ideas of Order* (1936), *The Man with the Blue Guitar* (1937), and *The Auroras of Autumn* (1950). He married Elsie Kachel and lived with from 1909 to 1955. Holly Stevens was his only child. He died on 2nd August, 1956 in Saint Francis Hospital, Hartford, Connecticut.

THIRTEEN WAYS OF LOOKING AT A BLACK BIRD

I

Among twenty snowy mountains,
The only moving thing
Was the eye of the blackbird

II

I was of three minds
Like a tree
In which there are three blackbirds

III

The blackbird whirled in the autumn winds.
It was a small part of the pantomime.

IV

A man and a woman
Are one.
A man and a woman and a blackbird
Are one.

V

I do not know which to prefer,
The beauty of inflections
Or the beauty of innuendoes,
The blackbird whistling
Or just after.

VI

Icicles filled the long window
With barbaric glass.
The shadow of the blackbird

Crossed it, to and fro.
The mood
Traced in the shadow
An indecipherable cause.

VII

O thin men of Haddam,
Why do you imagine golden birds?
Do you not see how the blackbird
Walks around the feet
Of the women about you?

VIII

I know noble accents
And lucid, inescapable rhythms;
But I know, too,
That the blackbird is involved
In what I know.

IX

When the blackbird flew out of sight,
It marked the edge
Of one of many circles.

X

At the sight of blackbirds
Flying in a green light,
Even the bawds of euphony
Would cry out sharply.

XI

He rode over Connecticut
In a glass coach.
Once, a fear pierced him,
In that he mistook

The shadow of his equipage
For blackbirds.

XII

The river is moving
The blackbird must be flying.

XIII

It was evening all afternoon.
It was snowing
And it was going to snow.
The blackbird sat
In the cedar-limbs.

THE EMPEROR OF THE ICE-CREAM

Call the roller of big cigars,
The muscular one, and bid him whip
In kitchen cups concupiscent curds.
Let the wenches dawdle in such dress
As they are used to wear, and let the boys
Bring flowers in last month's newspapers.
Let be finale of seem.
The only emperor is the emperor of ice-cream.

Take from the dresser of deal,
Lacking the three glass knobs, that sheet
On which she embroidered fantails once
And spread it so as to cover her face.
If her horny feet protrude, they come
To show how cold she is, and dumb.
Let the lamp affix its beam.
The only emperor is the emperor of ice-cream.

GUBBINAL

That strange flower, the sun,
Is just what you say.
Have it your way.

The world is ugly,
And the people are sad.

That tuft of jungle feathers,
That animal eye,
Is just what you say.

That savage of fire,
That seed,
Have it your way.

The world is ugly,
And the people are sad.

THE SNOW MAN

Launch Audio in a New Window
One must have a mind of winter
To regard the frost and the boughs
Of the pine-trees crusted with snow;

And have been cold a long time
To behold the junipers shagged with ice,
The spruces rough in the distant glitter

Of the January sun; and not to think
Of any misery in the sound of the wind,
In the sound of a few leaves,

Which is the sound of the land
Full of the same wind
That is blowing in the same bare place

For the listener, who listens in the snow,
And, nothing himself, beholds
Nothing that is not there and the nothing that is.

ANECDOTE OF THE JAR

I placed a jar in Tennessee,
And round it was, upon a hill.
It made the slovenly wilderness
Surround that hill.

The wilderness rose up to it.
And sprawled around, no longer wild,
The jar was round upon the ground
And tall and of a port in air.

It took domination everywhere.
The jar was gray and bare.
It did not give of bird or bush,
Like nothing else in Tennessee.

09

HAROLD MUNRO (1879-1932)

Harold Munro was born on 14th March, 1879 in Brussels in Belgium. He was the proprietor of a bookshop in London. Edward Munro, a civil engineer and Arable Sophia, also a civil engineer, were his parents. He was educated in Radley College and Gonville and Caius College, Cambridge. He edited a poetry magazine regularly and published his first collection *Poems* in 1906. *Chronicle of a Pilgrimage,* (1909), *Children of Love* (1915), *Strange Meetings* (1917) and *Collected Poems* (1970) were published later. He helped many poets to publish poetry and grow famous. He died on 16th March, 1932 at Cliff Combe Nursing Home Broadstairs, Kent, England.

THE CHILDREN OF LOVE

The holy boy
Went from his mother out in the cool of the day
Over the sun-parched fields
And in among the olives shining green and shining
grey.

There was no sound,
No smallest voice of any shivering stream.
Poor sinless little boy,
He desired to play and to sing; he could only sigh and
dream.

Suddenly came
Running along to him naked, with curly hair,
That rogue of the lovely world,
That other beautiful child whom the virgin Venus bare.

The holy boy
Gazed with those sad blue eyes that all men know.
Impudent Cupid stood
Panting, holding an arrow and pointing his bow.

(Will you not play?
Jesus, run to him, run to him, swift for our joy.
Is he not holy, like you?
Are you afraid of his arrows, O beautiful dreaming
boy?)

And now they stand
Watching one another with timid gaze;
Youth has met youth in the wood,
But holiness will not change its melancholy ways.

Cupid at last
Draws his bow and softly lets fly a dart.
Smile for a moment, sad world! –
It has grazed the white skin and drawn blood from the
sorrowful heart.

Now, for delight,
Cupid tosses his locks and goes wantonly near;
But the child that was born to the cross
Has let fall on his cheek, for the sadness of life, a
compassionate tear.

Marvellous dream!
Cupid has offered his arrows for Jesus to try
He as offered his bow for the game.
But Jesus went weeping away, and left him there
wondering why.

DOG

You little friend, your nose is ready; you sniff,
Asking for that expected walk,
(Your nostrils full of the happy rabbit-whiff)
And almost talk.

And so the moment becomes a moving force;
Coats glide down from their pegs in the humble dark;
The sticks grow live to the stride of their vagrant course.
You scamper the stairs,
Your body informed with the scent and the track and
the mark
Of stoats and weasels, moles and badgers and hares.

We are going out. You know the pitch of the word,
Probing the tone of thought as it comes through fog
And reaches by devious means (half-smelt, half-heard)
The four-legged brain of a walk-ecstatic dog.

Out in the garden your head is already low.
(Can you smell the rose? Ah, no.)
But your limbs can draw
Life from the earth through the touch of your padded
paw.

Now, sending a little look to us behind,
Who follow slowly the track of your lovely play,
You carry our bodies forward away from mind
Into the light and fun of your useless day.

Thus, for your walk, we took ourselves, and went
Out by the hedge and the tree to the open ground.
You ran, in delightful strata of wafted scent,
Over the hill without seeing the view;
Beauty is smell upon primitive smell to you:
To you, as to us, it is distant and rarely found.

Home ... and further joy will be surely there:
Supper waiting full of the taste of bone.
You throw up your nose again, and sniff, and stare
For the rapture known
Of the quick wild gorge of food and the still lie-down
While your people talk above you in the light
Of candles, and your dreams will merge and drown
Into the bed-delicious hours of night.

MILK FOR THE CAT

When the tea is brought at five o'clock,
And all the neat curtains are drawn with care,
The little black cat with bright green eyes
Is suddenly purring there.

At first she pretends, having nothing to do,
She has come in merely to blink by the grate,
But, though tea may be late or the milk may be sour,
She is never late.

And presently her agate eyes
Take a soft large milky haze,
And her independent casual glance
Becomes a stiff, hard gaze.

Then she stamps her claws or lifts her ears,
Or twists her tail and begins to stir,
Till suddenly all her lithe body becomes
One breathing, trembling purr.

The children eat and wriggle and laugh;
The two old ladies stroke their silk:
But the cat is grown small and thin with desire,
Transformed to a creeping lust for milk.

The white saucer like some full moon descends
At last from the clouds of the table above;
She sighs and dreams and thrills and glows,
Transfigured with love.

She nestles over the shining rim,
Buries her chin in the creamy sea;
Her tail hangs loose; each drowsy paw
Is doubled under each bending knee.

A long, dim ecstasy holds her life;
Her world is an infinite shapeless white,
Till her tongue has curled the last holy drop,
Then she sinks back into the night,

Draws and dips her body to heap
Her sleepy nerves in the great arm-chair,
Lies defeated and buried deep
Three or four hours unconscious there.

10

JAMES JOYCE (1882-1941)

He was born on 2nd February, 1882 in Rathgar, Dublin, Ireland. He was an Irish novelist, poet and literary critic. He contributed to the modernist *avant – garde* movement and is regarded as one of the most influential writers of the contemporary times. He admitted to a Jesuit Grammar School in Dublin and Belvedere College, without fees. He left the college without completing his degreee and lost his faith in Roman Catholic Church. *Ulysses* (1922) and *Finnegans Wake* (1939) are two main fictional works. He also wrote poetry. He married Nora Barnacle and lived from 1931 – 1941. He died on 13th January, 1941 in Zurich, Switzerland.

SIMPLES

O bella bionda,
Sei come l'onda!

Of cool sweet dew and radiance mild
The moon a web of silence weaves
In the still garden where a child
Gathers the simple salad leaves.

A moondew stars her hanging hair
And moonlight kisses her young brow
And, gathering, she sings an air:
Fair as the wave is, fair, art thou!

Be mine, I pray, a waxen ear
To shield me from her childish croon
And mine a shielded heart for her
Who gathers simples of the moon.

A FLOWER GIVEN TO MY DAUGHTER

Frail the white rose and frail are
Her hands that gave
Whose soul is sere and paler
Than time's wan wave.

Rosefrail and fair – yet frailest
A wonder wild
In gentle eyes thou veilest,
My blue veined child.

BE NOT SAD

Be not sad because all men
Prefer a lying clamour before you:
Sweetheart, be at peace again –
Can they dishonour you?

They are sadder than all tears;
Their lives ascend as a continual sigh.
Proudly answer to their tears:
As they deny, deny.

11

WILLIAMS CAROL WILLIAMS
(1883-1941)

Williams Carol Williams was born on 17th September, 1883 in Rutherford, New Jersey, USA. He was a physician by profession of Latin American descent. His parents were Williams George Williams, an English and his mother Raquel Helene Williams is from Puerto Rico and of French extraction. He studied first at Rutherford and later in France at Lycee Condorcet in Paris. He married Florence Williams and lived from 1912-1953. His main poetical works are – *Poems* (1909), *The Tempers* (1913), *Kora in Hell: Improvisations*. Being associated with modernism and imagism, he was influenced by Ezra Pound, Walt Whitman, and James Joyce. He died on 4th March, 1963 in Rutherford in New Jersey.

BLIZZARD

Snow:
years of anger following
hours that float idly down–
the blizzard
drifts its weight
deeper and deeper for three days
or sixty years, eh? Then
the sun! a clutter of
yellow and blue flakes–
Hairy looking trees stand out–
in long alleys
over a wild solitude.
The man turns and there–
his solitary track stretched out
upon the world.

THE RED WHEELBARROW

so much depends
upon

a red wheel
barrow

glazed with rain
water

beside the white
chickens.

THIS IS JUST TO SAY

I have eaten
the plums
that were in
the ice-box

and which
you were probably
saving
for breakfast

Forgive me
they were delicious
so sweet
and so cold.

LOVE SONG

I lie there thinking of you:–
stain of love
is upon the world!
Yellow, yellow, yellow
it eats into the leaves,
smears with saffron
the horned branches that lean
heavily
against a smooth purple sky!
There is no light
only a honey-thick stain
that drips from leaf to leaf
and limb to limb
spoiling colors
of the world–
you far off there under
the wine-red selvage of the west!

12

JAMES ELROY FLECKER (1984-1915)

James Elroy Flecker was born on 5th November, 1884 in Lewisham, London, United Kingdom. He was a British novelist, playwright, and poet whose poetry was most influenced by the Prussian poets. His father William Herman Flecker was the head master of Dean Close School, Cheltenham. His mother was Sarah. He studied in the same school and later in Trinity College, Oxford and Caius College, Cambridge. He married Helle Flecker who later edited her husband's letters. His poetical works are – *The Bridge of Fire* (1907), *Forty-Two Poems* (1910), and *Collected Poems* (1916). He died of Tuberculosis on 3rd Jan, 1915.

A FRAGMENT

O pouring weltering streams
Shouting that I have leapt the mountain bar,
Down curve on curve my journey's white way gleams –
My road along the river of return.

I know the countries where the white moons burn,
And heavy star on star
Dips on the pale and crystal desert hills.
I know the river of the sun that fills
With founts of gold the lakes of Orient sky.

. . . .

And I have heard a voice of broken seas
And from the cliffs a cry.
Ah still they learn, those cave-eared Cyclades,
The Triton's friendly or his fearful horn,
And why the deep sea-bells but seldom chime,
And how those waves with what spell-swept rhyme
In years of morning, on a summer's morn
Whispering round his castle on the coast,
Lured young Achilles from his haunted sleep
And drove him out to dive beyond those deep
Dim purple windows of the empty swell,
His ivory body flitting like a ghost
Over the holes where flat blind fishes dwell,
All to embrace his mother thronèd in her shell.

MARY MAGDALEN

O eyes that strip the souls of men!
There came to me the Magdalen.
Her blue robe with a cord was bound,

Her hair with Lenten lilies crowned.
"Arise," she said "God calls for thee,
Turned to new paths thy feet must be.
Leave the fever and the feast
Leave the friend thou lovest best:
For thou must walk in barefoot ways,
To give my dear Lord Jesus praise."
Then answered I— "Sweet Magdalen,
God's servant, once beloved of men,
Why didst thou change old ways for new,
Thy trailing red for corded blue,
Roses for lilies on thy brow,
Rich splendour for a barren vow?"

Gentle of speech she answered me:-
"Sir, I was sick with revelry.
True, I have scarred the night with sin,
A pale and tawdry heroine;
But once I heard a voice that said
'Who lives in sin is surely dead,
But whoso turns to follow me
Hath joy and immortality.'"

"O Mary, not for this," I cried,
"Didst thou renounce thy scented pride.
Not for a taste of endless years
Or barren joy apart from tears
Didst thou desert the courts of men.
Tell me thy truth, sweet Magdalen!"

She trembled, and her eyes grew dim:-
"For love of Him, for love of Him."

STILLNESS

When the words rustle no more,
And the last work's done,
When the bolt lies deep in the door,
And Fire, our Sun,
Falls on the dark-laned meadows of the floor;

When from the clock's last time to the next chime
Silence beats his drum,
And Space with gaunt grey eyes and her brother Time
Wheeling and whispering come,
She with the mould of form and he with the loom of
rhyme,

Then twittering out in the night my thought-birds flee,
I am emptied of all my dreams:
I only hear Earth turning, only see
Ether's long bankless streams,
And only know I should drown if you
Laid not your hand on me.

NO COWARD'S SONG

I am afraid to think about my death,
When it shall be, and whether in great pain
I shall rise up and fight the air for breath
Or calmly wait the bursting of my brain.
I am no coward who could seek in fear
A folk-lore solace or sweet Indian tales:
I know dead men are deaf and cannot hear
The singing of a thousand nightingales.
I know dead men are blind and cannot see
The friend that shuts in horror their big eyes,
And they are witless — O, I'd rather be
A living mouse than dead as a man dies.

D. H. LAWRENCE (1885-1930)

He was born on 11th September, 1885 in Eastwood, a village near Nottinghamshire, United Kingdom. He father, Arthur John Lawrence was an ordinary miner and his mother, Lydia Lawrence was a school teacher. As a precocious child, he attended the local school and later studied in College and University. He had an escapade with his teacher's wife in love. He wrote short stories, novels and poetry. Mainly he was regarded as a 'modern' novelist. *Sons and Lovers*, *The Rainbow* and *Women in Love* are his major novels. His poetry is highly emotional and descriptive, with the common themes of love, hatred and betrayal etc. He died on 2nd March, 1910 in Vance, France, 1930.

CONUNDRUMS

Tell me a word
that you've often heard,
yet it makes you squint
when you see it in print!

Tell me a thing
that you've often seen
yet if put in a book
it makes you turn green!

Tell me a thing
that you often do,
when described in a story
shocks you through and through!

Tell me what's wrong
with words or with you
that you don't mind the thing
yet the name is taboo.

PIANO

Softly, in the dusk, a woman is singing to me;
Taking me back down the vista of years, till I see
A child sitting under the piano, in the boom of the
tingling strings
And pressing the small, poised feet of a mother who
smiles as she
sings.

In spite of myself, the insidious mastery of song
Betrays me back, till the heart of me weeps to belong

To the old Sunday evenings at home, with winter outside
And hymns in the cozy parlour, the tinkling piano our guide.

So now it is vain for the singer to burst into clamour
With the great black piano appassionato. The glamour
Of childish days is upon me, my manhood is cast
Down in the flood of remembrance, I weep like a child for the past.
This poem is in the public domain.

WHALES WEEP NOT!

They say the sea is cold, but the sea contains
the hottest blood of all, and the wildest, the most urgent.

All the whales in the wider deeps, hot are they, as they urge
on and on, and dive beneath the icebergs.
The right whales, the sperm-whales, the hammer-heads, the killers
there they blow, there they blow, hot wild white breath out of
the sea!

And they rock, and they rock, through the sensual ageless ages
on the depths of the seven seas,
and through the salt they reel with drunk delight
and in the tropics tremble they with love
and roll with massive, strong desire, like gods.
Then the great bull lies up against his bride
in the blue deep bed of the sea,
as mountain pressing on mountain, in the zest of life:

and out of the inward roaring of the inner red ocean of
whale-blood
the long tip reaches strong, intense, like the maelstrom-
tip, and
comes to rest
in the clasp and the soft, wild clutch of a she-whale's
fathomless body.

And over the bridge of the whale's strong phallus,
linking the
wonder of whales
the burning archangels under the sea keep passing,
back and
forth,
keep passing, archangels of bliss
from him to her, from her to him, great Cherubim
that wait on whales in mid-ocean, suspended in the
waves of the sea
great heaven of whales in the waters, old hierarchies.

And enormous mother whales lie dreaming suckling
their whale-
tender young
and dreaming with strange whale eyes wide open in the
waters of
the beginning and the end.

And bull-whales gather their women and whale-calves
in a ring
when danger threatens, on the surface of the ceaseless
flood
and range themselves like great fierce Seraphim facing
the threat
encircling their huddled monsters of love.
And all this happens in the sea, in the salt
where God is also love, but without words:

and Aphrodite is the wife of whales
most happy, happy she!

and Venus among the fishes skips and is a she-dolphin
she is the gay, delighted porpoise sporting with love
and the sea
she is the female tummy-fish, round and happy among
the males
and dense with happy blood, dark rainbow bliss in the
sea.

DISCORD IN CHILDHOOD

Outside the house an ash-tree hung its terrible whips,
And at night when the wind arose, the lash of the tree
Shrieked and lashed the wind, as a ship's
Weird rigging in a storm shrieks hideously.

Within the house two voices arose in anger, a slender
lash
Whistling delirious rage, and the dreadful sound
Of a thick lash booming and bruising until it drowned
The other voice in a silence of blood,' neath the noise of
the ash.

14

SIEGEFRIED SASSOON (1886-1967)

Siegfried Sassoon is one of the famous war poets. He was born in Matfield, United Kingdom on 8th September, in 1886. He was a poet, writer and a soldier. He was educated at The New Beacon Preparatory School, Kent, Marlborough College, and at Clare College, Cambridge. He married Hester Gatty and he was influenced by Robert Graves and Thomas Hardy and others. His main poetical works are- *The Daffodil Murder* (1913), *Glory of Women* (1917), *Satirical Poems* (1926), *Selected Poems* (1926), and *Collected Poems.* (1951). He died in Heytesbury, Wiltshire, United Kingdom.

SUICIDE IN THE TRENCHES

I knew a simple soldier boy
Who grinned at life in empty joy,
Slept soundly through the lonesome dark,
And whistled early with the lark.

In winter trenches, cowed and glum,
With cramps and lice and lack of rum,
He put a bullet through his brain,
No one spoke o him again.

You smug-faced crowds with kindling eye
Who cheer when soldier lads march by,
Sneak home and pray you'll never know
The hell where youth and laughter go.

ABSOLUTION

The anguish of the earth absolves our eyes
Till beauty shines in all that we can see.
War is our scourge; yet war has made us wise,
And, fighting for our freedom, we are free.

Horror of wounds and anger at the foe,
And loss of things desired; all these must pass.
We are the happy legion, for we know
Time's but a golden wind that shakes the grass.

There was an hour when we were loth to part
From life we longed to share no less than others.
Now, having claimed this heritage of heart,
What need we more, my comrades and my brothers?

ATTACK

At dawn the ridge emerges massed and dun
In the wild purple of the glow'ring sun,
Smouldering through spouts of drifting smoke that shroud
The menacing scarred slope; and, one by one,
Tanks creep and topple forward to the wire.
The barrage roars and lifts. Then, clumsily bowed
With bombs and guns and shovels and battle-gear,
Men jostle and climb to, meet the bristling fire.
Lines of grey, muttering faces, masked with fear,
They leave their trenches, going over the top,
While time ticks blank and busy on their wrists,
And hope, with furtive eyes and grappling fists,
Flounders in mud. O Jesus, make it stop!

THE DEATH BED

He drowsed and was aware of silence heaped
Round him, unshaken as the steadfast walls;
Aqueous like floating rays of amber light,
Soaring and quivering in the wings of sleep.
Silence and safety; and his mortal shore
Lipped by the inward, moonless waves of death.

Someone was holding water to his mouth.
He swallowed, unresisting; moaned and dropped
Through crimson gloom to darkness; and forgot
The opiate throb and ache that was his wound.
Water—calm, sliding green above the weir;
Water—a sky-lit alley for his boat,
Bird-voiced, and bordered with reflected flowers
And shaken hues of summer: drifting down,
He dipped contented oars, and sighed, and slept.

Night, with a gust of wind, was in the ward,
Blowing the curtain to a gummering curve.
Night. He was blind; he could not see the stars
Glinting among the wraiths of wandering cloud;
Queer blots of colour, purple, scarlet, green,
Flickered and faded in his drowning eyes.

Rain — he could hear it rustling through the dark;
Fragrance and passionless music woven as one;
Warm rain on drooping roses; pattering showers
That soak the woods; not the harsh rain that sweeps
Behind the thunder, but a trickling peace,
Gently and slowly washing life away.

He stirred, shifting his body; then the pain
Leaped like a prowling beast, and gripped and tore
His groping dreams with grinding claws and fangs.
But someone was beside him; soon he lay
Shuddering because that evil thing had passed.
And death, who'd stepped toward him, paused and
stared.

Light many lamps and gather round his bed.
Lend him your eyes, warm blood, and will to live.
Speak to him; rouse him; you may save him yet.
He's young; he hated war; how should he die
When cruel old campaigners win safe through?

But death replied: "I choose him." So he went,
And there was silence in the summer night;
Silence and safety; and the veils of sleep.
Then, far away, the thudding of the guns.

15

HILDA DOOLITTLE (1886-1961)

Hilda Doolittle was born on 10th September, 1886 in Moravian Community, Bethlehem, Pennsylvania. She was an American Modernist poet, novelist, and memoirist who wrote under the name "H.D.", throughout her life. She is in the tradition of Imagist poetry, meeting other imagist poets like, Ezra Pound and William Carol Williams. She was educated in Bryn Mawr College. Her parents-Charles, a professor and Helen, a member of Moravian brotherhood. She had wealthy parents. She married Richard Aldington, an imagist poet in 1913. Her main collections of poems are – *Sea Garden* (1912), *Hymen* (1921), *Collected poems of H.D* (1926). At the age of 75, she died on 27th September 1961 in Zurich, Switzerland.

HELEN

All Greece hates
the still eyes in the white face,
the lustre as of olives
where she stands,
and the white hands.

All Greece reviles
the wan face when she smiles,
hating it deeper still
when it grows wan and white,
remembering past enchantments
and past ills.

Greece sees, unmoved,
God's daughter, born of love,
the beauty of cool feet
and slenderest knees,
could love indeed the maid,
only if she were laid,
white ash amid funereal cypresses.

SEA POPPIES

Amber husk
fluted with gold,
fruit on the sand
marked with a rich grain,

treasure
spilled near the shrub-pines
to bleach on the boulders:

your stalk has caught root
among wet pebbles
and drift flung by the sea
and grated shells
and split conch-shells.

Beautiful, wide-spread,
fire upon leaf,
what meadow yields
so fragrant a leaf
as your bright leaf?

PEAR TREE

Silver dust
lifted from the earth,
higher than my arms reach,
you have mounted.
O silver,
higher than my arms reach
you front us with great mass;

no flower ever opened
so staunch a white leaf,
no flower ever parted silver
from such rare silver;

O white pear,
your flower-tufts,
thick on the branch,
bring summer and ripe fruits
in their purple hearts.

ORCHARD

I saw the first pear
as it fell–
the honey-seeking, golden-banded,
the yellow swarm
was not more fleet than I,
(spare us from loveliness)
and I fell prostrate
crying:

you have flayed us
with your blossoms,
spare us the beauty
of fruit-trees.

The honey-seeking
paused not,
the air thundered their song,
and I alone was prostrate.

O rough-hewn
god of the orchard,
I bring you an offering–
do you, alone unbeautiful,
son of the god,
spare us from loveliness:

these fallen hazel-nuts,
stripped late of their green sheaths,
grapes, red-purple,
their berries
dripping with wine,
pomegranates already broken,
and shrunken figs
and quinces untouched,
I bring you as offering.

16

ROBINSON JEFFERS (1887-1963)

Robinson Jeffers, known for his work about the Central California Coast, was born on 10th January, 1887 in Allegheny, Pennsylvania, U.S.A. He studied in Occidental College. His parents were – Dr. William Jeffers and Annie Robinson Tuttle. He married Una Call Kuster and lived with her from 1913-1950. His collections of poems are-*The Selected Poetry of Robinson Jeffers* (1938) and *The Collected Poetry of Robinson Jeffers* (2000). It is said that he was influenced by Euripides, Whitman, Wordsworth, and Nietzsche, the German philosopher. Much of his poetry was written in narrative and epic form. However, he died on 20th January, 1962 in Carmel – by – the-Sea.

THE BLOODY SIRE

It is not bad. Let them play.
Let the guns bark and the bombing-plane
Speak his prodigious blasphemies.
It is not bad, it is high time,
Stark violence is still the sire of all the world's values.

What but the wolf's tooth whittled so fine
The fleet limbs of the antelope?
What but fear winged the birds, and hunger
Jewelled with such eyes the great goshawk's head?
Violence has been the sire of all the world's values.

Who would remember Helen's face
Lacking the terrible halo of spears?
Who formed Christ but Herod and Caesar,
The cruel and bloody victories of Caesar?
Violence, the bloody sire of all the world's values.

Never weep, let them play,
Old violence is not too old to beget new values.

LOVE THE WILD SWAN

"I hate my verses, every line, every word.
Oh pale and brittle pencils ever to try
One grass-blade's curve, or the throat of one bird
That clings to twig, ruffled against white sky.
Oh cracked and twilight mirrors ever to catch
One color, one glinting
Hash, of the splendor of things.
Unlucky hunter, Oh bullets of wax,
The lion beauty, the wild-swan wings, the storm of the
wings."

–This wild swan of a world is no hunter's game.
Better bullets than yours would miss the white breast
Better mirrors than yours would crack in the flame.
Does it matter whether you hate your . . . self?
At least Love your eyes that can see, your mind that can
Hear the music, the thunder of the wings. Love the wild
swan.

SHIVA

There is a hawk that is picking the birds out of our sky,
She killed the pigeons of peace and security,
She has taken honesty and confidence from nations and
men,
She is hunting the lonely heron of liberty.
She loads the arts with nonsense, she is very cunning
Science with dreams and the state with powers to catch
them at last.
Nothing will escape her at last, flying nor running.
This is the hawk that picks out the star's eyes.
This is the only hunter that will ever catch the wild
swan;
The prey she will take last is the wild white swan of the
beauty of
things.
Then she will be alone, pure destruction, achieved and
supreme,
Empty darkness under the death-tent wings.
She will build a nest of the swan's bones and hatch a
new brood,
Hang new heavens with new birds, all be renewed.

VULTURE

I had walked since dawn and lay down to rest on a bare
hillside
Above the ocean. I saw through half-shut eyelids a
vulture wheeling
high up in heaven,
And presently it passed again, but lower and nearer,
its orbit
narrowing,
I understood then
That I was under inspection. I lay death-still and heard
the flight-
feathers
Whistle above me and make their circle and come
nearer.
I could see the naked red head between the great wings
Bear downward staring. I said, 'My dear bird, we are
wasting time
here.
These old bones will still work; they are not for you.'
But how
beautiful
he looked, gliding down
On those great sails; how beautiful he looked, veering
away in the
sea-light
over the precipice. I tell you solemnly
That I was sorry to have disappointed him. To be eaten
by that beak
and
become part of him, to share those wings and those
eyes–
What a sublime end of one's body, what an enskyment;
what a life
after death.

17

RUPERT BROOKE (1887-1915)

Rupert Brook was born on 3rd August, 1887 in Rugby, United Kingdom. He was one of the famous war poets, known for his idealistic war sonnets written during the First World War (1914-1918). His parents were – William Parker and Ruth Mary Brooke who were working in Fettes College, Edinburg. He was educated in School at Hillbrow and later in King's College, Cambridge. He served as a soldier in the World War I. He died of septicemia after two operation to remove abscess on 23rd April, 1915., and buried at Skyros Greece.

THE SOLDIER

If I should die, think only this of me:
That there's some corner of a foreign field
That is forever England. There shall be
In that rich earth a richer dust concealed;
A dust whom England bore, shaped, made aware,
Gave, once, her flowers to love, her ways to roam,
A body of England's, breathing English air,
Washed by the rivers, blest by suns of home.

And think, this heart, all evil shed away,
A pulse in the eternal mind, no less
Gives somewhere back the thoughts by England given;
Her sights and sounds; dreams happy as her day;
And laughter, learnt of friends; and gentleness,
In hearts at peace, under an English heaven.

THE DEAD

These hearts were woven of human joys and cares,
Washed marvellously with sorrow, swift to mirth.
The years had given them kindness. Dawn was theirs,
And sunset, and the colours of the earth.
These had seen movement, and heard music; known
Slumber and waking; loved; gone proudly friended;
Felt the quick stir of wonder; sat alone;
Touched flowers and furs and cheeks. All this is ended.

There are waters blown by changing winds to laughter
And lit by the rich skies, all day. And after,
Frost, with a gesture, stays the waves that dance
And wandering loveliness. He leaves a white
Unbroken glory, a gathered radiance,
A width, a shining peace, under the night.

THE GREAT LOVER

I have been so great a lover: filled my days
So proudly with the splendour of Love's praise,
The pain, the calm, and the astonishment,
Desire illimitable, and still content,

And all dear names men use, to cheat despair,
For the perplexed and viewless streams that bear
Our hearts at random down the dark of life.
Now, ere the unthinking silence on that strife
Steals down, I would cheat drowsy Death so far,

My night shall be remembered for a star
That outshone all the suns of all men's days.
Shall I not crown them with immortal praise
Whom I have loved, who have given me, dared with me
High secrets, and in darkness knelt to see
The inenarrable godhead of delight?

Love is a flame: — we have beaconed the world's night.
A city: — and we have built it, these and I.
An emperor: — we have taught the world to die.
So, for their sakes I loved, ere I go hence,
And the high cause of Love's magnificence,
And to keep loyalties young, I'll write those names

Golden forever, eagles, crying flames,
And set them as a banner, that men may know,
To dare the generations, burn, and blow
Out on the wind of Time, shining and streaming . . . .
These I have loved:

White plates and cups, clean-gleaming,
Ringed with blue lines; and feathery, fiery dust;
Wet roofs, beneath the lamp-light; the strong crust

Of friendly bread; and many-tasting food;
Rainbows; and the blue bitter smoke of wood;
And radiant raindrops couching in cool flowers;
And flowers themselves, that sway through sunny
hours,

Dreaming of moths that drink them under the moon;
Then, the cool kindliness of sheets, that soon
Smooth away trouble; and the rough male kiss
Of blankets; grainy wood; live hair that is
Shining and free; blue-massing clouds; the keen
Unpassioned beauty of a great machine;

The benison of hot water; furs to touch;
The good smell of old clothes; and other such —

The comfortable smell of friendly fingers,
Hair's fragrance, and the musty reek that lingers
About dead leaves and last year's ferns.

Dear names,
And thousand other throng to me! Royal flames;
Sweet water's dimpling laugh from tap or spring;
Holes in the ground; and voices that do sing;
Voices in laughter, too; and body's pain,
Soon turned to peace; and the deep-panting train;
Firm sands; the little dulling edge of foam

That browns and dwindles as the wave goes home;
And washed stones, gay for an hour; the cold
Graveness of iron; moist black earthen mould;
Sleep; and high places; footprints in the dew;
And oaks; and brown horse-chestnuts, glossy-new;
And new-peeled sticks; and shining pools on grass; —
All these have been my loves. And these shall pass,

Whatever passes not, in the great hour,
Nor all my passion, all my prayers, have power
To hold them with me through the gate of Death.
They'll play deserter, turn with the traitor breath,

Break the high bond we made, and sell Love's trust
And sacramented covenant to the dust.
—Oh, never a doubt but, somewhere, I shall wake,
And give what's left of love again, and make
New friends, now strangers. . . .

But the best I've known
Stays here, and changes, breaks, grows old, is blown
About the winds of the world, and fades from brains
Of living men, and dies.
Nothing remains.

O dear my loves, O faithless, once again
This one last gift I give: that after men
Shall know, and later lovers, far-removed,
Praise you, 'All these were lovely'; say, 'He loved.'

You dragged your feet when you went out.
By the gate now, the moss is grown, the different
mosses,
Too deep to clear them away!
The leaves fall early this autumn, in wind.
The paired butterflies are already yellow with August
Over the grass in the West garden;
They hurt me.
I grow older.
If you are coming down through the narrows of the
river Kiang,
Please let me know beforehand,
And I will come out to meet you
As far as Chō-fū-Sa.

A PACT

I make truce with you, Walt Whitman–
I have detested you long enough.
I come to you as a grown child
Who has had a pig-headed father;
I am old enough now to make friends.
It was you that broke the new wood,
Now is a time for carving.
We have one sap and one root–
Let there be commerce between us.'

18

EDITH SITWELL (1887-1964)

She was born at Scarborough, the daughter of Sir George Sitwell. Being was six feet tall and habitually dressed in medieval fashions, she was a British poet of 'profound human concerns'. She reacted badly to her eccentric, unloving parents and lived much of her life with the governess. In 1933, she was awarded the medal of FRSL and in 1954, DGCO BE. She was the eldest of three Sitwells. Her collections of poems are – *The Mother* (1920), *The Wooden Pegasus* (1920)*The Sleeping Beauty* (1924) and *Street Songs* (1941). She died on 9th December, 1964 in London.

BY CANDLE LIGHT

Houses red as flower of bean,
Flickering leaves and shadows lean!
Pantalone, like a parrot,
Sat and grumbled in the garret—
Sat and growled and grumbled till
Moon upon the window-sill
Like a red geranium
Scented his bald cranium.
Said Brighella, meaning well:
"Pack your box and—go to Hell!
Heat will cure your rheumatism!" . . .
Silence crowned this optimism—
Not a sound and not a wail:
But the fire (lush leafy vales)
Watched the angry feathers fly.
Pantalone 'gan to cry—
Could not, *would* not, pack his box!
Shadows (curtseying hens and cocks)
Pecking in the attic gloom
Tried to smother his tail-plume . . .
Till a cockscomb candle-flame
Crowing loudly, died: Dawn came.

AT THE FAIR

Springing Jack

Green wooden leaves clap light away,
Severely practical, as they

Shelter the children candy-pale,
The chestnut-candles flicker, fail . . .

The showman's face is cubed clear as
The shapes reflected in a glass

Of water — (glog, glut, a ghost's speech
Fumbling for space from each to each).

The fusty showman fumbles, must
Fit in a particle of dust

The universe, for fear it gain
Its freedom from my cube of brain.

Yet dust bears seeds that grow to grace
Behind my crude-striped wooden face

As I, a puppet tinsel-pink
Leap on my springs, learn how to think —

Till like the trembling golden stalk
Of some long-petalled star, I walk

Through the dark heavens, and the dew
Falls on my eyes and sense thrills through.

II. The Ape Watches "Aunt Sally"

The apples are an angel's meat;
The shining dark leaves make clear sweet

The juice; green wooden fruits alway
Fall on these flowers as white as day —

(Clear angel-face on hairy stalk:
Soul grown from flesh, an ape's young talk!)

And in this green and lovely ground
The Fair, world-like, turns round and round

And bumpkins throw their pence to shed
Aunt Sally's wooden clear-striped head. —

I do not care if men should throw
Round sun and moon to make me go —

As bright as gold and silver pence . . .
They cannot drive their black shade hence!

WHAT THE GOOSE-GIRL SAID
ABOUT THE DEAN

Turn again, turn again,
Goose Clothilda, Goosie Jane.

Bright wooden waves of people creak
From houses built with coloured straws
Of heat; Dean Pasppus' long nose snores
Harsh as a hautbois, marshy-weak.

The wooden waves of people creak
Through the fields all water-sleek.

And in among the straws of light
Those bumpkin hautbois-sounds take flight.

Whence he lies snoring like the moon
Clownish-white all afternoon.

Beneath the trees' arsenical
Sharp woodwind tunes; heretical —

Blown like the wind's mane
(Creaking woodenly again).

His wandering thoughts escape like geese
Till he, their gooseherd, sets up chase,
And clouds of wool join the bright race
For scattered old simplicities.

19

MARIANNE MOORE (1887-1972)

Marianne Moore was the modernist poet, critic, editor, and translator. She was born in Presbyterian family on 15th November, 1887, in Kirkwood, Missouri, USA. Her parents were – John Milton Moore, an mechanical engineer and Mary Warner Moore. She was educated in Bryn Mawr College, (B.A.). Her collections of poems-*Poems* (1921), *The Pangolin and Other Verse* (1936), *Nevertheless* (1944), *Collected Poems* (1951), *Selected Poems* (1960), *The Complete Poems* (1982), and *Complete Poems* (1994). Her poetry is noted for its for its innovation, precise diction, irony and wit. She got the Pulitzer Prize and Bollingen Prize in 1951. She was nominated for the Nobel Prize in 1968. She died on 5th February, 1972, in New York.

POETRY

I too, dislike it: there are things that are important
beyond all this fiddle.
Reading it, however, with a perfect contempt for it,
one discovers that there is in it after all, a place for the
genuine.
Hands that can grasp, eyes
that can dilate, hair that can rise
if it must, these things are important not because a
high-sounding interpretation can be put upon them but
because they are
useful; when they become so derivative as to become
unintelligible, the
same thing may be said for all of us — that we
do not admire what
we cannot understand. The bat,
holding on upside down or in quest of something to
eat, elephants pushing, a wild horse taking a roll, a
tireless wolf under
a tree, the immovable critic twinkling his skin like a horse
that feels a flea, the base — ball fan, the statistician — case
after case
could be cited did
one wish it; nor is it valid
to discriminate against "business documents and
school-books"; all these phenomena are important. One
must make a distinction
however: when dragged into prominence by half poets,
the result is not poetry, nor till the autocrats among us
can be
"literalists of
the imagination" — above
insolence and triviality and can present
for inspection, imaginary gardens with real toads in
them, shall we have

it. In the meantime, if you demand on the one hand, in
defiance of their opinion —
the raw material of poetry in
all its rawness, and
that which is on the other hand,
genuine, then you are interested in poetry.

BLACK EARTH

Openly, yes,
With the naturalness
Of the hippopotamus or the alligator
When it climbs out on the bank to experience the

Sun, I do these
Things which I do, which please
No one but myself. Now I breathe and now I am sub-
Merged; the blemishes stand up and shout when the
object

In view was a
Renaissance; shall I say
The contrary? The sediment of the river which
Encrusts my joints, makes me very gray but I am used

To it, it may
Remain there; do away
With it and I am myself done away with, for the
Patina of circumstance can but enrich what was

There to begin
With. This elephant skin
Which I inhabit, fibered over like the shell of
The coco-nut, this piece of black glass through which
no light

Can filter—cut
Into checkers by rut
Upon rut of unpreventable experience—
It is a manual for the peanut-tongued and the

Hairy toed. Black
But beautiful, my back
Is full of the history of power. Of power? What
Is powerful and what is not? My soul shall never

Be cut into
By a wooden spear; through-
Out childhood to the present time, the unity of
Life and death has been expressed by the circumference

Described by my
Trunk; nevertheless, I
Perceive feats of strength to be inexplicable after
All; and I am on my guard; external poise, it

Has its centre
Well nurtured—we know
Where—in pride, but spiritual poise, it has its centre
where ?
My ears are sensitized to more than the sound of

The wind. I see
And I hear, unlike the
Wandlike body of which one hears so much, which was
made
To see and not to see; to hear and not to hear,

That tree trunk without
Roots, accustomed to shout
Its own thoughts to itself like a shell, maintained intact
By who knows what strange pressure of the atmosphere;
that

Spiritual
Brother to the coral
Plant, absorbed into which, the equable sapphire light
Becomes a nebulous green. The I of each is to

The I of each,
A kind of fretful speech
Which sets a limit on itself; the elephant is?
Black earth preceded by a tendril? It is to that

Phenomenon
The above formation,
Translucent like the atmosphere—a cortex merely—
That on which darts cannot strike decisively the first

Time, a substance
Needful as an instance
Of the indestructibility of matter; it
Has looked at the electricity and at the earth-

Quake and is still
Here; the name means thick. Will
Depth be depth, thick skin be thick, to one who can see
no
Beautiful element of unreason under it?

A GRAVEYARD

Man, looking into the sea—
taking the view from those who have as much right to it
as you have it to yourself—
it is human nature to stand in the middle of a thing
but you cannot stand in the middle of this:
the sea has nothing to give but a well excavated grave.

The firs stand in a procession—each with an emerald
turkey-foot at the top—
reserved as their contours, saying nothing;
repression, however, is not the most obvious
characteristic of the sea;
the sea is a collector, quick to return a rapacious look.
There are others besides you who have worn that look—
whose expression is no longer a protest; the fish no
longer investigate them
for their bones have not lasted;
men lower nets, unconscious of the fact that they are
desecrating a grave,
and row quickly away—the blades of the oars
moving together like the feet of water-spiders as if there
were no such thing as death.
The wrinkles progress upon themselves in a phalanx—
beautiful under networks of foam,
and fade breathlessly while the sea rustles in and out of
the seaweed;
the birds swim through the air at top speed, emitting
cat-calls as heretofore—
the tortoise-shell scourges about the feet of the cliffs, in
motion beneath them
and the ocean, under the pulsation of light-houses and
noise of bell-buoys,
advances as usual, looking as if it were not that ocean in
which dropped things are bound to sink—
in which if they turn and twist, it is neither with volition
nor consciousness.

TO A SNAIL

If ' compression is the first grace of style,"
you have it. Contractibility is a virtue
as modesty is a virtue.

It is not acquisition of nay one thing
that is able to adorn,
or the incidental quality that occurs
as a concomitant of something well said,
that we value in style,
but the principle that is hid;
in the absence of feet,' a method of conclusions";
"a knowledge of principles,"
in the curious phenomenon of your occipital horn.

20

JOHN CROWE RANSOM (1888-1974)

J.C. Ransom was a famous American educator and scholar, poet, essayist and editor. He was born on 30th April, 1888 in Pulaski, Tennessee, USA. He is considered to be the founder of New Criticism during 1960s. He obtained, B.A., in Vanderbilt University (1909) M.A., in Christ College, Cambridge, and later in University of Oxford. He was the editor of *The Kenyon Review*. His collections of poems are – *Poems about God* (1919), *Chills and Fever* (1924), *Grace after Meat* (1924), etc. He won the Bollingen Prize for 'fugitive' poetry. He died on 3rd July, 1974 in Gambier, Ohio.

BELLS FOR JOHN WHITESIDE'S DAUGHTER

There was such speed in her little body,
And such lightness in her footfall,
It is no wonder her brown study
Astonishes us all.

Her wars were bruited in our high window.
We looked among orchard trees and beyond
Where she took arms against her shadow,
Or harried unto the pond

The lazy geese, like a snow cloud
Dripping their snow on the green grass,
Tricking and stopping, sleepy and proud,
Who cried in goose, Alas,

For the tireless heart within the little
Lady with rod that made them rise
From their noon apple-dreams and scuttle
Goose-fashion under the skies!

But now go the bells, and we are ready,
In one house we are sternly stopped
To say we are vexed at her brown study,
Lying so primly propped.

JANET WAKING

Beautifully Janet slept
Till it was deeply morning. She woke then
And thought about her dainty-feathered hen,
To see how it had kept.

One kiss she gave her mother,
Only a small one gave she to her daddy
Who would have kissed each curl of his shining baby;
No kiss at all for her brother.

"Old Chucky, Old Chucky!" she cried,
Running across the world upon the grass
To Chucky's house, and listening. But alas,
Her Chucky had died.

It was a transmogrifying bee
Came droning down on Chucky's old bald head
And sat and put the poison. It scarcely bled,
But how exceedingly

And purply did the knot
Swell with the venom and communicate
Its rigour! Now the poor comb stood up straight
But Chucky did not.

So there was Janet
Kneeling on the wet grass, crying her brown hen
(Translated far beyond the daughters of men)
To rise and walk upon it.

And weeping fast as she had breath
Janet implored us, "Wake her from her sleep!"
And would not be instructed in how deep
Was the forgetful kingdom of death.

WINTER REMEMBERED

Two evils, monstrous either one apart,
Possessed me, and were long and loath at going:
A cry of Absence, Absence, in the heart,
And in the wood the furious winter blowing.

Think not, when fire was bright upon my bricks,
And past the tight boards hardly a wind could enter,
I glowed like them, the simple burning sticks,
Far from my cause, my proper heat and center.

Better to walk forth in the frozen air
And wash my wound in the snows; that would be
healing;
Because my heart would throb less painful there,
Being caked with cold, and past the smart of feeling.

And where I walked, the murderous winter blast
Would have this body bowed, these eyeballs streaming,
And though I think this heart's blood froze not fast
It ran too small to spare one drop for dreaming.

Dear love, these fingers that had known your touch,
And tied our separate forces first together,
Were ten poor idiot fingers not worth much,
Ten frozen parsnips hanging in the weather.

DEAD BOY

The little cousin is dead, by foul subtraction,
A green bough from Virginia's aged tree,
And none of the county kin like the transaction,
Nor some of the world of outer dark, like me.

A boy not beautiful, nor good, nor clever,
A black cloud full of storms too hot for keeping,
A sword beneath his mother's heart–yet never
Woman bewept her babe as this is weeping.

A pig with pasty face, so I had said,
Squealing for cookies, kinned by poor pretense

With a noble house. But the little man quite dead,
I see the forebears' antique lineaments.

The elder men have strode by the box of death
To the wide flag porch, and muttering low send round
The brunt of the day. O friendly waste of breath!
Their hearts are hurt with a deep dynastic wound.

He was pale and little, the foolish neighbors say;
The first fruits, saith the Preacher, the Lord has taken;
But this was the old tree's late branch wrenched away,
Grieving the sapless limbs, the shorn and shaken.
(1927)

21

T.S. ELIOT (1888-1965)

T.S.Eliot, OM, was a poet-critic, essayist, and playwright. He was born on 26th September, 1888 in St Louis Missouri, USA. He is considered to be one of the great poets of 20th century. His strictly Catholic parents were-Henry Ware Eliot and Charlotte Champe Stearns. From America, he migrated to England. He did his B.A., and M.A., in Harvard University and also in Merton College, Oxford. His famous works are – *The Love Song of Alfred Prufrock and Other Poems* (1915), *The Waste Land* (1922), *The Hollow Men* (1925), *Ash Wednesday* (1930), and *Four Quartets* (1943) He died on 4th January, 1965, in London, United Kingdom. He won the Nobel Prize for Literature in 1948.

THE LOVE SONG OF J.ALFRED PRUFROCK

S'io credesse che mia risposta fosse
A persona che mai tornasse al mondo,
Questa fiamma staria senza piu scosse.
Ma percioche giammai di questo fondo
Non torno vivo alcun, s'i'odo il vero,
Senza tema d'infamia ti rispondo.

Let us go then, you and I,
When the evening is spread out against the sky
Like a patient etherized upon a table;
Let us go, through certain half-deserted streets,
The muttering retreats
Of restless nights in one-night cheap hotels
And sawdust restaurants with oyster-shells:
Streets that follow like a tedious argument
Of insidious intent
To lead you to an overwhelming question ...
Oh, do not ask, "What is it?"
Let us go and make our visit.

In the room the women come and go
Talking of Michelangelo.

The yellow fog that rubs its back upon the window-
panes,
The yellow smoke that rubs its muzzle on the window-
panes,
Licked its tongue into the corners of the evening,
Lingered upon the pools that stand in drains,
Let fall upon its back the soot that falls from chimneys,
Slipped by the terrace, made a sudden leap,
And seeing that it was a soft October night,
Curled once about the house, and fell asleep.

And indeed there will be time
For the yellow smoke that slides along the street,
Rubbing its back upon the window-panes;
There will be time, there will be time
To prepare a face to meet the faces that you meet;
There will be time to murder and create,
And time for all the works and days of hands
That lift and drop a question on your plate;
Time for you and time for me,
And time yet for a hundred indecisions,
And for a hundred visions and revisions,
Before the taking of a toast and tea.

In the room the women come and go
Talking of Michelangelo.

And indeed there will be time
To wonder, "Do I dare?" and, "Do I dare?"
Time to turn back and descend the stair,
With a bald spot in the middle of my hair —
(They will say: "How his hair is growing thin!")
My morning coat, my collar mounting firmly to the chin,
My necktie rich and modest, but asserted by a simple pin —
(They will say: "But how his arms and legs are thin!")
Do I dare
Disturb the universe?
In a minute there is time
For decisions and revisions which a minute will reverse.

For I have known them all already, known them all:
Have known the evenings, mornings, afternoons,
I have measured out my life with coffee spoons;
I know the voices dying with a dying fall

Beneath the music from a farther room.
So how should I presume?

And I have known the eyes already, known them all—
The eyes that fix you in a formulated phrase,
And when I am formulated, sprawling on a pin,
When I am pinned and wriggling on the wall,
Then how should I begin
To spit out all the butt-ends of my days and ways?
And how should I presume?

And I have known the arms already, known them all—
Arms that are braceleted and white and bare
(But in the lamplight, downed with light brown hair!)
Is it perfume from a dress
That makes me so digress?
Arms that lie along a table, or wrap about a shawl.
And should I then presume?
And how should I begin?

Shall I say, I have gone at dusk through narrow streets
And watched the smoke that rises from the pipes
Of lonely men in shirt-sleeves, leaning out of windows?
...

I should have been a pair of ragged claws
Scuttling across the floors of silent seas.

And the afternoon, the evening, sleeps so peacefully!
Smoothed by long fingers,
Asleep ... tired ... or it malingers,
Stretched on the floor, here beside you and me.
Should I, after tea and cakes and ices,
Have the strength to force the moment to its crisis?
But though I have wept and fasted, wept and prayed,

Though I have seen my head (grown slightly bald)
brought in upon a platter,
I am no prophet — and here's no great matter;
I have seen the moment of my greatness flicker,
And I have seen the eternal Footman hold my coat, and
snicker,
And in short, I was afraid.

And would it have been worth it, after all,
After the cups, the marmalade, the tea,
Among the porcelain, among some talk of you and me,
Would it have been worthwhile,
To have bitten off the matter with a smile,
To have squeezed the universe into a ball
To roll it towards some overwhelming question,
To say: "I am Lazarus, come from the dead,
Come back to tell you all, I shall tell you all" —
If one, settling a pillow by her head
Should say: "That is not what I meant at all;
That is not it, at all."

And would it have been worth it, after all,
Would it have been worthwhile,
After the sunsets and the dooryards and the sprinkled
streets,
After the novels, after the teacups, after the skirts that
trail along the floor —
And this, and so much more? —
It is impossible to say just what I mean!
But as if a magic lantern threw the nerves in patterns
on a screen:
Would it have been worth while
If one, settling a pillow or throwing off a shawl,
And turning toward the window, should say:
"That is not it at all,
That is not what I meant, at all."

No! I am not Prince Hamlet, nor was meant to be;
Am an attendant lord, one that will do
To swell a progress, start a scene or two,
Advise the prince; no doubt, an easy tool,
Deferential, glad to be of use,
Politic, cautious, and meticulous;
Full of high sentence, but a bit obtuse;
At times, indeed, almost ridiculous —
Almost, at times, the Fool.

I grow old ... I grow old ...
I shall wear the bottoms of my trousers rolled.

Shall I part my hair behind? Do I dare to eat a peach?
I shall wear white flannel trousers, and walk upon the
beach.
I have heard the mermaids singing, each to each.

I do not think that they will sing to me.

I have seen them riding seaward on the waves
Combing the white hair of the waves blown back
When the wind blows the water white and black.
We have lingered in the chambers of the sea
By sea-girls wreathed with seaweed red and brown
Till human voices wake us, and we drown.

PRELUDES

I

The winter evening settles down
With smell of steaks in passageways.
Six o'clock.
The burnt-out ends of smoky days.

And now a gusty shower wraps
The grimy scraps
Of withered leaves about your feet
And newspapers from vacant lots;
The showers beat
On broken blinds and chimney-pots,
And at the corner of the street
A lonely cab-horse steams and stamps.
And then the lighting of the lamps.

II

The morning comes to consciousness
Of faint stale smells of beer
From the sawdust-trampled street
With all its muddy feet that press
To early coffee-stands.
With the other masquerades
That time resumes,
One thinks of all the hands
That are raising dingy shades
In a thousand furnished rooms.

III

You tossed a blanket from the bed,
You lay upon your back, and waited;
You dozed, and watched the night revealing
The thousand sordid images
Of which your soul was constituted;
They flickered against the ceiling.
And when all the world came back
And the light crept up between the shutters
And you heard the sparrows in the gutters,
You had such a vision of the street

As the street hardly understands;
Sitting along the bed's edge, where
You curled the papers from your hair,
Or clasped the yellow soles of feet
In the palms of both soiled hands.

IV

His soul stretched tight across the skies
That fade behind a city block,
Or trampled by insistent feet
At four and five and six o'clock;
And short square fingers stuffing pipes,
And evening newspapers, and eyes
Assured of certain certainties,
The conscience of a blackened street
Impatient to assume the world.

I am moved by fancies that are curled
Around these images, and cling:
The notion of some infinitely gentle
Infinitely suffering thing.

Wipe your hand across your mouth, and laugh;
The worlds revolve like ancient women
Gathering fuel in vacant lots.

GERONTION

Thou hast nor youth nor age
But as it were an after dinner sleep
Dreaming of both.

Here I am, an old man in a dry month,
Being read to by a boy, waiting for rain.

I was neither at the hot gates
Nor fought in the warm rain
Nor knee deep in the salt marsh, heaving a cutlass,
Bitten by flies, fought.
My house is a decayed house,
And the Jew squats on the window sill, the owner,
Spawned in some estaminet of Antwerp,
Blistered in Brussels, patched and peeled in London.
The goat coughs at night in the field overhead;
Rocks, moss, stonecrop, iron, meads.
The woman keeps the kitchen, makes tea,
Sneezes at evening, poking the peevish gutter.
I an old man,
A dull head among windy spaces.

Signs are taken for wonders. 'We would see a sign!'
The word within a word, unable to speak a word,
Swaddled with darkness. In the juvescence of the year
Came Christ the tiger

In depraved May, dogwood and chestnut, flowering
Judas,
To be eaten, to be divided, to be drunk
Among whispers; by Mr.Silvero
With caressing hands, at Limoges
Who walked all night in the next room;

By Hakagawa, bowing among the Titians;
By Madame de Tornquist, in the dark room
Shifting the candles; Fräulein von Kulp
Who turned in the hall, one hand on the door.
Vacant shuttles
Weave the wind. I have no ghosts,
An old man in a draughty house
Under a windy knob.

After such knowledge, what forgiveness? Think now
History has many cunning passages, contrived corridors
And issues, deceives with whispering ambitions,
Guides us by vanities. Think now
She gives when our attention is distracted
And what she gives, gives with such supple confusions
That the giving famishes the craving. Gives too late
What's not believed in, or is still believed,
In memory only, reconsidered passion. Gives too soon
Into weak hands, what's thought can be dispensed with
Till the refusal propagates a fear. Think
Neither fear nor courage saves us. Unnatural vices
Are fathered by our heroism. Virtues
Are forced upon us by our impudent crimes.
These tears are shaken from the wrath-bearing tree.

The tiger springs in the new year. Us he devours. Think
at last
We have not reached conclusion, when I
Stiffen in a rented house. Think at last
I have not made this show purposelessly
And it is not by any concentration
Of the backward devils.
I would meet you upon this honestly.
I that was near your heart was removed there from
To lose beauty in terror, terror in inquisition.
I have lost my passion: why should I need to keep it
Since what is kept must be adulterated?
I have lost my sight, smell, hearing, taste and touch:
How should I use it for your closer contact?

These with a thousand small deliberations
Protract the profit of their chilled delirium,
Excite the membrane, when the sense has cooled,
With pungent sauces, multiply variety
In a wilderness of mirrors. What will the spider do

Suspend its operations, will the weevil
Delay? De Bailhache, Fresca, Mrs. Cammel, whirled
Beyond the circuit of the shuddering Bear
In fractured atoms. Gull against the wind, in the windy straits
Of Belle Isle, or running on the Horn,
White feathers in the snow, the Gulf claims,
And an old man driven by the Trades
To a sleepy corner.

Tenants of the house,
Thoughts of a dry brain in a dry season.

JOURNEY OF THE MAGI

"A cold coming we had of it,
Just the worst time of the year
For a journey, and such a long journey:
The ways deep and the weather sharp,
The very dead of winter."
And the camels galled, sore-footed, refractory,
Lying down in the melting snow.
There were times we regretted
The summer palaces on slopes, the terraces,
And the silken girls bringing sherbet.
Then the camel men cursing and grumbling
And running away, and wanting their liquor and women,
And the night-fires going out, and the lack of shelters,
And the cities hostile and the towns unfriendly
And the villages dirty and charging high prices:
A hard time we had of it.
At the end we preferred to travel all night,
Sleeping in snatches,
With the voices singing in our ears, saying

That this was all folly.
Then at dawn we came down to a temperate valley,
Wet, below the snow line, smelling of vegetation;
With a running stream and a water-mill beating the darkness,
And three trees on the low sky,
And an old white horse galloped away in the meadow.
Then we came to a tavern with vine-leaves over the lintel,
Six hands at an open door dicing for pieces of silver,
And feet kicking the empty wine-skins.
But there was no information, and so we continued
And arrived at evening, not a moment too soon
Finding the place; it was (you may say) satisfactory.
All this was a long time ago, I remember,
And I would do it again, but set down
This set down
This: were we led all that way for
Birth or Death? There was a Birth, certainly,
We had evidence and no doubt. I had seen birth and death,
But had thought they were different; this Birth was
Hard and bitter agony for us, like Death, our death.
We returned to our places, these Kingdoms,
But no longer at ease here, in the old dispensation,
With an alien people clutching their gods.
I should be glad of another death.

22

EZRA POUND (1885-1972)

Ezra Pound, a great American poet-critic, is widely known for the use of imagism. He was born on 30th October, 1885 in Hailey Idaho, United States of America. He was an expatriate poet and critic, a major figure in the early Modernist Poetry Movement, especially imagism. It was Pound who perfectly edited 1400 lines of *The Waste Land* and brought to its present size of 446 lines. His poetical works are – *In a Station of the Metro* (1913) *Cathay* (1915), *Hugh Selwyn Mauberley* (1920), *The Cantos* (1925), and *Pisan Cantos* (1948). He was influenced by W.B.Yeats, Walt Whitman, Dante, and Robert Browning. He died on 1st November, 1972 in Venice, Italy.

HISTORIAN

No man hath dared to write this thing as yet,
And yet I know, how that the souls of all men great
At times pass through us,
And we are melted into them, and are not
Save reflexions of their souls.
Thus am I Dante for a space and am
One Francois Villon, ballad-lord and thief,
Or am such holy ones I may not write
Lest blasphemy be writ against my name;
This for an instant and the flame is gone.
'Tis as in midmost us there glows a sphere
Translucent, molten gold, that is the "I"
And into this some form projects itself:
Christ us, or John, or eke the Florentine;
And as the clear space is not if a form's
Imposed thereon,
So cease we from all being for the time,
And these, the Masters of the Soul, live on.

Epilogue
I bring you the spoils, my nation,
I, who went out in exile,
Am returned to thee with gifts.
I, who have labored long in the tombs
Am come back there from with riches

Behold my spices and robes, my nation,
My gifts of Tyre

Here are my rimes of the south;
Here are strange fashions of music;
Here is my knowledge
Behold, I am come with patterns

Behold, I return with devices,
Cunning the craft, cunning the work, the fashion.

THE RIVER-MERCHANT'S WIFE:
A LETTER

While my hair was still cut straight across my forehead
I played about the front gate, pulling flowers.
You came by on bamboo stilts, playing horse,
You walked about my seat, playing with blue plums.
And we went on living in the village of Chōkan:
Two small people, without dislike or suspicion.
At fourteen I married My Lord you.
I never laughed, being bashful.
Lowering my head, I looked at the wall.
Called to, a thousand times, I never looked back.

At fifteen I stopped scowling,
I desired my dust to be mingled with yours
Forever and forever, and forever.
Why should I climb the look out?

At sixteen you departed
You went into far Ku-tō-en, by the river of swirling
eddies,
And you have been gone five months.
The monkeys make sorrowful noise overhead.

You dragged your feet when you went out.
By the gate now, the moss is grown, the different
mosses,
Too deep to clear them away!
The leaves fall early this autumn, in wind.
The paired butterflies are already yellow with August
Over the grass in the West garden;

They hurt me.
I grow older.
If you are coming down through the narrows of the
river Kiang,
Please let me know beforehand,
And I will come out to meet you
As far as Chō-fū-Sa.

A PACT

I make truce with you, Walt Whitman–
I have detested you long enough.
I come to you as a grown child
Who has had a pig-headed father;
I am old enough now to make friends.
It was you that broke the new wood,
Now is a time for carving.
We have one sap and one root–
Let there be commerce between us.'

23

EDNA ST. VINCENT MILAY
(1892-1950)

Edna St. Vincent Milay was born on 22nd September, 1892 in Rockland, Maine, USA. She was an American lyrical poet and playwright. Milay was recognized as a social figure and noted feminist in the Roaring Twenties. Her parents were Henry Tollman Milay, and Cora Lounella. She studied B.A., with English Literature in Vassar College. Her collections of poems are – *Poetry Foundation* (1922), *Epstein* (2001), *Lofty Dogmas* (2005) etc. In 1923, she won the Pulitzer Prize for poetry. She died on 19th October, 1950 in Austerlitz, New York.

ASHES OF LIFE

Love has gone and left me and the days are all alike;
Eat I must, and sleep I will, — and would that night
were here!
But ah! — to lie awake and hear the slow hours strike!
Would that it were day again! — with twilight near!

Love has gone and left me and I don't know what to do;
This or that or what you will is all the same to me;
But all the things that I begin I leave before I'm through, —
There's little use in anything as far as I can see.

Love has gone and left me, — and the neighbors knock
and borrow,
And life goes on forever like the gnawing of a mouse, —
And to-morrow and to-morrow and to-morrow and to-
morrow
There's this little street and this little house.

I, BEING A WOMAN

I, being born a woman and distressed
By all the needs and notions of my kind,
Am urged by your propinquity to find
Your person fair, and feel a certain zest
To bear your body's weight upon my breast:
So subtly is the fume of life designed,
To clarify the pulse and cloud the mind,
And leave me once again undone, possessed
Think not for this, however, the poor treason
Of my stout blood against my staggering brain,
I shall remember you with love, or season
My scorn with pity,- – let me make it plain:

I find this frenzy insufficient reason
For conversation when we meet again.

CHILDHOOD IS THE KINGDOM
WHERE NOBODY DIES

Childhood is not from birth to a certain age and aat a
certain age
The child is grown, and puts away childish things.
Childhood is the kingdom where nobody dies.

Nobody that matters, that is. Distant relatives of
course
Die, whom one never has seen or has seen for an hoiur,
And they gave on candy in a pink – and – green striped
bag, or a jack-knife.
And went away, and cannot really he said to have lived
at all.

And cats die. They lie on the floor and lash their tails,
And their reticent fur is suddenly all in motion
With fleas that one never knew were there,
Polished and brown, knowing all there is to know,
Trekking off into the living world.
You fetch a shoe-box, but it's much too small, because
she wont curl up now:
So you find a bigger box, and bury her in the yard, and
weep.

But you do not wake up a month from the, two
months,
A year from then, two years . to the middle of the night
And weep, with your knuckles in your mouth, and say
Oh, God! Oh, God!

Childhood is the kingdom where nobody dies that
matters – -mothers and fathers don't die.

And if you have said," For Heaven's sake, must you
always be kissing a person?"
Or, " I do wish to gracious you'd stop tapping on the
window with your thimble!"

Tomorrow, or even the day after tomorrow if you're
busy having fun,
Is plenty of time to say," "I'm sorry, mother."

To be grown up is to sit at the table with people who
have died, who neither listen nor speak;
Who do not drink their tea, though they always said
Tea was such a comfort.

Run down into the cellar and bring up the last jar of
raspberries; they are not tempted.
Flatter them, ask them what was it they said exactly
Mrs Mason;
They are not taken in.
Shout at them, get rid in the face, rise,
Drag them up out of their chairs by their stiff
shoulders and shake them and yell at them;
They are not startled, they are not even embarrassed;
they slide back into their chairs.

Your tea is cold now.
You drink is standing up,
And leave the house.
(1934)

LOVE IS NOT ALL: IT IS NOT MEAT OR DRINK

Love is not all; it is not meat or drink
Nor slumber nor a roof against the rain;
Nor yet a floating spar to men that sink
And rise and sink and rise and sink again;
Love cannot fill the thickened lung with breath,
Nor clean the blood, nor set the fractured bone;
Yet many a man is making friends with death
Even as I speak, for lack of love alone.
It well may be that in a difficult hour,
Pinned down by pain and moaning for release,
Or nagged by want past resolution's power,
I might be driven to sell your love for peace,
Or trade the memory of this night for food.
It well may be. I do not think I would.
(1926)

I SHALL NOT FORGET YOU PRESENTLY, MY DEAR

I shall not forget you presently, my dear,
So make the most of this, your little day,
Your little mouth, your little half a year,
Ere I forget, or die, or move away.
And we are done forever; by and by
I shall forget you, as I said, but now
If you entreat me with your loveliest lie
I will protest you with my favorite vow,
I would indeed that love were longer-lived,
And vows were not so brittle as they are,
But so it is, and nature has contrived
To struggle on without a break thus for,-
Is idle, biologically speaking.
(1934)

DOROTHY PARKER (1893-1967)

Dorothy Parker was born on 22nd August, 1893 in Long Branch, New Jersey, USA. Based in New York, she was an American poet and writer of fiction, plays and screenplays. She had schooling in the Roman Catholic cemetery school; she did not have the college education. Her parents were – Jacob Henry Rothschild and Eliza Annie Rothschild. She got married to Alan Campbell. Critics state that she was influenced by Robert Benchley, Sarah Murphy and M.W. Thackeray, the great Victorian novelist. Unfortunately, she died of a heart attack on 7th January, 1967.

LOVE SONG

My own dear love, he is strong and bold
And he cares not what comes after.
His words ring sweet as a chime of gold,
And his eyes are lit with laughter.
He is jubilant as a flag unfurled —
Oh, a girl, she'd not forget him.
My own dear love, he is all my world, —
And I wish I'd never met him.

My love, he's mad, and my love, he's fleet,
And a wild young wood-thing bore him!
The ways are fair to his roaming feet,
And the skies are sunlit for him.
As sharply sweet to my heart he seems
As the fragrance of acacia.
My own dear love, he is all my dreams, —
And I wish he were in Asia.

My love runs by like a day in June,
And he makes no friends of sorrows.
He'll tread his galloping rigadoon
In the pathway of the morrows.
He'll live his days where the sunbeams start,
Nor could storm or wind uproot him.
My own dear love, he is all my heart, —
And I wish somebody'd shoot him.

INTERVIEW

The ladies men admire, I've heard,
Would shudder at a wicked word.
Their candle gives a single light;
They'd rather stay at home at night.

They do not keep awake till three,
Nor read erotic poetry.
They never sanction the impure,
Nor recognize an overture.
They shrink from powders and from paints ...
So far, I've had no complaints.

RESUMÉ

Razors pain you;
Rivers are damp;
Acids stain you;
And drugs cause cramp.
Guns aren't lawful;
Nooses give;
Gas smells awful;
You might as well live.

ONE PERFECT ROSE

A single flow'r he sent to me, since we met.
All tenderly his messenger he chose;
Deep-hearted, pure, with scented dew still wet–
One perfect rose.

I knew the language of the floweret;
"My fragile leaves, "it said," his heart enclose."
Love long has taken for his amulet
One perfect rose.

Why is it no one ever sent me yet
One perfect limousine, do you suppose?
Ah no, it's always just my luck to get
One perfect rose.

25

WILFRED OWEN (1893-1918)

Wilfred Owen, one of significant war poets, was born on 18th March, 1893 in Oswestry, United Kingdom. His parents – Harriet Susan Shaw, the mother and Thomas Owen, the father. He was educated in Local School and College. He was enlisted in the war in 1915. Many of his poems carried anti-war sentiments. His collections of poems are-*Poems of Wilfred Owen, Poems* (1920), *Collected Poems of Wilfred Owen* (1963), and *The Complete Poems and Fragments* (1991). He, being an MC, was also a soldier in the active service of war. He died of a shell shock in Craiglockhart War on 4th November, 1918 in Sambre-Oise-Canal, France.

EXPOSURE

Our brains ache, in the merciless iced east winds that
knive us...
Wearied we keep awake because the night is silent...
Low drooping flares confuse our memory of the
salient...
Worried by silence, sentries whisper, curious, nervous,
But nothing happens.

Watching, we hear the mad gusts tugging on the wire,
Like twitching agonies of men among its brambles.
Northward, incessantly, the flickering gunnery rumbles,
Far off, like a dull rumour of some other war.
What are we doing here?

The poignant misery of dawn begins to grow...
We only know war lasts, rain soaks, and clouds sag
stormy.
Dawn massing in the east her melancholy army
Attacks once more in ranks on shivering ranks of grey,
But nothing happens.

Sudden successive flights of bullets streak the silence.
Less deadly than the air that shudders black with snow,
With sidelong flowing flakes that flock, pause, and
renew,
We watch them wandering up and down the wind's
nonchalance,
But nothing happens.

Pale flakes with fingering stealth come feeling for our
faces —
We cringe in holes, back on forgotten dreams, and stare,
snow- dazed,
Deep into grassier ditches. So we drowse, sun-dozed,

Littered with blossoms trickling where the blackbird
fusses.
— Is it that we are dying?

Slowly our ghosts drag home: glimpsing the sunk fires,
glozed
With crusted dark-red jewels; crickets jingle there;
For hours the innocent mice rejoice: the house is theirs;
Shutters and doors, all closed: on us the doors are
closed, —
We turn back to our dying.

Since we believe not otherwise can kind fires burn;
Now ever suns smile true on child, or field, or fruit.
For God's invincible spring our love is made afraid;
Therefore, not loath, we lie out here; therefore were
born,
For love of God seems dying.

Tonight, this frost will fasten on this mud and us,
Shrivelling many hands, and puckering foreheads crisp.
The burying-party, picks and shovels in shaking grasp,
Pause over half-known faces. All their eyes are ice,
But nothing happens.

ANTHEM FOR DOOMED YOUTH

What passing-bells for these who die as cattle?
Only the monstrous anger of the guns.
Only the stuttering rifles' rapid rattle
Can patter out their hasty orisons.
No mockeries now for them; no prayers nor bells;
Nor any voice of mourning save the choirs, —
The shrill, demented choirs of wailing shells;
And bugles calling for them from sad shires.

What candles may be held to speed them all?
Not in the hands of boys, but in their eyes
Shall shine the holy glimmers of goodbyes.
The pallor of girls' brows shall be their pall;
Their flowers the tenderness of patient minds,
And each slow dusk a drawing-down of blinds.

STRANGE MEETING

It seemed that out of the battle I escaped
Down some profound dull tunnel, long since scooped
Through granites which Titanic wars had groined.
Yet also there encumbered sleepers groaned,
Too fast in thought or death to be bestirred.
Then, as I probed them, one sprang up, and stared
With piteous recognition in fixed eyes,
Lifting distressful hands as if to bless.
And by his smile, I knew that sullen hall;
By his dead smile I knew we stood in Hell.
With a thousand fears that vision's face was grained;
Yet no blood reached there from the upper ground,
And no guns thumped, or down the flues made moan.
'Strange, friend,' I said, 'Here is no cause to mourn.'
'None,' said the other, 'Save the undone years,
The hopelessness. Whatever hope is yours,
Was my life also; I went hunting wild
After the wildest beauty in the world,
Which lies not calm in eyes, or braided hair,
But mocks the steady running of the hour,
And if it grieves, grieves richlier than here.
For by my glee might many men have laughed,
And of my weeping something has been left,
Which must die now. I mean the truth untold,
The pity of war, the pity war distilled.
Now men will go content with what we spoiled.

Or, discontent, boil bloody, and be spilled.
They will be swift with swiftness of the tigress,
None will break ranks, though nations trek from
progress.
Courage was mine, and I had mystery;
Wisdom was mine, and I had mastery;
To miss the march of this retreating world
Into vain citadels that are not walled.
Then, when much blood had clogged their chariot-
wheels
I would go up and wash them from sweet wells,
Even with truths that lie too deep for taint.
I would have poured my spirit without stint
But not through wounds; not on the cess of war.
Foreheads of men have bled where no wounds were.
I am the enemy you killed, my friend.
I knew you in this dark; for so you frowned
Yesterday through me as you jabbed and killed.
I parried; but my hands were loath and cold.
Let us sleep now ...

WITH AN IDENTITY DISC

If ever I dreamed of my dead name
High in the heart of London, unsurpassed
By Time for ever, and the Fugitive, Fame,
There seeking a long sanctuary at last,

I better that; and recollect with shame
How once I longed to hide it from life's heats
Under those holy cypresses, the same
That shade always the quiet place of Keats,

Now rather thank I God there is no risk
Of gravers scoring it with florid screed,

But let my death be memoried on this disc.
Wear it, sweet friend. Inscribe no date nor deed.
But may thy heart-beat kiss it night and day,
Until the name grow vague and wear away.

FUTILITY

Move him into the sun —
Gently its touch awoke him once,
At home, whispering of fields half-sown.
Always it woke him, even in France,
Until this morning and this snow.
If anything might rouse him now
The kind old sun will know.

Think how it wakes the seeds —
Woke once the clays of a cold star.
Are limbs, so dear-achieved, are sides
Full-nerved, still warm, too hard to stir?
Was it for this the clay grew tall?
—O what made fatuous sunbeams toil
To break earth's sleep at all?

26

ROBERT GRAVES (1895-1985)

Robert Graves was born on 24th July, 1895 in Wimbledon, Surrey, England. He was an English poet, soldier, historical novelist and critic. His father was Alfred Perceval Graves, a celebrated Irish poet and figure in the Gaelic Revival. His mother, Elisabeth Sophie von Ronke was his father's second wife. He was educated in St John's College, Oxford. He served in the World War I. His collections of poems are – *Poems* (1925), *Poems 1930-1933* (1933), *No More Ghosts: Selected Poems* (1940), *Collected Poems 1914-1947* (1948). Being lived for 100 years, he died on 7th December, 1985 in Dela, Majorca, Spain.

A BOY IN CHURCH

'Gabble-gabble, . . . brethren, . . . gabble-gabble!'
My window frames forest and heather.
I hardly hear the tuneful babble,
Not knowing nor much caring whether
The text is praise or exhortation,
Prayer or thanksgiving, or damn
Outside it blows wetter and wetter,
The tossing trees never stay still.
I shift my elbows to catch better
The full round sweep of heathered hill.
The tortured copse bends to and fro
In silence like a shadow-show.

The parson's voice runs like a river
Over smooth rocks, I like this church:
The pews are staid, they never shiver,
They never bend or sway or lurch.
'Prayer,' says the kind voice, 'is a chain
That draws down Grace from Heaven again.'

I add the hymns up, over and over,
Until there's not the least mistake.
Seven-seventy-one. (Look! there's a plover!
It's gone!) Who's that Saint by the lake?
The red light from his mantle passes
Across the broad memorial brasses.

It's pleasant here for dreams and thinking,
Lolling and letting reason nod,
With ugly serious people linking
Sad prayers to a forgiving God . . . .
But a dumb blast sets the trees swaying
With furious zeal like madmen praying.

THE GOD CALLED POETRY

Now I begin to know at last,
These nights when I sit down to rhyme,
The form and measure of that vast
God we call Poetry, he who stoops
And leaps me through his paper hoops
A little higher every time.

Tempts me to think I'll grow a proper
Singing cricket or grass-hopper
Making prodigious jumps in air
While shaken crowds about me stare
Aghast, and I sing, growing bolder
To fly up on my master's shoulder
Rustling the thick stands of his hair.

He is older than the seas,
Older than the plains and hills,
And older than the light that spills
From the sun's hot wheel on these.
He wakes the gale that tears your trees,
He sings to you from window sills.

At you he roars, or he will coo,
He shouts and screams when hell is hot,
Riding on the shell and shot.
He smites you down, he succours you,
And where you seek him, he is not.

To-day I see he has two heads
Like Janus—calm, benignant, this;
That, grim and scowling: his beard spreads
From chin to chin: this god has power
Immeasurable at every hour:
He first taught lovers how to kiss,

He brings down sunshine after shower,
Thunder and hate are his also,
He is YES and he is NO.

The black beard spoke and said to me,
'Human frailty though you be,
Yet shout and crack your whip, be harsh!
They'll obey you in the end:
Hill and field, river and marsh
Shall obey you, hop and skip
At the terror of your whip,
To your gales of anger bend.'

The pale beard spoke and said in turn
'True: a prize goes to the stern,
But sing and laugh and easily run
Through the wide airs of my plain,
Bathe in my waters, drink my sun,
And draw my creatures with soft song;
They shall follow you along
Graciously with no doubt or pain.'

Then speaking from his double head
The glorious fearful monster said
'I am YES and I am NO,
Black as pitch and white as snow,
Love me, hate me, reconcile
Hate with love, perfect with vile,
So equal justice shall be done
And life shared between moon and sun.
Nature for you shall curse or smile:
A poet you shall be, my son.'

27

EDMUND BLUNDEN (1896-1974)

Edmund Blunden, CBE MC, was born on 1st November, 1896 in London, United Kingdom. He was an English poet, author and critic. Like his friend Siegfried Sassoon, he also wrote poems out of his experiences of fighting in the World War I. His parents were Charles Blunden and Georgina Margaret, both teachers at Yalding School. He studied in Maidstone Grammar School, Merton College and later in University of Oxford, Oxford. He got married Mary Daines. He ended as the Professor of Poetry at the University of Oxford. His collections of poems are-*Poems 1913and 1914(1914)*, *Three Poems* (194), *The Harbingers* (1916), *Poems 1930-1940* (1940), *Poems of Many Years* (1957), and *Poems from Japan* (1967). He died on 20th January,1974 in Long Melford, United Kingdom.

FESTUBERT, 1916

Tired with dull grief, grown old before my day,
I sit in solitude and only hear
Long silent laughters, murmurings of dismay,
The lost intensities of hope and fear;
In those old marshes yet the rifles lie,
On the thin breastwork flutter the grey rags,
The very books I read are there—and I
Dead as the men I loved, wait while life drags

Its wounded length from those sad streets of war
Into green places here, that were my own;
But now what once was mine is mine no more,
I seek such neighbours here and I find none.
With such strong gentleness and tireless will
Those ruined houses seared themselves in me,
Passionate I look for their dumb story still,
And the charred stub outspeaks the living tree.

I rise up at the singing of a bird
And scarcely knowing slink along the lane,
I dare not give a soul a look or word
For all have homes and none's at home in vain:
Deep red the rose burned in the grim redoubt,
The self-sown wheat around was like a flood,
In the hot path the lizards lolled time out,
The saints in broken shrines were bright as blood.

Sweet Mary's shrine between the sycamores!
There we would go, my friend of friends and I,
And snatch long moments from the grudging wars;
Whose dark made light intense to see them by ...
Shrewd bit the morning fog, the whining shots
Spun from the wrangling wire; then in warm swoon

The sun hushed all but the cool orchard plots,
We crept in the tall grass and slept till noon.

HARVEST

So there's my year, the twelvemonth duly told
Since last I climbed this brow and gloated round
Upon the lands heaped with their wheaten gold,
And now again they spread with wealth imbrowned –
And thriftless I meanwhile,
What honeycombs have I to take, what sheaves to pile?

I see some shrivelled fruits upon my tree,
And gladly would self-kindness feign them sweet;
The bloom smelled heavenly, can these stragglers be
The fruit of that bright birth and this wry wheat,
Can this be from those spires
Which I, or fancy, saw leap to the spring sun's fires?

I peer, I count, but anxious is not rich,
My harvest is not come, the weeds run high;
Even poison-berries, ramping from the ditch
Have stormed the undefended ridges by;
What Michaelmas is mine!
The fields I sought to serve, for sturdier tillage pine.

But hush – Earth's valleys sweet in leisure lie;
And I among them wandering up and down
Will taste their berries, like the bird or fly,
And of their gleanings make both feast and crown.
The Sun's eye laughing looks.
And Earth accuses none that goes among her stooks.

THE SURVIVAL

To-day's house makes to-morrow's road;
I knew these heaps of stone
When they were walls of grace and might,
The country's honour, art's delight
That over fountain'd silence show'd-9
Fame's final bastion.
Inheritance has found fresh work,
Disunion union breeds;
Beauty the strong, its difference lost,
Has matter fit for flood and frost.
Here's the true blood that will not shirk
Life's new-commanding needs.
With curious costly zeal, O man,
Raise ornery and ode;
How shines your tower, the only one
Of that especial site and stone!
And even the dream's confusion can
Sustain to-morrow's road.

FOREFATHERS

Here they went with smock and crook,
Toiled in the sun, lolled in the shade,
Here they mudded out the brook
And here their hatchet cleared the glade:
Harvest-supper woke their wit,
Huntsmen's moon their wooings lit.

From this church they led their brides,
From this church themselves were led
Shoulder-high; on these waysides

Sat to take their beer and bread.
Names are gone – what men they were
These their cottages declare.

Names are vanished, save the few
In the old brown Bible scrawled;
These were men of pith and thew,
Whom the city never called;
Scarce could read or hold a quill,
Built the barn, the forge, the mill.

On the green they watched their sons
Playing till too dark to see,
As their fathers watched them once,
As my father once watched me;
While the bat and beetle flew
On the warm air webbed with dew.

Unrecorded, unrenowned,
Men from whom my ways begin,
Here I know you by your ground
But I know you not within –
There is silence, there survives
Not a moment of your lives.

Like the bee that now is blown
Honey-heavy on my hand,
From his toppling tansy-throne
In the green tempestuous land –
I'm in clover now, nor know
Who made honey long ago.

28

LOUSIE BOGAN (1897-1970)

Lousie Bogan was born on 11th August, 1897 in Livermore Falls, Maine, USA. She was the wife of the famous poet Theodore Roethke. Her parents helped her to look after her daughter. She attended Mount St Mary's Academy and Girls' Latin School for five years and later Boston University. She began writing poetry at an early age. She got married to Curt Alexander who died of pneumonia in 1920. Her collections of poems are – *Body of this Death: Poems* (1923), *Collected Poems 1923-1953* (1954), *The Blue Estuaries:Poems 1923-1968* (1968. In 1955, She got the Bollingen Prize for poetry. She was appointed and the fourth Poet Laureate to the Library of Congress in 1945. She was the first woman to hold this title. She died on 4th February, 1970 in New York, USA.

THE DAEMON

Must I tell you again
In the words I know
For the ears of men
The flesh, the blow?

Must I show outright
The bruise in the side,
The halt in the night,
And how death cried?

Must I speak to the lot
Who little bore?
It said *why not?*
It said *Once more.*

MEDUSA

I had come to the house, in a circle f trees,
Facing a sheer sky
Everything moved,-a bell hung ready to strike,
Sun and reflection wheeled by.

When the bare eyes were before me
and the hissing hair
Held up at a window, seen through the door,
the stiff bald eyes, the serpents on the forehead
Formed in the air.

This is a dead scene forever now.
Nothing will ever stir.
The end will never brighten it more than this,
Nor the rain blur.

The water will always fall, and will not fall,
And the tipped bell make no sound
The grass will always be growing for hay
Deep on the ground.

And I shall stand here like a shadow
Under the great balanced day,
My eyes on the yellow dust, that was lifting in this wind,
And does not drift away.

WOMEN

Women have no wilderness in them,
They are provident instead,
Content in the tight hot cell of their hearts
To eat dusty bread.

They do not see cattle cropping red winter grass,
They do not hear
Snow water going down under culverts
Shallow and clear.

They wait, when they should turn to journeys,
They stiffen, when they should bend.
They use against themselves that benevolence
To which no man is friend.

They cannot think of so many crops to a field
Or of clean wood cleft by an axe.
Their love is an eager meaninglessness
Too tense, or too lax.

They hear in every whisper that speaks to them
A shout and a cry.
As like as not, when they take life over their door-sills
They should let it go by.

SONG FOR THE LAST ACT

Now that I have your face by heart, I look
Less at its features than its darkening frame
Where quince and melon, yellow as young flame,
Lie with quilted dahlias and the shepherd's crook.
Beyond, a garden. There, in insolent ease
The lead and marble figures watch the show
Of yet another summer loath to go
Although the scythes hang in the apple trees.

Now that I have your face by heart, I look.

Now that I have your voice by heart, I read
In the black chords upon a dulling page
Music that is not meant for music's cage,
Whose emblems mix with words that shake and bleed.
The staves are shuttled over with a stark
Unprinted silence. In a double dream
I must spell out the storm, the running stream.
The beat's too swift. The notes shift in the dark.

Now that I have your voice by heart, I read.

Now that I have your heart by heart, I see
The wharves with their great ships and architraves;
The rigging and the cargo and the slaves
On a strange beach under a broken sky.
not departure, but a voyage done!

The bales stand on the stone; the anchor weeps
Its red rust downward, and the long vine creeps
Beside the salt herb, in the lengthening sun.

Now that I have your heart by heart, I see.

29

E.E.CUMMINGS (1894-1962)

E.E.Cummings was born on 14th October, 1894, in Cambridge, Massachusetts. Having studied in Cambridge school and Latin School, he later enrolled in Harvard University. He did his B.A. with English Literature and Classics. During the war, he did some odd jobs for some years. His father had a teaching position before becoming a Unitarian minister. In 1924, he married Elaine Orr, wife of his friend and begot daughter named Nancy. Most known is his collection of poems *Eimi* (1933). He died on 3rd September, 1962, after widely travelling in Spain, Italy and Greece.

SINCE FEELING IS FIRST

since feeling is first
who pays any attention
to the syntax of things
will never wholly kiss you;

wholly to be a fool
while Spring is in the world

my blood approves,
and kisses are a better fate
than wisdom
lady I swear by all flowers. Don't cry
– the best gesture of my brain is less than
your eyelids' flutter which says

we are for each other; then
laugh, leaning back in my arms
for life's not a paragraph

And death I think is no parenthesis

THE BIGNESS OF CANNON

the bigness of cannon
is skilful,

but i have seen
death's clever enormous voice
which hides in a fragility
of poppies. . . .

i say that sometimes
on these long talkative animals
are laid fists of huger silence.

I have seen all the silence
filled with vivid noiseless boys

at Roupy
i have seen
between barrages,

the night utter ripe unspeaking girls.

IN JUST-

in just
spring hen the world is mud
luscious the little
lame baloonman

whistles far and wee

and eddiandbill come
running from marbles and
piracies and it's
spring
when the world is puddle-wonderful

the queer
the old balloonman whistles
far and wee
and betty and isabel come dancing

from hop-scotch and jump-rope and
it's

spring
and
the

goat-footed

ballooonMan whistles
far
and
wee
(1923)

MEVIN B.TOLSON (1898-1966)

Melvin B. Tolson was an American poet, columnist, politician, and educator. He was born on 6th February, 1898 in Moberly, Missouri. As a poet he was influenced by the modernism and language experiences of Africa. He was debate coach in Wily College, in Marshall, Texas. His parents were Rev., Alonzo and Lera Ann Hurt Tolson. He studied in Fisk University, Lincoln University and Columbia University. His collections of poems-*Harlem Gallery: Book One*, *The Curator* (1965), *Libretto for the Republic of Liberia* (1953), *Rendezvous with America* (1963). At the age of 68, he died on 29th August, 1966 in Dallas, Texas, United States of America.

THE SEA-TURTLE AND THE SHARK

Strange but true is the story
of the sea-turtle and the shark – the instinctive drive of
the weak to survive in the oceanic dark.
Driven,
driven by hunger from abyss to shoal, sometime the
shark swallows the sea-turtle whole.
The sly reptilian marine
withdraw, into the shell of his undersea craft,
his leathery head and the rapacious claws
that can rip a rhinoceros' hide or strip a crocodile to
fare-thee-well;
now inside the shark,
the sea-turtle begins the churning seesaw
of his decent into pelagic hell;
then...then with ravenous jaws that cut sheet steel
scrap,
the sea-turtle gnaws...and gnaws...and gnaws...his
way to freedom,
beyond the vomiting dark, beyond the stomach walls
of the shark.

THE BIRTH OF JOHN HENRY

The night John Henry is born
an ax of lightning splits the sky,
and a hammer of thunder pounds the earth,
and the eagles and panthers cry!

John Henry-he says to his Ma and Pa:
"Get a gallon of barleycorn.
I want to start right, like a he-man child,
the night that I am born!"

Says: "I want some ham hocks, ribs, and jowls,
a pot of cabbage and greens;
some hoecakes, jam, and buttermilk,   -
a platter of pork and beans!"

John Henry's Ma-she wrings her hands,
and his Pa-he scratches his head.
John Henry-he curses in giraffe-tall words,
flops over, and kicks down the bed.

He's burning mad, like a bear on fire-
so he tears to the riverside.
As he stoops to drink, Old Man River gets scared
and runs upstream to hide!

Some say he was born in Georgia-O Lord!
Some say in Alabam.
But it's writ on the rock at the Big Bend Tunnel:
"Lousyana was my home, So scram"!!!!!!

UNCLE RUFUS

The Harlem Advocate fell between his legs.
The story was incredible!
Taking off his glasses,
Uncle Rufus rubbed the lenses and thought…though.

Yes, his son had always been a prodigal son,
Drinking home brew and chasing sin-loving women
And staying away from church at revival times.

Then he had gone to Selma, Alabama,
With that Blackwood woman
Who had lived with a dozen different sweet men.

The Harlem Advocate said
Eddie had cut up the Blackwood woman in a dance hall;
And when the jury had found him guilty
He'd struck a prosecuting attorney in the jaw;
And it had taken the jurors and a deputy sheriff
To pin him to the floor and handcuff him.

Uncle Rufus bowed his head and groaned.
He remembered now that people used to say
Eddie was a little off...a little off.

"De boy musta been crazy," Uncle Rufus mused aloud,
"Yes, he musta been crazy...
Him hittin' a white lawyah
In a white man's courthouse,
Befor' a white jedge an' a white jury
Down in Alabama"...

31

LAURA (RIDING) JACKSON
(1900-1991)

Laura Jackson was born in New York city on 16th January,1900. Her original name was Laura Reichenthal. Her resentment against her Marxist father, she favoured poetry to politics. In 1918, she joined Cornell University and got married to Louis Gottschalk and also changed her name to Laura Gottschalk in 1923. Her first collection, *The Close Couplet* (1926) came out well and wrote *A Survey of Modernist Poetry* with Robert Graves. Her *Collected Poems* was published in 1938. In 1991, she received the Bollinger Prize for her lifetime contribution to American poetry.

VOCABLES OF LOVE

Vocables of love,
zones of dreamt responses
Where wing on wing folds in
The negro centuries of sleep
And the thick lips compress
Compediums of silence...

Throats claw the mirror blind triumph,
Eyes pursue sight into the heart of terror.
Call within call
Succumbs to the indistinguishable
Wall within wall
Embracing the last crushed vocable,
The spoken unity of efforts.

vocables of love,
The end of an end is an echo,
A last cry follows a last cry
Finality of finality
Is perfection's touch of folly.
Ruin unfolds from ruin.
A remnant breeds a universe of fragment.
Horizons spread intelligibility
And once more it is yesterday.

TAKE HANDS

Take hands.
There is no love now.
But there are hands.
There is no joining now,
But a joining has been
Of the fastening of fingers

And their opening.
More than the clasp even, the kiss
Speaks loneliness,
How we dwell apart,
And how love triumphs in this.

DEATH AS DEATH

To conceive death as death
Is difficulty come by easily,
A blankness fallen among
Images of understanding.
Death like a quick cold hand
On the hot slow head of suicide
So is it come by easily
For one instant. Then again furnaces
Roar in the ears, then again hell revolves,
And the elastic eye holds paradise
At visible length from blindness,
And dazedly the body echoes
"Like this, like this, like nothing else."

Like nothing – a similarity
Without resemblance. The prophetic eye,
Closing upon difficulty,
Halving the actuality
As a gift too plain, for which
Gratitude has no language,
Foresight no vision.

32

LANGSTON HUGHES (1901-1967)

Langston Hughes was born on 1st February, 1902 in Joplin, Missouri. He studied in Central High School and college in Cleveland. He attended B.A., in Lincoln University and M.A. in Columbia University. He had a poor relationship with his father whom he rarely saw. His first collection of poems *Weary Blues* was published in 1926. *Fine Clothes to the Jew* (1922), *Dear Lovely Death* (1932) and *Lenin* (1946) are his other collections. He was an Afro-American poet, playwright, short story writer and novelist of high order. He died on 22nd May, 1967 in Stuyvesant Polyclinic.

THE NEGRO SPEAKS OF RIVERS

I've known rivers:
I've known rivers ancient as the world and older than
the flow of human blood in human veins.

My soul has grown deep like the rivers.

I bathed in the Euphrates when dawns were young.
I built my hut near the Congo and it lulled me to sleep.
I looked upon the Nile and raised the pyramids above it.
I heard the singing of the Mississippi when Abe Lincoln
went down to New Orleans, and I've seen its muddy
bosom turn all golden in the sunset.

I've known rivers:
Ancient, dusky rivers.

My soul has grown deep like the rivers.

BALLAD OF THE LANDLORD

Landlord, landlord,
My roof has sprung a leak.
Don't you 'member I told you about it
Way last week? Landlord, landlord,
These steps is broken down.
When you come up yourself
It's a wonder you don't fall down.
Ten Bucks you say I owe you?
Ten Bucks you say is due?
Well, that's Ten Bucks more'n I'll pay you
Till you fix this house up new.
What? You gonna get eviction orders?
You gonna cut off my heat?

You gonna take my furniture and
Throw it in the street? Um-huh!
You talking high and mighty.
Talk on — till you get through.
You ain't gonna be able to say a word
If I land my fist on you.

Police! Police!
Come and get this man!
He's trying to ruin the government
And overturn the land!

Copper's Whistle!
Patrol bell!
Arrest

Precinct Station
Iron cell
Headlines in press:

MAN THREATENS LANDLORD

TENANT HELD NO BAIL

JUDGE GIVES NEGRO 90 DAYS IN COUNTY JAIL

NECESSITY

Work?
I don't have to do nothing
but eat, drink, stay black, and die.
This little old furnished room's
so small I can't whip a cat
without getting fur in my mouth
and my landlady's so old

her features is all run together
and God knows she sure can overcharge—
Which is why I reckon I *does*
have to work after all.

I, TOO

I, too, sing America.

I am the darker brother.
They send me to eat in the kitchen
When company comes,
But I laugh,
And eat well,
And grow strong.

Tomorrow,
I'll be at the table
When company comes.
Nobody'll dare
Say to me,
"Eat in the kitchen,"
Then.

Besides,
They'll see how beautiful I am
And be ashamed —
I, too, am America.

NOTE ON COMMERCIAL THEATRE

You've taken my blues and gone —
You sing 'em on Broadway
And you sing 'em in Hollywood Bowl,

And you mixed 'em up with symphonies
And you fixed 'em
So they don't sound like me.
Yep, you done taken my blues and gone.

You also took my spirituals and gone.
You put me in Macbeth and Carmen Jones
And all kinds of Swing Mikados
And in everything but what's about me —
But someday somebody'll
Stand up and talk about me,
And write about me —
Black and beautiful —
And sing about me,
And put on plays about me!
I reckon it'll be
Me myself!

Yes, it'll be me.

HARLEM

What happens to a dream deferred?
Doers it dry up
like a raisin in the sun?
Or fester like a sore-
And then run?
Does it stink like rotten meat?
Or crust and sugar over-
like a syrupy sweet?

May be just sags
like a heavy load.

Or does it explode?

33

OGDEN NASH (1902-1971)

Ogden Nash (1902-1971) was born in a prominent Southern family on 19th August,1902. After attending St George School, he enrolled at Harvard University in 1920 but he had to discontinue due to financial problems. He drifted through several odd jobs and became publicist for Doubleday Page publishing house, and thereby he began to write poetry seriously. *Hard Lines* (1931) was his first collection of poems. *Free Wheeling* (1932), *Happy Days* (1933), *The Primrose Path* (1935) and *I'm a Stranger Here Myself* (1938) are his other collections; he went on writing in 1950s and 1960s. At the age of 69, he died in Baltimore on 19th May, 1971.

THE TROUBLE WITH WOMEN IS MEN

A husband is man who two minutes after his head
touches the pillow is snoring like an overloaded
omnibus.
Particularly on those occasions when between the
humidity and the mosquitoes your own bed is no
sensitive to the faintest gleam.
But if by any chance you are asleep and he wakeful, he
is not slow to rouse you with the complaint that he
can't close his eyes, what about slipping downstairs
and freezing him a cooling dish of pistachio ice
cream.
His touch with a bottle opener is sure,
But he cannot help you get a tight dress over your head
without catching those hooks and a button in your
coiffure. Nor can he so much as wash his ears without
leaving an
inch of water on the bathroom linoleum,
But if you mention it you evoke not a promise to splash
no more but a mood of deep melancholium.
Indeed each time he transgresses your chance of
correcting his faults grows lesser,
Because he produces either a maddingly logical
explanation or a look of martyrdom which leaves you
instead of him feeling the remorse of the
transgressor.
Such are husbandly foibles, but there are moments
when a foible ceases to be a foible.
Next time you ask for a glass of water and when he
brings it to you have a needle almost threaded and
instead of setting it down he stands there holding it
out to you, just kick him fairly hard in the stomach,
you will find it thoroughly enjoyable.

I MUST TELL YOU ABOUT MY NOVEL

My grandpa wasn't salty,
No hero he of fable,
His English wasn't faulty,
He wore a coat at table.
His character lacked the color
Of either saint or satyr,
His life was rather duller
Than that of Walter Pater.

Look at Grandpa, take a look!
How can I write a book!

His temper wan't crusty,
He shone not forth majestic
For barroom exploits lusty,
Or tyranny domestic.
He swung not on the gallows
But went to his salvation
While toasting stale marshmallows,
His only dissipation.

Look at Grandpa, take a look!
How can I write a book!

My Uncle John was cautious,
He never slipped his anchor,
His probity was nauseous,
In fact he was a banker.
He hubbed no hubba hubbas,
And buckled he no swashes,
He wore a pair of rubbers
Inside of his galoshes.

Look at my uncle, a look!
How can I write a book!

My other uncle, Herbie,
Just once enlarged his orbit,
The day he crushed his derby
While cheering James J.Corbett.
No toper he, or wencher,
He backed nor horse nor houri,
His racist adventure
A summons to the jury.

Look at my uncles, take a look!
How can I write a book!

Round my ancestral menfolk,
There hangs no spicy aura,
I have no racy kinfolk
From Rome or Gloccamora.
Not nitwits, not Napoleons,
The mill they were the run of,
My family weren't Mangolians;
Then whom can I make fun of ?

Look!
No book!   (1949)

34

CECIL DAY LEWIS (1904-1972)

Cecil Day Lewis, CBE, was born on 27th April,1904 in Ballintubert, Ireland. He was an Anglo-Irish poet and the Poet Laureate of England from 1968 till his death in 1972. He was educated in Sherborne School and later in Wadham College, Oxford in 1946. Being a lecturer in Cambridge University, he married Jill Balcon in 1951. Divorcing her, he remarried Constance Mary King in 1928. His collections of poems are – *Malice in the Wonderland* (1940), *The Beast Must Die* (1952), *This Man Must Die* (1969) , *The Dreadful Hollow* (1953), *The Widow's Cruise* (1959), and *The Sad Variety* (1964). A the age of 68, he died on 22nd May, 1972 in Lemmons, Barnet, United Kingdom.

WINTER NIGHT

This evening holds her breath
And makes a crystal pause;
The streams of light are frozen,
Shining above their source.

Now if ever might one
Break through the sensual gate;
Seraph's wing glimpse far-glinting.
Is it, is it too late?

We look up at the sky
Yes, it is mirror clear;
Too well we recognise
The physiognomy there.

Friend, let us look at earth,
Be stubborn, act and sleep.
Here at our feet the skull
Keeps a stiff upper lip;

Feeling the weight of winter,
Grimaces underground;
But does not need to know
Why spirit was flesh-bound.

ELEGY BEFORE DEATH

Come to the orangery. Sit down awhile,
The sun is setting; the verandah frames
An illuminated leaf of Italy.
Gold and green and blue, stroke upon stroke,
Seem to tell what nature and man could make of it

If only their marriage were made in heaven. But see
Even as we hold the picture,
The colors are fading already, the lines collapsing
Fainting into the dream they will soon be.

Again? Again we are baffled who have sought
So long in a melting Now the formula
Of Always. There is no fast dye. Always?-
That is the word the sirens sing
On bone island. Oh, stop your ears, and stop
All this vain peering wherein we change and ripen,
And never mind for what. Let us even embrace
The shadows wheeling away our windfall days.

Again again again, the frogs are screeling
Down by the lily pond. Listen! I'll echo them—
gain gain gain... Could we compel
One grain of one vanishing moment to deliver
Its golden ghost, loss would be gain,
And Love step naked from illusion's shell.
Did we but dare to see it,
All things to us, you and I to each other,
Stand in this naked potency of farewell.

ADDRESS TO THE MOTHER

This was your world and this I owe you–
Room for growing, a site for building,
The braced sinew, the hands agreeing
Mind foreseeing and serve for facing.
You were my world, my breath, my seasons,
Where blood ran easy and springs failed
Kind was clover to feet exploring
A broad earth and all to discover.
Simple that world of two dimensions,

of stone mansions and good examples;
each image actual, nearness was no
Fear, and distance without a mirage.
Dawn like a greyhound leapt the hilltops,
A million leaves held up the noonday,
Evening was slow with bells pealing,
And night compelling to breast and pillow.
That was my world-Oh, this you gave me-
Safety for seed, petal uncured there;
Love asked no proving or price, a country
Sunny for play, for spring maneuvers.

Woman, ask no more of me,
Chill not the blood with jealous feud;
This is a separate country now;
Will pay respects but no tribute.
Demand no atavistic rites,
Preference in trade or tithe of grain;
Bound by the limiting matrix I
Increased you once, will not again.
My vision's patented, my plant
Set up, my constitution whole;
New fears, old tunes cannot induce
Nostalgia of the sickly soul.
Would you prolong your day, transfuse
Young blood into your veins? Beware
Lest one oppressed by autumn's weight
May thrill to feel death in the air.
Lest love be like a natural day
That folds her work and takes to bed;
Ploughland and tree stand out in black,
Enough memorial for the dead.

35

WILLIAM EMPSON (1906-1984)

He was born on 27th September, 1906 in Yokefleet, United Kingdom. Arthur Reginald Empson and Laura Mickelthwait were his parents. He was educated in Winchester school and Trinity College, Cambridge and did his B.A., and M.A., 1912 and 1815 respectively. He married Hetta and lived 1941-1984. He was a Professor English at various universities in the U.K., and the Far East and the noted writer for *Seven Types of Ambiguity*, an influential piece of literary criticism. He was most influential a critic known for the practice of close reading literary works. He believes in concentrating much meaning into few words. *Missing Dates* was written while he was teaching in China. At age of 78 he died on 15th April, 1984 in London.

MISSING DATES

Slowly the poison the whole blood stream fills.
It is not the effort nor the failure tires.
The waste remains, the waste remains and kills.

It is not your system or clear sight that mills
Down small to the consequence a life requires;
Slowly the poison the whole blood stream fills.

They bled an old dog dry yet the exchange rills
Of young dog blood gave but a month's desire.
The waste remains, the waste remains and kills.

It is the Chinese tombs and the slag hills
Usurp the soil, and not the soil retires.
Slowly the poison the whole blood stream fills.

Not to have fire is to be a skin that shrills.
The complete fire is death. From partial fires
The waste remains, the waste remains and kills.

It is the poems you have lost, the ills
From missing dates, at which the heart expires.
The waste remains, the waste remains and kills.
Slowly the poison the whole blood stream fills.

BACCHUS III

The god who fled down with a standard yard
(Surveying with that reed which was his guard
He showed St. John, the New Jerusalem;
It was a sugarcane containing rum
And hence the fire on which those works depend)
Taught and quivered strung upon the bend

An outmost crystal a recumbent flame
(He drinks all cups the tyrant could acclaim;
He still is dumb, illimitably wined,
Burns still his nose and liver for mankind)
It is an ether, such an agony.
In the thin choking air of Caucasus
He under operation lies forever
Smelling the chlorine in the chloroform.
The pains around him flood with the destroyers
Pasturing the stallions in the standing corn.

36

JOHN BETJEMAN (1906-1984)

John Betjeman, CBE, was born on 28th August, 1906 in London, United Kingdom. He was an English poet, writer, and broadcaster. His parents Mabel and Earnest Betjeman. He studied in High Gate School and later Marlborough College, London. He married Penelope Chetwode in 1933 and lived with her 1984. His collections of poems are – *Mount Zion* (1933), *Collected Poems* (1958), *High and Low* (1966), *A Nip in the Air* (1974), *Uncollected Poems* (1981). He was the Poet Laureate from 1972 to 1984 and was a founding member of the Victorian Society. On 19th May, 1984 he died in Trebetherick, United Kingdom and buried in St Enodoc Church Trebetherick, United Kingdom.

A SHROPSHIRE LAD

The gas was on in the Institute,
The flare was up in the gym,
A man was running a mineral line,
A lass was singing a hymn,
When Captain Webb the Dawley man,
Captain Webb from Dawley,
Came swimming along the old canal
That carried the bricks to Lawley.
Swimming along –
Swimming along –
Swimming along from Severn,
And paying a call at Dawley Bank while swimming
along to Heaven.

The sun shone low on the railway line
And over the bricks and stacks
And in at the upstairs windows
Of the Dawley houses' backs
When we saw the ghost of Captain Webb,
Webb in a water sheeting,
Come dripping along in a bathing dress
To the Saturday evening meeting.
Dripping along –
Dripping along –
To the Congregational Hall;
Dripping and still he rose over the sill and faded away
in a wall.

There wasn't a man in Oakengates
That hadn't got hold of the tale,
And over the valley in Ironbridge,
And round by Coalbrookdale,
How Captain Webb the Dawley man,
Captain Webb from Dawley,

Rose rigid and dead from the old canal
That carries the bricks to Lawley.
Rigid and dead –
Rigid and dead –
To the Saturday congregation,
Paying a call at Dawley Bank on the way to his
destination.

IN WESTMINSTER ABBEY

Let me take this other glove off
As the vox humana swells,
And the beauteous fields of Eden
Bask beneath the Abbey bells.
Here, where England's statesmen lie,
Listen to a lady's cry.

Gracious Lord, oh bomb the Germans,
Spare their women for Thy Sake,
And if that is not too easy
We will pardon Thy Mistake.
But, gracious Lord, whate'er shall be,
Don't let anyone bomb me.

Keep our Empire undismembered
Guide our Forces by Thy Hand,
Gallant blacks from far Jamaica,
Honduras and Togoland;
Protect them Lord in all their fights,
And, even more, protect the whites.

Think of what our Nation stands for,
Books from Boots' and country lanes,
Free speech, free passes, class distinction,
Democracy and proper drains.

Lord, put beneath Thy special care
One-eighty-nine Cadogan Square.

Although dear Lord I am a sinner,
I have done no major crime;
Now I'll come to Evening Service
Whensoever I have the time.
So, Lord, reserve for me a crown,
And do not let my shares go down.

I will labour for Thy Kingdom,
Help our lads to win the war,
Send white feathers to the cowards
Join the Women's Army Corps,
Then wash the steps around Thy Throne
In the Eternal Safety Zone.

Now I feel a little better,
What a treat to hear Thy Word,
Where the bones of leading statesmen
Have so often been interr'd.
And now, dear Lord, I cannot wait
Because I have a luncheon date.

BUSINESS GIRLS

From the geyser ventilators
Autumn winds are blowing down
On a thousand business women
Having baths in Camden Town

Waste pipes chuckle into runnels,
Steam's escaping here and there,
Morning trains through Camden cutting
Shake the Crescent and the Square.

Early nip of changeful autumn,
Dahlias glimpsed through garden doors,
At the back precarious bathrooms
Jutting out from upper floors;

And behind their frail partitions
Business women lie and soak,
Seeing through the draughty skylight
Flying clouds and railway smoke.

Rest you there, poor unbelov'd ones,
Lap your loneliness in heat.
All too soon the tiny breakfast,
Trolley-bus and windy street.

THE OLYMPIC GIRL

The sort of girl I like to see
Smiles down from her great height at me.
She stands in strong, athletic pose
And wrinkles her retroussé nose.
Is it distaste that makes her frown,
So furious and freckled, down
On an unhealthy worm like me?
Or am I what she likes to see?
I do not know, though much I care,
.....would I were
(Forgive me, shade of Rupert Brooke)
An object fit to claim her look.
Oh! would I were her racket press'd
With hard excitement to her breast
And swished into the sunlit air
Arm-high above her tousled hair,
And banged against the bounding ball

"Oh! Plung!" my tauten'd strings would call,
"Oh! Plung! my darling, break my strings
For you I will do brilliant things."
And when the match is over, I
Would flop beside you, hear you sigh;
And then with what supreme caress,
You'd tuck me up into my press.
Fair tigress of the tennis courts,
So short in sleeve and strong in shorts,
Little, alas, to you I mean,
For I am bald and old and green.

37

W.H. AUDEN (1907-1973)

Born on 21st February, 1907, Wystan Hugh Auden attended St.Edmund School in Hindhead; then, he moved to Gresham School in Norfolk, where he began to write poetry. He attended Christ Church College at Oxford. After the graduation he moved to Berlin. In 1939, Auden left England to America. *The Shield of Achilles* (1955) is the most popular collection of poems. In his best of the poems, his extraordinary intelligence never detaches from his emotions. The poems have imaginative brilliance and penetrating candor. W.H.Auden is the most famous Anglo-American poet widely known for his leftist inclination.

FUNERAL BLUES

Stop all the clocks, cut off the telephones,
Prevent the dog from barking with a juicy bone,
Silence the pianos and with muffled drum
Bring out the coffin, let the mourners come.

Let aero planes circle moaning overhead
Scribbling on the sky the message He Is dead
Put crepe bows round the white necks of the public doves,
Let the traffic policemen wear black cotton gloves.

He was my north, my South, my East and West
My working week and my Sunday rest,
My noon, my midnight, my talk, my song;
I thought that love would last forever: I was wrong.

The stars are not wanted now: put out everyone;
Pack up the moon and dismantle the sun;
Pour away the ocean and sweep up the wood;
For nothing now can ever come to any good.

CONSIDER THIS AND IN OUR TIME

As the hawk sees it or the helmeted airman:
The clouds rift suddenly – look there
At cigarette-end smoldering on a border
At the first garden party of the year.
Pass on, admire the view of the massif
Through plate-glass windows of the Sport hotel;
Join there the insufficient units
Dangerous, easy, in furs, in uniform
And constellated at reserved tables
Supplied with feelings by an efficient band

Relayed elsewhere to farmers and their dogs
Sitting in kitchens in the stormy fens.

Long ago, supreme Antagonist,
More powerful than the great northern whale
Ancient and sorry at life's limiting defect,
In Cornwall, Mendip, or the Pennine moor
Your comments on the highborn mining-captains,
Found they no answer, made them wish to die
– Lie since in barrows out of harm.
You talk to your admirers every day
By silted harbours, derelict works,
In strangled orchard, and the silent comb
Where dogs have worried or a bird was shot.
Order the ill that they attack at once:
Visit the ports and, interrupting
The leisurely conversation in the bar
Within a stone's throw of the sunlit water,
Beckon your chosen out. Summon
Those handsome and diseased youngsters, those
women
Your solitary agents in the country parishes;
And mobilize the powerful forces latent
In soils that make the farmer brutal
In the infected sinus, and the eyes of stoats.
Then, ready, start your rumour, soft
But horrifying in its capacity to disgust
Which, spreading magnified, shall come to be
A polar peril, a prodigious alarm,
Scattering the people, as torn up paper
Rags and utensils in a sudden gust,
Seized with immeasurable neurotic dread.

Financier, leaving your little room
Where the money is made but not spent,
You'll need your typist and your boy no more;

The game is up for you and for the others,
Who, thinking, pace in slippers on the lawns
Of College Quad or Cathedral Close,
Who are born nurses, who live in shorts
Sleeping with people and playing fives.
Seekers after happiness, all who follow
The convolutions of your simple wish,
It is later than you think; nearer that day
Far other than that distant afternoon
Amid rustle of frocks and stamping feet
They gave the prizes to the ruined boys.
You cannot be away, then, no
Not though you pack to leave within an hour,
Escaping humming down arterial roads:
The date was yours; the prey to fugues,
Irregular breathing and alternate ascendancies
After some haunted migratory years
To disintegrate on an instant in the explosion of mania
Or lapse for ever into a classic fatigue.

IN MEMORY OF W.B.YEATS

(d. January 1939)
I

He disappeared in the dead of winter:
The brooks were frozen, the airports almost deserted,
And snow disfigured the public statues;
The mercury sank in the mouth of the dying day.
` What instruments we have agree
The day of his death was a dark cold day.
Far from his illness
The wolves ran on through the evergreen forests,
The peasant river was untempted by the fashionable
quays;

By mourning tongues
The death of the poet was kept from his poems.
But for him it was his last afternoon as himself,
An afternoon of nurses and rumours;
The provinces of his body revolted,
The squares of his mind were empty,
Silence invaded the suburbs,
The current of his feeling failed; he became his admirers.
Now he is scattered among a hundred cities
And wholly given over to unfamiliar affections,
To find his happiness in another kind of wood
And be punished under a foreign code of conscience.
The words of a dead man
Are modified in the guts of the living.
But in the importance and noise of tomorrow
When the brokers are roaring like beasts on the floor of
the bourse,
And the poor have the sufferings to which they are
fairly accustomed
And each in the cell of himself is almost convinced of
his freedom
A few thousand will think of this day
As one thinks of a day when one did something slightly
unusual.
What instruments we have agree
The day of his death was a dark cold day.

II

You were silly like us; your gift survived it all:
The parish of rich women, physical decay,
Yourself. Mad Ireland hurt you into poetry.
Now Ireland has her madness and her weather still,
For poetry makes nothing happen: it survives
In the valley of its making where executives
Would never want to tamper, flows on south

From ranches of isolation and the busy griefs,
Raw towns that we believe and die in; it survives,
A way of happening, a mouth.

III

Earth, receive an honoured guest:
William Yeats is laid to rest.
Let the Irish vessel lie
Emptied of its poetry.
In the nightmare of the dark
All the dogs of Europe bark,
And the living nations wait,
Each sequestered in its hate;
Intellectual disgrace
Stares from every human face,
And the seas of pity lie
Locked and frozen in each eye.
Follow, poet, follow right
To the bottom of the night,
With your unconstraining voice
Still persuade us to rejoice;
With the farming of a verse
Make a vineyard of the curse,
Sing of human unsuccess
In a rapture of distress;
In the deserts of the heart
Let the healing fountain start,
In the prison of his days
Teach the free man how to praise.

IN TRANSIT

Let out where two fears intersect, a point selected
Jointly by general staffs and engineers, In a wet land,
facing rough oceans, never invaded
By Caesars or a Cartesian doubt, I stand, Pale, half
asleep, inhaling its new fresh air that smells
So strongly of soil and grass, of toil and gender, But not
for long: a professional friend is at hand
Who smiling leads us indoors; we follow in file,
Obeying that fond peremptory tone reserved for those
Nervously sick and children one cannot trust, 10 Who
might be tempted by ponds or learn some disgusting
Trick from a ragamuffin. Through modern panes I
admire a limestone hill I have no permission to climb
And the pearly clouds of a sunset dint seems oddly
early to me: maybe an ambitious lad stares back,
Dreaming of elsewhere and our godlike freedom.
Somewhere are places where we have really been, dear
spates
Of our deeds and faces, scenes we remember As
unchanging because there we changed, where shops
have names,
Dogs bark in die dark at a stranger's footfall 20 And
crops grow ripe and cattle fatten under the kind
Protection of a godling or goddessling.
Whose affection has been assigned them, to heed their
needs and
Plead in heaven the special case of their place.
Somewhere, too, unique for each, his frontier dividing
Past from future, reached and crossed without warning:
That bridge where an ageing destroyer takes his last
salute, In his rear all rivals fawning, in cages
Or dead, ahead a field of wradi; and that narrow pass
where,
Late from a sullen childhood, a fresh creator

Yields, glowing, to a boyish rapture, wild gothic peaks
above him, Below, Italian sunshine, Italian flesh.
But here we are nowhere, unrelated to day or to Mother
Earth in love or in hate; our occupation Leaves no trace
on this place or each odier who do not
Meet in its mere enclosure but are exposed As objects
for speculation, aggressive creatures
On their way to their prey but now quite docile, Told
to wait and controlled by a voice that from time to time
calls
Some class of souls to foregather at die gate. 40
It calls me again to our plane and soon we are floating
above
A possessed congested surface, a world; down there
Motives and natural processes are stirred by spring
And wrongs and graves grow greenly; slaves in quarries
Against their wills feel the will to live renewed by the
song
Of a loose bird, maculate cities are spared Through the
prayers of illiterate saints, and an ancient
Feud re-opens with the debacle of a river.

FIRST THINGS FIRST

Woken, I lay in the arms of my own warmth and listened
To a storm enjoying its storminess in the winter dark
Till my ear, as it can when half-asleep or half-sober,
Set to work to unscramble diat interjectory uproar,
Construing its airy vowels and watery consonants Into
a love-speech indicative of a Proper Name.
Scarcely the tongue I should have chosen, yet, as well
As harshness and clumsiness would allow, it spoke in
your praise-,
Kenning you a god-child of the Moon and die West
Wind

With power to tame both real and imaginary monsters, 10
Likening your poise of being to an upland county,
Here green on purpose, there pure blue for luck.
Loud though it was, alone as it certainly found me, It
reconstructed a day of peculiar silence
When a sneeze could be heard a mile off, and had me
walking
On a headland of lava beside you, your presence exactly
So once, so valuable, so very now.

This, moreover, at an hour when only too often
A smirking devil annoys me in beautiful English,
Predicting a world where every sacred location
Is a sand-buried site all cultured Texans do,
Misinformed and thoroughly fleeced by their guides,
And gentle hearts are extinct like Hegelian Bishops.

Grateful, I slept till a morning that would not say
How much it believed of what I said the storm had said
But quietly drew my attention to what had been done
—So many cubic metres the more in my cistern
Against a leonine summer—, putting first things first:
Thousands have lived without love, not one without
water.

IF I COULD TELL YOU

Time will say nothing but I told you so,
Time only knows the price we have to pay;
I could tell you I would let you know

If we should weep when clowns put on their show,
If we should stumble when musicians play,
Time will say nothing but I told you so.

But there are no fortunes to be told, although,
Because I love you more than I can say,
If I could tell you I would let you know.

The winds must come from somewhere when they
blow,
There must be reasons why the leaves decay;
Time will say nothing but I told you so.

Perhaps the roses really want to grow,
The vision seriously intends to say;
If I could tell you I would let you know.

Suppose the lions all get up and go,
And all the brooks and soldiers run away;
Will Time say nothing but I told you so?
If I could tell you I would let you know.

38

LOUIS MACNEICE (1907-1963)

Louis MacNiece, CBE, was born on 12th September,1907 in Belfast, Ireland, and spent most of his childhood in the rural harbour town of Carrickfergus. His father was clergyman and his mother died when Mac Niece was six years old. He attended Sherborne Prep School in Dorset. In 1926 he entered Merton College at Oxford and studied Classics and Philosophy. He became a poet, playwright and producer for BBC. *Blind Fireworks* was his first collection of poems. He married Mary Ezra in 1930 and Hedli Anderson in 1942. His volumes of poetry are – *Poems* (1935), *Solstices* (1961) and *The Burning Perch* (1963). His poetry speaks "a completely original and authentic voice." He died in London on 3rd September, 1963.

MEETING POINT

Time was away and somewhere else,
There were two glasses and two hairs
And two people with the one pulse
(Somebody stopped the moving stairs)
Time was away and somewhere else.

And there were neither up nor down,
The stream's music did not stop
Flowing through heather, limpid brown,
Although they sat in a coffee shop
And they were neither up nor down.

The bell was silent in the air
Holding its inverted poise-
Between the clang and clang a flower,
A brazen calyx of no noise
The bell was silent in the air.

The camels crossed miles of sand
That stretched around the cups and plates;
The desert was their own, they planned
To portion out the stars and dates;
The camels crossed the miles of sand.

Time was away and somewhere else
That bloomed again in tropic trees;
Not caring if the markets crash
When they had forests such as these,
Her fingers flicked away the ash.

God or whatever means the Good
Be praised that time can stop like this,
That what the heart has understood

Can verify in the body's peace
God or whatever means the Good.

Time was away and she was here
And life no longer what it was,
The bell was silent in the air
And all the room a glow because
Time was away and she was here.
(1941)

CONVERSATION

Ordinary people are peculiar too:
Watch the vagrant in their eyes
Who sneaks away while they are talking with you
Into some black wood behind the skull,
Following un – or other, realities,
Fishing for shadows in a pool.

But sometimes the vagrant comes the other way
Out of their eyes and into yours
Having mistaken you perhaps for yesterday
Or for tomorrow night, a wood in which
He may pick up among the pine-needles and burrs
The lost purse, the dropped stitch.

Vagrancy however is forbidden; ordinary men
Soon come back to normal, look you straight
In the eyes as if to say 'It will not happen again',
Put up a barrage of common sense to baulk
Intimacy but by mistake interpolate
Swear-words like roses in their talk.

STAR-GAZER

Forty years ago (to me if to no one else
The number is of some interest) it was a brilliant
starry night.
And the westward train was empty and had no
corridors.
So darting from side to side I could catch the unwonted
sight.
Of those almost intolerably bright
Holes, punched in the sky, which excited me partly
because
Of their Latin names and partly because I had read
in the textbooks.
How very far off they were, it seemed their light
Had left them (some at least) long years before I was.

And this remembering now I mark that what
Light was leaving some of them at least then,
Forty-two years ago, will never arrive
In time for me to catch it, which light when
It does get here may find that there is not
Anyone left alive.
To run from side to side in a late night train
Admiring it and adding nougats in vein.
(1963)

BIRMINGHAM

Smoke from the train-gulf hid by hoardings blunders
upward, the brakes of cars
Pipe as the policeman pivoting round raises his flat
hand, bars

With his figure of a monolith Pharaoh the queue of
fidgety machines
(Chromium dogs on the bonnet, faces behind the triplex
screens).
Behind him the streets run away between the proud
glass of shops,
Cubical scent-bottles artificial legs arctic foxes and
electric mops,
But beyond this centre the slumward vista thins like a
diagram:
There, unvisited, are Vulcan's forges who doesn't care
a tinker's damn.

Splayed outwards through the suburbs houses, houses
for rest
Seducingly rigged by the builder, half-timbered houses
with lips pressed
So tightly and eyes staring at the traffic through bleary
haws
And only a six-inch grip of the racing earth in their
concrete claws;
In these houses men as in a dream pursue the Platonic
Forms
With wireless and cairn terriers and gadgets
approximating to the fickle norms
And endeavour to find God and score one over the
neighbour
By climbing tentatively upward on jerry-built beauty
and sweated labour.

The lunch hour: the shops empty, the shop girls' faces
relax
Diaphanous as green glass, empty as old almanacs
As incoherent with ticketed gewgaws tiered behind
their heads

As the Burne-Jones windows in St. Philip's broken by
crawling leads;
Insipid colour, patches of emotion, Saturday thrills
(This theatre is sprayed with 'June') – the gutter take our
old playbills,
Next week-end it is likely in the heart's funfair we shall
pull
Strong enough on the handle to get back our money; or
at any rate it is possible.

On shining lines the trams like vast sarcophagi move
Into the sky, plum after sunset, merging to duck's egg,
barred with mauve
Zeppelin clouds, and Pentecost-like the cars' headlights
bud
Out from side roads and the traffic signals, crême-de-
menthe or bull's blood,
Tell one to stop, the engine gently breathing, or to go on
To where like black pipes of organs in the frayed and
fading zone
Of the West the factory chimneys on sullen sentry will
all night wait
To call, in the harsh morning, sleep-stupid faces through
the daily gate.

BAGPIPE MUSIC

It's no go the merry-go-round, it's no go the rickshaw,
All we want is a limousine and a ticket for the peepshow.
Their knickers are made of crêpe-de-chine, their shoes
are made of python,
Their halls are lined with tiger rugs and their walls with
heads of bison.
John MacDonald found a corpse, put it under the sofa,
Waited till it came to life and hit it with a poker,

Sold its eyes for souvenirs, sold its blood for whisky,
Kept its bones for dumb-bells to use when he was fifty.
It's no go the Yogi-Man, it's no go Blavatsky,
All we want is a bank balance and a bit of skirt in a taxi.
Annie MacDougall went to milk, caught her foot in the
heather,
Woke to hear a dance record playing of Old Vienna.
It's no go your maidenheads, it's no go your culture,
All we want is a Dunlop tyre and the devil mend the
puncture.
The Laird o'Phelps spent Hogmanay declaring he was
sober,
Counted his feet to prove the fact and found he had one
foot over.
Mrs Carmichael had her fifth, looked at the job with
repulsion,
Said to the midwife 'Take it away; I'm through with
over-production'.
It's no go the gossip column, it's no go the Ceilidh,
All we want is a mother's help and a sugar-stick for the
baby.
Willie Murray cut his thumb, couldn't count the
damage,
Took the hide of an Ayrshire cow and used it for a
bandage.
His brother caught three hundred cran when the seas
were lavish,
Threw the bleeders back in the sea and went upon the
parish.
It's no go the Herring Board, it's no go the Bible,
All we want is a packet of fags when our hands are idle.
It's no go the picture palace, it's no go the stadium,
It's no go the country cot with a pot of pink geraniums,
It's no go the Government grants, it's no go the elections,
Sit on your arse for fifty years and hang your hat on a
pension.

It's no go my honey love, it's no go my poppet;
Work your hands from day to day, the winds will blow the profit.
The glass is falling hour by hour, the glass will fall forever,
But if you break the bloody glass you won't hold up the weather.

TRAIN TO DUBLIN

Our half-thought thoughts divide in sifted wisps
Against the basic facts repatterned without pause,
I can no more gather my mind up in my fist
Than the shadow of the smoke of this train upon the grass –
This is the way that animals' lives pass.

The train's rhythm never relents, the telephone posts
Go striding backwards like the legs of time to where
In a Georgian house you turn at the carpet's edge
Turning a sentence while, outside my window here,
The smoke makes broken queries in the air.

The train keeps moving and the rain holds off,
I count the buttons on the seat, I hear a shell
Held hollow to the ear, the mere
Reiteration of integers, the bell
That tolls and tolls, the monotony of fear.

At times we are doctrinaire, at times we are frivolous,
Plastering over the cracks, a gesture making good,
But the strength of us does not come out of us.
It is we, I think, are the idols and it is God
Has set us up as men who are painted wood,

And the trains carry us about. But not consistently so,
For during a tiny portion of our lives we are not in
trains,
The idol living for a moment, not muscle-bound
But walking freely through the slanting rain,
Its ankles wet, its grimace relaxed again.

All over the world people are toasting the King,
Red lozenges of light as each one lifts his glass,
But I will not give you any idol or idea, creed or king,
I give you the incidental things which pass
Outward through space exactly as each was.

I give you the disproportion between labour spent
And joy at random; the laughter of the Galway sea
Juggling with spars and bones irresponsibly,
I give you the toy Liffey and the vast gulls,
I give you fuchsia hedges and whitewashed walls.

I give you the smell of Norman stone, the squelch
Of bog beneath your boots, the red bog-grass,
The vivid cheque of the Antrim hills, the trough of dark
Golden water for the cart-horses, the brass
Belt of serene sun upon the plough.

And I give you the faces, not the permanent masks,
But the faces balanced in the toppling wave –
His glint of joy in cunning as the farmer asks
Twenty per cent too much, or a girl's, forgetting to be
suave,
A trio choosing stuffs, preferring mauve.

And I give you the sea and yet again the sea's
Tumultuous marble,
With Thor's thunder or taking his ease akimbo,

Lumbering torso, but finger-tips a marvel
Of surgeon's accuracy.

I would like to give you more but I cannot hold
This stuff within my hands and the train goes on;
I know that there are further syntheses to which,
As you have perhaps, people at last attain
And find that they are rich and breathing gold.

39

THEODORE ROETHKE (1908-1963)

Theodore Roethke was born on 25th May, 1908 in Saginaw, Michigan, USA. As a child he spent his time in his father's greenhouse. His father died when he was quite young. The death brought him trauma that was with him for a long time. He enrolled in the University of Michigan in 1825 and graduated in 1929 after which he took classes in the University of Michigan and Harvard University. In 1931 – 'the year of the Great Depression' he began teaching in Lafayette College. During this period, he began to write poetry seriously and publish in local magazines and journals. *Open House (1941),* and *The Lost Son and Other Poems* (1948) *The Words for the Wind* (1958), *The Far Field* (1964) – are his other collections. For *Waking Poems 1933-1953* (1953), he got the Pulitzer Prize. He died on 1st August, 1963 in Bainbridge, Island, Washington.

THE SLOTH

In moving slow, he has no Peer.
You ask him something in his Ear,
He thinks about it for a Year;

And, then, before he says a Wore
There, upside down (unlike a Bird),
He will assume that you have Heard–

A most Ex-as-per-at–ing Lug.
But should you call his manner Smug,
He'll sigh and give his Branch a Hug;

Then off again to Sleep he goes,
Still swaying gently by his Toes,
And you just know he knows he knows.
(1958)

THE WAKING

I wake to sleep, and take my waking slow.
I feel my fate in what I cannot fear.
I learn by going where I have to.

We think by feeling. What is there to know?
I hear my being dance from ear to ear,
I wake to sleep, and take my waking slow.

those so close beside me, which are you?
God bless the Ground! I shall walk softly there,
And learn by going where I have to go.

Light takes the Trees; but who can tell us how?
The lowly worm climbs up a winding stair;

I wake to sleep, and take my waking slow.

Great Nature has no other thing to do
To you and me; so take the lively air,
And, lovely learn by going where to go.

This shaking keeps me steady. I should know
What falls away is always. And is near.
I wake to sleep, and take my waking slow,
I learn by going where I have to go.
(1953)

MY PAPA'S WALTZ

The whiskey on your breath
Could make a small boy dizzy;
But I hung on like death;
Such waltzing was not easy.

We romped until the pans
Slid from the kitchen shelf;
My mother's countenance
Could not unfrown itself.

The hand that held my wrist
Was battered on one knuckle;
At every step you missed
My right ear scraped a buckle.

You beat time on my head
With a palm asked her by dirt,
Then waltzed me off to bed
Still clinging to your shirt.

I KNEW A WOMAN

I knew a woman, lovely in her bones,
When small birds sighed, who would sigh back at them;
Ah, when she moved, she moved more ways than one;
The shapes a bright container can contain!
Of her choice virtues only gods should speak,
Or English poets who grew up on Greek
(I'd have them sing in chorus, cheek to cheek).

How well her wishes went! She stroked my chin,
She taught me Turn, and Counter-turn, and Stand;
She taught me Touch, and undulant hand;
I nibbled meekly from her proffered hand;
She was the sickle; I , poor I, rake,
Coming behind her for her pretty sake,
(But what prodigious mowing we did make).

Love likes a gander, and adores a goose:
Her full lips pursed, the errant note to seize;
She played it quick, she it light and loose;
My eyes they dazzled at her flowing knees;
Her several parts could keep a pure repose,
Or one hip quiver with a mobile nose
(She moved in circles, and those circles moved).

Let seed be grass, and grass turn into hay:
I'm martyr to a motion not my own;
What's freedom for? To know eternity.
I swear she cast a shadow white as stone.
But who would count eternity in days?
These old bones live to learn her wanton ways;
(I measure time by how a body sways).
(1958)

IN A DARK TIME

In a dark time, the eye begins to see,
I meet my shadow in the deepening shade;
I hear my echo in the chopping wood–
A Lord of nature weeping to a tree,
I live between the heron and the wren,
Beasts of the hill and serpents of the den.

What's madness but nobility of soul
At odds with circumstance? The day's on fire!
I know the purity of pure despair,
My shadow pinned against a sweating wall.
That place among the rocks–is its cave,
Or winding path? The edge is what I have.

A steady storm of correspondences!
A night flowing with birds, a ragged moon,
And in broad day the midnight come again!
A man goes far to find out what he is–
Death of the self in a long, tearless night,
All natured shapes blazing unnatural light.

Dark, dark my light, and darker my desire.
My soul, like some heat-maddened summer fly.
Keeps buzzing at the sill. Which I is *I* ?
A fallen man, I climb out of my fear.
The mind enters itself, and God the mind,
And one is One, free in the tearing wind.

(1964)

40

STEPHEN SPENDER (1909-1995)

Born on 28th February, 1909 in Kensington, London United kingdom, Stephen Spender, CBE, was an English poet, novelist, and essayist whose work was concerned with themes of social justice and class-struggle. His parents were Harold Spender and Violet Hilda Schuster, a painter and a poet of German-Jewish heritage. He studied in University College, Oxford. He married Natasha in 1941 and lived with her till 1995. His collections of poems are-*Twenty Poems* (1930), *Ruins and Visions* (1942), *Collected Poems 1928-1953* (1955), *Selected Poems* (1955), *Recent Poems* (1978), and *Collected poems 1928-1985* (1986). He died on 16th July,1995 in St John's Wood, London.

AUDEN'S FUNERAL

I

One among friends who stood above your grave
I cast a clod of earth from those heaped there
Down on the great brass-handled coffin lid.
It rattled on the oak like a door knocker
And at that sound I saw your face beneath
Wedged in an oblong shadow under ground.
Flesh creased, eyes shut, jaw jutting
And on the mouth a grin: triumph of one
Who has escaped from life-long colleagues roaring
For him to join their throng. He's still half with us
Conniving slyly, yet he knows he's gone
Into that cellar where they'll never find him,
Happy to be alone, his last work done,
Word freed from world, into a different wood.

II

But we, with feet on grass, feeling the wind
Whip blood up in our cheeks, walk back along
The hillside road we earlier climbed today
Following the hearse and tinkling village band.
The white October sun circles Kirchstetten
With colours of chrysanthemums in gardens,
And bronze and golden under wiry boughs,
A few last apples gleam like jewels.
Back in the village inn, we sit on benches
For the last toast to you, the honoured ghost
Whose absence now becomes incarnate in us.
Tasting the meats, we imitate your voice
Speaking in flat benign objective tones
The night before you died. In the packed hall
You are your words. Your listeners see

Written on your face the poems they hear
Like letters carved in a tree's bark
The sight and sound of solitudes endured.
And looking down on them, you see
Your image echoed in their eyes
Enchanted by your language to be theirs.
And then, your last word said, hallooing hands
Hold up above their heads your farewell bow.
Then many stomp the platform, entreating
Each for his horde, your still warm signing hand.
But you have hidden away in your hotel
And locked the door and lain down on the bed
And fallen from their praise, dead on the floor.

III

(Ghost of a ghost, of you when young, you waken
In me my ghost when young, us both at Oxford.
You, the tow-haired undergraduate
With jaunty liftings of the head.
Angular forward stride, cross-questioning glance,
A Buster Keaton-faced pale *gravitas*.
Saying aloud your poems whose letters bit
Ink-deep into my fingers when I set
Them up upon my five-pound printing press:
'*An evening like a coloured photograph*
A music stultified across the water
The heel upon the finishing blade of grass.')

IV

Back to your room still growing memories –
Handwriting, bottles half-drunk, and us – drunk –
Chester, in prayers, still prayed for your 'dear C.',
Hunched as Rigoletto, spluttering

Ecstatic sobs, already slanted
Down towards you, his ten-months-hence
Grave in Athens – remembers
Opera, your camped-on heaven, odourless
Resurrection of your bodies singing
Passionate duets whose chords resolve
Your rows in harmonies. Remembers
Some tragi-jesting wish of yours and puts
'Siegfried's Funeral March' on the machine.
Wagner who drives out every thought but tears –
Down-crashing drums and cymbals cataclysmic
End-of-world brass exalt on drunken waves
The poet's corpse borne on a bier beyond
The foundering finalities, his world,
To that Valhalla where the imaginings
Of the dead makers are their lives.
The dreamer sleeps forever with the dreamed.

AN ELEMENTARY SCHOOL CLASSROOM
IN A SLUM

Far far from gusty waves these children's faces.
Like rootless weeds, the hair torn round their pallor:
The tall girl with her weighed-down head. The paper-
seeming boy, with rat's eyes. The stunted, unlucky heir
Of twisted bones, reciting a father's gnarled disease,
His lesson, from his desk. At back of the dim class
One unnoted, sweet and young. His eyes live in a dream
Of squirrel's game, in tree room, other than this.

On sour cream walls, donations. Shakespeare's head,
Cloudless at dawn, civilized dome riding all cities.
Belled, flowery, Tyrolese valley. Open-handed map
Awarding the world its world. And yet, for these
Children, these windows, not this map, their world,

Where all their future's painted with a fog,
A narrow street sealed in with a lead sky
Far, far from rivers, capes, and stars of words.

Surely, Shakespeare is wicked, the map a bad example.
With ships and sun and love tempting them to steal —
For lives that slyly turn in their cramped holes
From fog to endless night? On their slag heap, these children
Wear skins peeped through by bones and spectacles of steel
With mended glass, like bottle bits on stones.
All of their time and space are foggy slum.
So blot their maps with slums as big as doom.

Unless, governor, inspector, visitor,
This map becomes their window and these windows
That shut upon their lives like catacombs,
Break O break open till they break the town
And show the children to green fields, and make their world
Run azure on gold sands, and let their tongues
Run naked into books the white and green leaves open
History theirs whose language is the sun.

THE EXPRESS

After the first powerful plain manifesto
The black statement of pistons, without more fuss
But gliding like a queen, she leaves the station.
Without bowing and with restrained unconcern
She passes the houses which humbly crowd outside,
The gasworks and at last the heavy page
Of death, printed by gravestones in the cemetery.
Beyond the town there lies the open country

Where, gathering speed, she acquires mystery,
The luminous self-possession of ships on ocean.
It is now she begins to sing – at first quite low
Then loud, and at last, with jazzy madness–
The song of her whistle screaming at curves,
Of deafening tunnels, brakes and innumerable bolts.
And always light, aerial, underneath
Goes the elate metre of her wheels
Steaming through metal landscape o her lines
She plunges new eras of wild happiness
Where speed throws up strange shapes, broad curves
And parallels clean like the steel of guns
At last, further than Edinburg or Rome.
Beyond the crest of the world, she reaches night
Where only a low streamline brightness
Of phosphorus on the tossing hills is white.
Ah, like a comet through flame, she moves entranced
Wrapt in her music no bird song, no, nor bough
Breaking with honey buds, shall ever equal.

MY PARENTS

My parents kept me from children who were rough
Who threw words like stones and wore torn clothes
Their thighs showed through rags they ran in the street
And climbed cliffs and stripped by the country streams.

I feared more than tigers their muscles like iron
Their jerking hands and their knees tight on my arms
I feared the salt coarse pointing of those boys
Who copied my lisp behind me on the road.

They were lithe they sprang out behind hedges
Like dogs to bark at my world. They threw mud
While I looked the other way, pretending to smile.
I longed to forgive them but they never smiled.

41

CHARLES OLSON (1910-1970)

Charles Olson was born on 27ᵗʰ December,1910 in Worcester, Massachusetts, USA. He was of the second generation American modernist poet and a link between early modernist figures and later one, like, William Carlos Williams. He was with poets of the Black Mountain School and the Beat Generation. His parents were Karl Joseph and Mary Hines Olson. He did his B.A., in Wesleyan University in 1932 and M.A. in 1933 in Harvard University. He married twice – Constance Wilcock and Elizabeth Kaiser. *The Distances* (1960) and *The Maximus Poems* (1960) are his most important collections of poems. He died on 10ᵗʰ January, 1970 in New York, United States of America.

THE LIBRARIAN

The landscape (the landscape!) again: Gloucester,
the shore one of me is (duplicates), and from which
(from offshore, I, Maximus) am removed, observe.

In this night I moved on the territory with combinations
(new mixtures) of old and known personages: the
leader,
my father, in an old guise, here selling books and
manuscripts.

My thought was, as I looked in the window of his shop,
there should be materials here for Maximus, when,
then,
I saw he was the young musician has been there (been
before me)

before. It turned out it wasn't a shop, it was a loft (wharf-
house) in which, as he walked me around, a year ago
came back (I had been there before, with my wife and
son,

I didn't remember, he presented me insinuations via
himself and his girl) both of whom I had known for
years.
But never in Gloucester. I had moved them in, to my
country.

His previous appearance had been in my parents'
bedroom where I
found him intimate with my former wife: this boy
was now the Librarian of Gloucester, Massachusetts!

Black space,
old fish-house.

Motions
of ghosts.
I,
dogging
his steps.
He
(not my father,
by name himself
with his face
twisted
at birth)
possessed of knowledge
pretentious
giving me
what in the instant
I knew better of.

But the somber
place, the flooring
crude like a wharf's
and a barn's
space

I was struck by the fact I was in Gloucester, and that my
daughter
was there — that I would see her! She was over the Cut. I
hadn't even connected her with my being there, that she
was

here. That she was there (in the Promised Land — the
Cut!
But there was this business, of poets, that all my Jews
were in the fish-house too, that the Librarian had made
a party

I was to read. They were. There were many of them,
slumped

around. It was not for me. I was outside. It was the Fort.
The Fort was in East Gloucester — old Gorton's Wharf,
where the Library

was. It was a region of coal houses, bins. In one a gang
was beating someone to death, in a corner of the labyrinth
of fences. I could see their arms and shoulders whacking

down. But not the victim. I got out of there. But cops
tailed me along the Fort beach toward the Tavern

The places still
half-dark, mud,
coal dust.

There is no light
east
of the Bridge

Only on the headland
toward the harbor
from Cressy's

have I seen it (once
when my daughter ran
out on a spit of sand

isn't even there.) Where
is Bristow? when does I-A
get me home? I am caught

in Gloucester. (What's buried
behind Lufkin's
Diner? Who is

Frank Moore?

42

ELIZABETH BISHOP (1911-1979)

Elizabeth Bishop was born on 8th February,1911 and had a weathered childhood. Her father died when she was less than a year old and her mother had several nervous collapses. She was shifted to Worcester, Massachusetts where her aunt and uncle lived. Between 1927 and 1930 she attended Walnut Hill School outside, Boston and enrolled in Vassar College from which she graduated in 1924. Accidentally she met Marian Moore, the famous poet and they became lifelong friends though there was twenty years gap between the two. In 1936, she brought out her collection *Trial Balances, North and South* in 1938 and *Poems: North and South-A Cold Spring* in 1955 with more poems.

ARMADILLO

This is the time of year
when almost every night
the frail, illegal fire balloons appear.
Climbing the mountain height.

rising toward a saint
still honoured in these parts
the paper chambers flush and fill with light
that comes and goes, like hearts.

Once up against the sky it's hard
to tell them from the stars–
planets, that is – -the tinted ones;
Venus going down, or Mars.

or the pale green one. With a wind
they flare and falter, wobble and toss;
but if it's still they steer between
the kite sticks of the Southern Cross.

receding, dwindling, solemnly
and steadily forsaking us,
or, in the down draft from a peak,
suddenly turning dangerous.

Last night another big one fell.
It splattered like an egg of fire
against the cliff behind the house.
he flame ran down. We saw the pair

of owls who nest there flying up
and up, their whirling black-and-white
stained bright pink underneath, until
they shrieked up out of sight.

The ancient owls' nest must have burned.
Hastily, all alone,
a glistening armadillo left the scene,
rose-flecked, head down, tail down.

and then a baby rabbit jumped out,
short-eared, to our surprise.
So soft!–a handful of intangible ash
with fixed, ignited eyes.

Too pretty, dreamlike mimicry!
of falling fire and piercing cry
and panic, and a weak mailed fist
clenched ignorant against the sky!
(1965)

THE MAP

Land lies in water; it is shadowed green
Shadows, or are they shallows, at its edges
showing the line of long sea-weed ledges
where weeds hang to the simple blue from green.
Or does the land lean down to left the sea from under,
drawing it unperturbed around itself?
Along the fine tan sandy shelf
is the land tugging at the sea from under?

The shadow of Newfoundland lies flat and still.
Labrador's yellow, where the moony Eskimo
has oiled it. We can stroke these lovely bays,
under a glass as if they were expected to blossom,
or as if to provide a clean cage for invisible fish.
The names of sea-shore towns run out to sea.
the names of cities cross the neighboring mountains

–the printer here experiencing the same excitement
as when emotion too far exceeds its cause.
These peninsulas take the water between thumb and finger
like woman feeling for the smoothness of yard-goods.

Mapped waters are more quiet than the land is,
lending the land their waves' own conformation:
and Norway's hare runs south in agitation,
profiles investigate the sea, where land is.
Are they assigned, or can the countries pick their colors?
–What suits the character or the native waters best.
Topography displays no favorites; North's as near as West
More delicate than the historians are the map-makers' colors.
(1946)

43

CHARLES MADGE (1912-1996)

Charles Madge was born on 10th Oct, 1912 in Johannesburg in South Africa. He was a famous poet, journalist and sociologist. He studied in Winchester College in Oxford, and Magdalene College, University of Cambridge in England. In 1938, he was married to Kathleen Raine. His main poetical works are-*The Disappearing Castle* (1937) *The Father Found* (1941) and *Of Love, Time and Places* (1994). His prose works are – *Inner City Poverty in Paris and London* (1981), *Britain By Mass* (1939), *Village Communities* (1955), etc. He is now remembered as the founder of Mass – Observation. He died on 17th January, 1996 in Borough of Haringey, London, United Kingdom.

IN CONJUNCTION

Now in the circulating torrent of the stars
Certain events are drawn correct and clear
Faces that wear expressions of anguish and delight

Signs unmistakable of the heavenly progress
The flying planet leaves the night house
The two twined figures fill the highest hemisphere

From which we conclude peace, and grateful offerings
While the bird of war, thunderless on leaden roof
No shadow shows on the galactic brilliance of the
streaming breast

And beyond the fated, tragic, foursquare, immovable
house
Evenings under trees of calm, descending evening of
rest
Relenting over battlefields, evenings upholding us
Among alarms, rust and the dead, waiting to be blest.

TO MAKE A BRIDGE

To make a bridge
Between poetry and prose

To make a movable bridge
Between this year and next year

To know the male from the female embryo
By auscultation

To enable the plotting of barometric areas

To make a bridge
Between heaven and earth
To make a bridge
Between man and man
And between men and men
A bridge across the grey dividing river
A skeleton bridge
(Their bones fly electrically
To arch themselves in a system of stresses
Exactly and patiently
Between the lines of the two camps)

A flying bridge
In the dark 'air
Sensible of the currents

A bridge between you and me

To make such a bridge
Foresight and cunning
The development of additional organs

In peace
The building of new brains
Lobe by lobe
In the wide spaces and the free pathways of the wind

The collection of materials
The sorting of minerals
The naming of substances
The enumeration of all these
And the congratulation of all those
Who live in a certain part of a certain place

The co-ordinates of pleasure

In the category of bridges
We have this bridge and that bridge
But whatever the bridge
And wherever the bridge
There is only one space
Hungry, roaring and indivisible
Under the bridge

To be kind to each other
To help in construction
To be sorry
To be aware of the difficulties
To give treatment
To arrange food supplies
To make shelters and centres for the construction of
bridge
To allow time
To put together and to take to pieces
Talking quietly and thinking loudly
We have undertaken.

THE BIRDS OF TIN

The birds of tin
We cannot eat.

We play with them
They cost us nothing
The birds of tin
Municipal

They fly, they float
They wave to us
From far away
They come to rest

Perfectly flat
medals
Of innumerable sizes
On the surface of the sea.
Some are enormously large
Some are six feet high
Some you can hold
Some you can put in your mouth
Some slip through your fingers
And there are microscopic
tiny birds.
In vain we speak to them
In vain we call to them
Or entreat them to open their wings.
They are affixed to walls
Pinned to the sky
Attached by screws
Tied by chains
The birds of tin
Are dead.

DELUSIONS VI

Without surprise, on that not distant shore
Wandering feet mounting towards the trees
A pilgrim guide, until, just as before
The infant brook and half-hid house he sees.

The same, the inarticulate music moves
Depending foliage of annual green
And mutters through the fastness of his groves
Meaningless comment on the well-known scene.

He listens, ears pricked up, and strains his eyes
On to the polar image of his heart.

A retina matured with other skies
Receives the impressions that the woods impart.

Oh wanderer, do not turn back your feet
To the green haunt and the imprisoned wood.
Enough that trickling streams ever repeat
Their senseless noise to perfect solitude.

44

MAY SWENSON (1913-1989)

May Swenson was born on 28th May, 1913 in Logan Utah, USA. She was an American poet and playwright. Herald Bloom considered her as one of the most important original poetesses of the times. She was the eldest of ten children of Margaret and Dan Arthur Swenson. Having attended Utah State University in Logan she passed with the first class in 1934 with the Bachelor Degree. She began to teach poetry in Bryn Mawr College, the University of North Carolina. From 1959 to 1966 she worked as a manuscript reviewer at New Directions Publishing. Her poetry is known for its engaging imagery, intricate wordplay and eccentric use of typography. She published her *Collected Poems* in 2013. She died 4 December, 1989 in Bethany Beach, Delaware, USA.

FOUR-WORD:LINES

Your eyes are just,
like bees, and I
feel like a flower.
Their brown power makes
a breeze go over
my skin. When your
lashes ride down and
rise like brown bees'
legs, your prolonged gaze
makes my eyes gauze.
I wish we were
in some shade and
no swarm of other
eyes to know that
I'm a flower breathing
bare, laid open to
your bees' warm stare.
I'd let you wade
in me and seize
with your eager brown
bees' power a sweet
glistening at my core.

QUESTION

Body my house
my horse my hound
what will I do
when your are fallen.

Where will I sleep
How ill I ride
What will I hunt

Where can I go
without my mount
all eager and quick
How will I know
in thicket ahead
is danger or treasure
when Body my good
bright dog is dead

How will it be
to lie in the sky
without roof or door
and wind for an eye

With cloud for shift
how will I hide?

THE WOODS AT NIGHT

The binocular owl,
fastened to a limb
like a lantern
all night long,

SEES WHERE ALL
the other birds sleep:
towhee under leaves
titmouse deep

in a twig house,
sapsucker gripped
to a knothole lip,
redwing in the reeds,

swallow in the willow
flicker in the oak–
but cannot see poor
whippoorwill!

under the hill
in deadbrush nest,
who's awake, too–
with striken eye

flayed by the moon
her brindled breast
repeats, repeats, repeats is plea
for cruelty.

45

ROBERT HAYDEN (1913-1989)

Robert Heyden was born on 4th August, 1913 in Detroit, Michigan, USA. He was an American poet, essayist and educator. Ruth Sheffey and Asa Sheffy were his parents. He studied in Northern Senior High School, and later in the University of Michigan, and Wayne State University. He married Erma Morris in 1940. *Heart Shape in the Dust* (1940) is his first collection of poems. *Kaleidoscope Poems* (1967), *Collected Poems* (1989), *Words in the Mourning Time* (1970) were the later. He served as Consultant in Poetry to the Library of Congress from 1976 to 1978, today known as Poet Laureate of America. He died on 25th February, 1980 in Ann Arbor, Michigan.

THE BALLAD OF NAT TURNER

Then fled, O brethren, the wicked juba
and wandered, wandered far
from curfew joys in the Dismal's night.
Fool of St. Elmo's fire

In scary night I wandered, praying,
Lord God my hastener,
speak to me now or let me die;
speak, Lord, to this mourner.

And came at length to livid trees
where Ibo warriors
hung shadowless, turning in wind
that moaned like Africa,

Their bell tongue bodies dead, their eyes
alive with the anger deep
in my own heart. Is this the sign,
the sign for promised me?

The spirits vanished. Afraid and lonely
I wandered on in blackness.
Speak to me now or let me die.
Die, whispered the blackness.

And wild things gasped and scuffled in
the night; seething shapes
of evil frolicked upon the air.
I reeled with fear, I prayed.

Sudden brightness clove the preying
darkness, brightness that was
itself a golden darkness, brightness
so bright that it was darkness.

And there were angels, their faces hidden
from me, angels at war
with one another, angels in dazzling
combat. And oh the splendor,

The fearful splendor of that warring.
Hide me, I cried to rock and bramble.
Hide me, the rock, the bramble cried. . . .
How tell you of that holy battle?

The shock of wing on wing and sword
on sword was the tumult of
at taken city burning. I cannot
say how long they strove,

For the wheel in a turning wheel which is time
in eternity had ceased
its whirling, and owl and moccasin,
panther and nameless beast

And I were held like creatures fixed
in flaming, in fiery amber.
But I saw I saw oh many of
those mighty beings waver,

Waver and fall, go streaking down
into swamp water, and the water
hissed and steamed and bubbled and locked
shuddering shuddering over

The fallen and soon was motionless.
Then that massive light
began a-folding slowly in
upon itself, and I

Beheld the conqueror faces and, lo,
they were like mine, I saw
they were like mine and in joy and terror
wept, praising, praising Jehovah.

Oh praised my honor, hastener
till a sleep came over me,
a sleep heavy as death. And when
I awoke at last free

And purified, I rose and prayed
and returned after a time
to the blazing fields, to the humbleness.
And bided my time.

FREDERICK DOUGLASS

When it is finally ours, this freedom, this liberty, this
beautiful
and terrible thing, needful to man as air,
usable as earth; when it belongs at last to all,
when it is truly instinct, brain matter, diastole, systole,
reflex action; when it is finally won; when it is more
than the gaudy mumbo jumbo of politicians:
this man, this Douglass, this former slave, this Negro
beaten to his knees, exiled, visioning a world
where none is lonely, none hunted, alien,
this man, superb in love and logic, this man
shall be remembered. Oh, not with statues' rhetoric,

not with legends and poems and wreaths of bronze
alone,
but with the lives grown out of his life, the lives
fleshing his dream of the beautiful, needful thing.

THOSE WINTER SUNDAYS

Sundays too my father got up early
and put his clothes on in the blueblack cold,
then with cracked hands that ached
from labor in the weekday weather made
banked fires blaze. No one ever thanked him.

I'd wake and hear the cold splintering, breaking
When the rooms were warm, he'd call,
and slowly I would rise and dress,
fearing the chronic angers of that house,

Speaking indifferently to him,
who had driven out the cold
and polished my good shoes as well.
What did I know, what did I know
of love's austere and lonely offices?

46

MURIEL RUKEYSER (1913-1980)

She was born on 15th December, 1913 in New York. She was an American poet, essayist, biographer and political activist. She wrote poems about equality, feminism social justice and Judaism. Her parents were Lawrence and Myra Lyons Rukeyser. She attended the Ethical Culture Fieldstone School and then, in Vassar College in Poughkeepsie. From 1930 to 1932 she attended Columbia university. Her poetical works are – *The Book of the Dead* (1938), *A Turning Wind: Poems* (1939), *The Green Wave: Poems* (1948) and *29 Poems* (1972). She died on 12th February, 1980 in New York.

NIGHT FEEDING

Deeper than sleep but not so deep as death
I lay there sleeping and my magic head
remembered and forgot. On first cry I
remembered and forgot and did believe.
I knew love and I knew evil:
woke to the burning song and the tree burning blind,
despair of our days and the calm milk-giver who
knows sleep, knows growth, the sex of fire and grass,
and the black snake with gold bones.

Black sleeps, gold burns; on second cry I woke
fully and gave to feed and fed on feeding.
Gold seed, green pain, my wizards in the earth
walked through the house, black in the morning dark.
Shadows grew in my veins, my bright belief,
my head of dreams deeper than night and sleep.
Voices of all black animals crying to drink,
cries of all birth arise, simple as we,
found n the leaves, in clouds and dark, in dream,
deep as this hour, ready again to sleep.

THE POEM AS MASK

Orpheus
When I wrote of the women in their dances and
wildness, it was a mask
on their mountain, gold-hunting, singing, in orgy,
it was a mask; when I wrote of the god,
fragmented, exiled from himself, his life, the love gone
down with song,
it was myself, split open, unable to speak, in exile from
myself.
There is no mountain, there is no god, there is no
memory

of my torn life, myself split open in sleep, the rescued
child
beside med among the doctors, and a word
of rescue from the great eyes.

No more masks! No more mythologies!

Now, for the first time, the god lifts his hand,
the fragments join in me with their own music.

AKIBA

THE WAY OUT

The night is covered with signs. The body and face of
man,
with signs, and his journeys. Where the rock is split
and speaks to the water; the flame speaks to the cloud;
the red splatter, abstraction, on the door
speaks to the angel and the constellations.
The grains of sand on the sea-floor speak at last to the
noon.
And the loud hammering of the land behind
speaks ringing up the bones of our thighs, the hoofs,
we hear the hoofs over the seethe of the sea.

All night down the centuries, have heard, music of
passage.

Music of one child carried into the desert;
firstborn forbidden by law of the pyramid.
Drawn through the water with the water-drawn people
led by the water-drawn man to the smoke mountain.
The voice of the world speaking, the world covered by
signs,

the burning, the loving, the speaking, the opening.
Strong throat of sound from the smoking mountain.
Still flame, the spoken singing of a young child.
The meaning beginning to move, which is the song.

Music of those who have walked out of slavery.

Into that journey where all things speak to all things
refusing to accept the curse, and taking
for signs the signs of all things, the world, the body
which is part of the soul, and speaks to the world,
all creation being created in one image, creation.
This is not the past walking into the future,
the walk is painful, into the present, the dance
not visible as dance until much later.
These dancers are discoverers of God.

We knew we had all crossed over when we heard the
song.

Out of a life of building lack on lack:
the slaves refusing slavery, escaping into faith:
an army who came to the ocean: the walkers
who walked through the opposites, from I to opened
Thou,
city and cleave of the sea. Those at flaming Nauvoo,
the ice on the great river: the escaping Negroes,
swamp and wild city: the shivering children of Paris
and the glass black hearses; those on the Long March:
all those who together are the frontier, forehead of man.

Where the wilderness enters, the world, the song of the
world.

Akiba rescued, secretly, in the clothes of death
by his disciples carried from Jerusalem

in blackness journeying to find his journey
to whatever he was loving with his life.
The wilderness journey through which we move
under the whirlwind truth into the new,
the only accurate. A cluster of lights at night:
faces before the pillar of fire. A child watching
while the sea breaks open. This night. The way in.

Barbarian music, a new song.

Acknowledging opened water, possibility:
open like a woman to this meaning.
In a time of building statues of the stars,
valuing certain partial ferocious skills
while past us the chill and immense wilderness
spreads its one-color wings until we know
rock, water, flame, cloud, or the floor of the sea,
the world is a sign, a way of speaking. To find.
What shall we find? Energies, rhythms, journey.

Ways to discover. The song of the way in.

47

WILLIAM STAFFORD (1914-1993)

William Stafford was born on 17th January, 1914 in Hutchinson, Kansas, USA. He was an American poet and self-declared pacifist. He was father of a poet and essayist, Kim Stafford. He was appointed as the Consultant in Poetry to the Library of Congress. He studied B.A., in the University of Kansas, in 1937and was drafted into US army in 1941 and did in his M.A,, in the same University in 1947. He married Dorothy Hope Frantz. His collections of poems are – *West of Your City* (1960), *The Rescued Year* (1965), *Poems for Tennessee* (1971), *That Other Alone* (1973), and *Kansas Poems of William Stafford* (1990) edited by Denise Low. He died on 28th August, 1993 in Lake Oswego, Oregon.

ACROSS KANSAS

My family slept those level miles
but like a bell rung deep till dawn
I drove down an aisle of sound,
nothing real but in the bell,
past the town where I was born.

Once you cross a land like that
you own your face more: what the light
struck told a self; every rock
denied all the rest of the world.
We stopped at Sharon Springs and ate—

My state still dark, my dream too long to tell.

AT THE BOMB TESTING SITE

At noon in the desert a panting lizard
waited for history, its elbows tense,
watching the curve of a particular road
as if something might happen.

It was looking at something farther off
than people could see, an important scene
acted in stone for little selves
at the flute end of consequences.

There was just a continent without much on it
under a sky that never cared less.
Ready for a change, the elbows waited.
The hands gripped hard on the desert.

THIS LIFE

With Kit, Age 7, at the Beach
We would climb the highest dune,
from there to gaze and come down:
the ocean was performing;
we contributed our climb.

Waves leapfrogged and came
straight out of the storm.
What should our gaze mean?
Kit waited for me to decide.

Standing on such a hill,
what would you tell your child?
That was an absolute vista.
Those waves raced far, and cold.

"How far could you swim, Daddy,
in such a storm?"
"As far as was needed," I said,
and as I talked, I swam.

HOMEWORK

Homage Kenneth Koch

If I were doing my Laundry I'd wash my dirty Iran
I'd throw in my United States, and pour on the Ivory
Soap, scrub up Africa, put all the birds and elephants
back in the jungle,
I'd wash the Amazon river and clean the oily Carib &
Gulf of Mexico,
Rub that smog off the North Pole, wipe up all the
pipelines in Alaska,

Rub a dub dub for Rocky Flats and Los Alamos, Flush
that sparkly Cesium out of Love Canal
Rinse down the Acid Rain over the Parthenon & Sphinx,
Drain Sludge out of the Mediterranean basin & make it
azure again,
Put some blueing back into the sky over the Rhine,
bleach the little Clouds so snow return white as snow,
Cleanse the Hudson Thames & Neckar, Drain the Suds
out of Lake Erie
Then I'd throw big Asia in one giant Load & wash out
the blood & Agent Orange,
Dump the whole mess of Russia and China in the
wringer, squeeze out the tattle tail Gray of U.S. Central
American police state,
& put the planet in the drier & let it sit 20 minutes or an
Aeon till it came out clean.
Boulder, April 26, 1980

48

RANDALL JARRELL (1914-1965)

Randall Jarrell was born on 6th May, 1914 in Nashville, Tennessee, USA. He was an American poet, literary critic, children's author, essayist, and novelist. He studied B.A., in Vanderbilt University in 1935 under Robert Penn Warren. He married Mackie Langham in 1942 in the University of Texas where he taught English. His collections of poems are – *Selected Poems* (1955), *Woman at the Washington Zoo,* (1960), *The Lost World,* (1965), and *Complete Poems* (1969). He was appointed as the Consultant in Poetry to the Library Congress and bears the title of the Poet Laureate of USA. He died on 14th October,1965 in Chapel Hill, North Carolina.

THE DEATH OF THE BALL TURRET GUNNER

From my mother's sleep I fell into the State,
And I hunched in its belly till my wet fur froze.
Six miles from earth, loosed from its dream of life,
I woke to black flak and the nightmare fighters.
When I died they washed me out of the turret with a hose.

NORTH

At home, in my flannel gown, like a bear to its floe,
I clambered to bed; up the globe's impossible sides
I sailed all night—till at last, with my black beard,
My furs and my dogs, I stood at the northern pole.

There in the childish night my companions lay frozen,
The stiff furs knocked at my starveling throat,
And I gave my great sigh: the flakes came huddling,
Were they really my end? In the darkness I turned to my rest.

—Here, the flag snaps in the glare and silence
Of the unbroken ice. I stand here,
The dogs bark, my beard is black, and I stare
At the North Pole . . .
And now what? Why, go back.

Turn as I please, my step is to the south.
The world—my world spins on this final point
Of cold and wretchedness: all lines, all winds
End in this whirlpool I at last discover.

And it is meaningless. In the child's bed
After the night's voyage, in that warm world
Where people work and suffer for the end
That crowns the pain — in that Cloud-Cuckoo-Land

I reached my North and it had meaning.
Here at the actual pole of my existence,
Where all that I have done is meaningless,
Where I die or live by accident alone —

Where, living or dying, I am still alone;
Here where North, the night, the berg of death
Crowd me out of the ignorant darkness,
I see at last that all the knowledge

I wrung from the darkness — that the darkness flung
me —
Is worthless as ignorance: nothing comes from nothing,
The darkness from the darkness. Pain comes from the
darkness
And we call it wisdom. It is pain.
(1981)

FACE

Die alte Freu, die alte Marschallin!

Not good any more, not beautiful–
Not even young.
This isn't mine.
Where is the old one, the old ones?
Those were mine.

It's so: I have pictures,
Not such old ones; people behaved

Differently then.. When they meet me they say:
You haven't changed,
I want to say: You haven't looked.

This is what happens to everyone.
At first you get bigger, you knowmore,
Then something goes wrong.
You are, and you say: I am–
And you were...I've been too long.

I know, there's no saying no,
But just the same you say it. No.
I'll point to myself and say: I'm not like this.
I'm the same as always inside.
And even that's not so.

I thought: If nothing happens...
And nothing happened,
Here I am.

But it's not *right*.
If just living can do this,
Living is more dangerous than anything:

It is terrible to be alive.

AGING

I wake, but before I know it is done,
The day, I sleep...And of days like these the years,
A life are made, I nod, consenting to my life.
–But who can live in these quick-passing hours?
I need to find again, to make a life,
A child's Sunday afternoon, the Pleasure Drive
Where everything went by but time–the Study Hour

Spent at a desk with folded hands, in waiting.
In those I could make. Did I not make in them
Myself? the Grown One whose time shortness,
Breath quickens, heart beats faster, till at last
It catches, skips? Yet those hours that seemed, were endless
Were still not long enough to have remade
My childish heart: the heart that must have, always,
To make anything of anything, not time,
Not time but–
but, alas! eternity.

49

JOHN BERRYMAN (1914-1972)

John Berryman was born on 25th October,1914, in McAlester, Oklahoma, USA. He was an American poet and a scholar. He was a major figure in American poetry in the second half-of the 20th century. His parents were Martha, a school teacher and John Smith, a banker. He studied B.A., in Columbia University. He married three times – to Kate Donahue, Ann Levine and Eileen Simpson. His collections of poems are – *77 Dream Songs* (1964), *Dream Songs* (1969). *Homage to Mistress* (1956), *Berryman's Sonnets* (1967), and *Love and Fame* (1970). He won the Pulitzer Prize for poetry in 1964. He died on 7th January, 1972, in Minneapolis, Minnesota.

THE BALL POEM

What is the boy now, who has lost his ball.
What, what is he to do? I saw it go
Merrily bouncing, down the street, and then
Merrily over — there it is in the water!
No use to say 'O there are other balls':
An ultimate shaking grief fixes the boy
As he stands rigid, trembling, staring down
All his young days into the harbour where
His ball went. I would not intrude on him,
A dime, another ball, is worthless. Now
He senses first responsibility
In a world of possessions. People will take balls,
Balls will be lost always, little boy,
And no one buys a ball back. Money is external.
He is learning, well behind his desperate eyes,
The epistemology of loss, how to stand up
Knowing what every man must one day know
And most know many days, how to stand up
And gradually light returns to the street,
A whistle blows, the ball is out of sight.
Soon part of me will explore the deep and dark
Floor of the harbour . . I am everywhere,
I suffer and move, my mind and my heart move
With all that move me, under the water
Or whistling, I am not a little boy.

DREAM SONG 14

Life, friends, is boring. We must not say so.
After all, the sky flashes, the great sea yearns,
we ourselves flash and yearn,
and moreover my mother told me as a boy

(repeatingly) 'Ever to confess you're bored
means you have no

Inner Resources.' I conclude now I have no
inner resources, because I am heavy bored.
Peoples bore me,
literature bores me, especially great literature,
Henry bores me, with his plights & gripes
as bad as Achilles,

who loves people and valiant art, which bores me.
And the tranquil hills, & gin, look like a drag
and somehow a dog
has taken itself & its tail considerably away
into mountains or sea or sky, leaving
behind: me, wag.

50

DYLAN THOMAS (1914-1953)

Dylan Thomas was born on 27th October, in 1914 in Uplands, Swansea, Wales, United Kingdom. He was a Welsh poet and writer. He had the bilingual parents – his father, David John or Jack Thomas and his mother, Florence Hannah, a seamstress, speaking Welsh and English. He studied in Swansea Grammar School, and after joined the field of journalism at the early age. He married Caitlin Thomas and lived from 1937 to 1953. His poetical works are – *Under Milk wood* (1955), *Collected Poems of Dylan Thomas* (2014), and *On the Air with Dylan Thomas* (1991). He died on 9th November, in 1953 in St Vincent's Catholic Medical Center, New York, United States. He was influenced by T.S.Eliot, James Joyce, and W.B.Yeats.

THE FORCE THAT THROUGH THE GREEN FUSE DRIVES THE FLOWER

The force that through the green fuse drives the flower
Drives my green age; that blasts the roots of trees
Is my destroyer.
And I am dumb to tell the crooked rose
My youth is bent by the same wintry fever.
The force that drives the water through the rocks
Drives my red blood; that dries the mouthing streams
Turns mine to wax.
And I am dumb to mouth unto my veins
How at the mountain spring the same mouth sucks.
The hand that whirls the water in the pool
Stirs the quicksand; that ropes the blowing wind
Hauls my shroud sail.
And I am dumb to tell the hanging man
How of my clay is made the hangman's lime.
The lips of time leech to the fountain head;
Love drips and gathers, but the fallen blood
Shall calm her sores.
And I am dumb to tell a weather's wind
How time has ticked a heaven round the stars.
And I am dumb to tell the lover's tomb
How at my sheet goes the same crooked worm.

THE HUNCHBACK IN THE PARK

The hunchback in the park
A solitary mister
Propped between trees and water
From the opening of the garden lock
That lets the trees and water enter
Until the Sunday sombre bell at dark

Eating bread from a newspaper
Drinking water from the chained cup
That the children filled with gravel
In the fountain basin where I sailed my ship
Slept at night in a dog kennel
But nobody chained him up.

Like the park birds he came early
Like the water he sat down
And Mister they called Hey mister
The truant boys from the town
Running when he had heard them clearly
On out of sound

Past lake and rockery
Laughing when he shook his paper
Hunchbacked in mockery
Through the loud zoo of the willow groves
Dodging the park keeper
With his stick that picked up leaves.

And the old dog sleeper
Alone between nurses and swans
While the boys among willows
Made the tigers jump out of their eyes
To roar on the rockery stones
And the groves were blue with sailors

Made all day until bell time
A woman figure without fault
Straight as a young elm
Straight and tall from his crooked bones
That she might stand in the night
After the locks and chains

All night in the unmade park
After the railings and shrubberies
The birds the grass the trees the lake
And the wild boys innocent as strawberries
Had followed the hunchback
To his kennel in the dark.

POEM IN OCTOBER

It was my thirtieth year to heaven
Woke to my hearing from harbour and neighbour wood
And the mussel pooled and the heron
Priested shore

The morning beckon
With water praying and call of seagull and rook
And the knock of sailing boats on the net webbed wall
Myself to set foot
That second
In the still sleeping town and set forth.

My birthday began with the water-
Birds and the birds of the winged trees flying my name
Above the farms and the white horses
And I rose
In rainy autumn
And walked abroad in a shower of all my days.
High tide and the heron dived when I took the road
Over the border
And the gates
Of the town closed as the town awoke.

A springful of larks in a rolling
Cloud and the roadside bushes brimming with whistling
Blackbirds and the sun of October

Summery
On the hill's shoulder,
Here were fond climates and sweet singers suddenly
Come in the morning where I wandered and listened
To the rain wringing
Wind blow cold
In the wood faraway under me.

Pale rain over the dwindling harbour
And over the sea wet church the size of a snail
With its horns through mist and the castle
Brown as owls
But all the gardens
Of spring and summer were blooming in the tall tales
Beyond the border and under the lark full cloud.
There could I marvel
My birthday
Away but the weather turned around.

It turned away from the blithe country
And down the other air and the blue altered sky
Streamed again a wonder of summer
With apples
Pears and red currants
And I saw in the turning so clearly a child's
Forgotten mornings when he walked with his mother
Through the parables
Of sun light
And the legends of the green chapels

And the twice told fields of infancy
That his tears burned my cheeks and his heart moved
in mine.
These were the woods the river and sea
Where a boy
In the listening

Summertime of the dead whispered the truth of his joy
To the trees and the stones and the fish in the tide.
And the mystery
Sang alive
Still in the water and singing birds.

And there could I marvel my birthday
Away but the weather turned around. And the true
Joy of the long dead child sang burning
In the sun.
It was my thirtieth
Year to heaven stood there then in the summer noon
Though the town below lay leaved with October blood.
O may my heart's truth
Still be sung
On this high hill in a year's turning.

51

TERENCE TILLER (1916-1987)

Terence Tiller was born on 19th September, 1916, in Truro, United Kingdom. He was an English poet and radio announcer in BBC. He was educated in Latymer Upper School, Hammersmith. Seriously he studied in the Jesus College, Cambridge and got his B.A., in 1937. He won the Chancellor's Medal for his first verse in 1937. His collections of poems are – *Poems* (1941), *Reading a Medal and Other Poems* (1957), *New Poems* (1960). *The Singing Mesh and Other Poems* (1979). At the age of 71, he died on 24th December 1987, in London, United Kingdom.

ADAM

He split upon the seamless box of silver
important hands; thrust in his father's face
the silence of the glittering revolver,
dragged wounded limbs along a narrow place
between two horrors: till he saw the dream
pursuer, on the naked side of him.

The hair and the dark blood, the sidelong looks,
the tingling of pursuit, the dead weapon,
lay behind. Before, meaningless rocks,
rose sharply, empty, and he felt them ripen
like things growing. His long desire was there,
the buried flute that whistled him to her.

He felt a father's teeth upon his throat;
the chisel broke on the dividing wall;
the fountain's blade was crumpled. Then remote
as a bird's cry, daylight, the wonderful
escape, the tunnel; pierced. But in his side
death's pain, and a spring of blood.

THE BIRDS

When, drawn behind his lamplight and shut doors,
his windows dumb and his day carpeted,
the miser contemplation glowers within
his jealous web (and winding silence pores
on toys of Nothing in that golden shade),
or falls to mapping knowledge by the coin,
or counts himself in poems; when he stands
in his own image on the glass of prayer:
whatever asks a secrecy of hands,
or wedded patience of the tower of cards,

his wild familiars trouble; he will hear
the mouse-eyed amorous eavesdropping birds.

Oh, birds whose homely wings flutter his pane,
cry back your brothers on the weather's wing
wrestling in red air, tassel-hovering, twined
in the blue patterns of the shoals of sun;
cry back the whistle of their flight, their song
in the torn evening trailing like threads of wind.
He knows their picaresque employment; he
has watched from the wife-lintel of his door
that eloquence of breath, and how the tree
streams bowing through its amethyst: but all
his care and cunning have been bound (no more
those echoing coloured miles) within the wall.

ALEXANDER

The Caesar of the world cast his crown
into the heaven's flood,
thinking fiery spaces watched his toy
and saw it drown.
But the seventh heaven would be God:
the perfect hour looks for infinity:
into a hope beyond their spheres
looked upward, stars.

There is an image in the death of trees:
men creep into their bone;
and the birds sing, because ambitious fail,
in their dead boughs.
Our living is a shell between
the crooked beggar and the nightingale;
and Caesar into circling waves
cast eyes, not leaves.

FOR LOST LOVERS

Next unto this Planate of love
The bright Sonne stant above
(John Gower: *Confessio Amantis*, vii, 801-2)

The sun stands in the abyss of giving, and gives;
all in his corridor among the receding stars,
the vaporous yield of the field of wild fire, lives
by his yielding. The keen path of Mars,
Earth's powdered highway upon emptiness,
and Venus's glittering zone, hold from his deep,
music of bounty, balance of duress
by which together being spun they sleep.

Standing where all is well, he draws to him
by gravity of love what else would lie
rolled in those flying caverns on whose rim
of segregation they both seek and fly
the ardour of possession – and yet swing
forever home; neither can reel nor break
their tense their singing distance; they must sing
to the rocked windless and the vibrant lake.

For every broken coupling lashes hard
even in breaking, the act the memory
of its united status: there is one chord
by which all planets and all stars are free
in consort who would die in unison.
Follow the paths of the receding stars:
even the centre of your light is one,
and may not turn aside to follow yours.

52

ROBERT LOWELL (1917-1977)

Robert Lowell (1917-1977) was born 1st March, 1917 in the prominent Boston Brahmin family in Boston. He attended Boston Private School and and St Marks Preparatory School, Kenyon College, and then enrolled in the Harvard University, Harvard and Louisiana University. He married three times – first, the novelist and short story writer Jean Stafford, the second with Lady Caroline Blackwood and the third, with Elizabeth Hardwick. His collections of poems are – *The Dolphin* (1974) for which he won the second Pulitzer Prize. *For the Union Dead* and *Collected Poems* were published in 1964 and 1997. He died on 12th September, 1977 in New York.

WATER

Water
is clearly
a mystery
to me.

A solid?
A liquid?
A gas?
It's all three.

Freeze it.
Warm it.
Boil it.
You'll see.

Water
is clearly
a mystery
to me.

RANDALL JARRELL

The dream went like a rake of sliced bamboo,
slats of dust distracted by a down draw;
I woke and knew I held a cigarette;
I looked, there was none, could have been none;
I slept off years before I woke again,
palming the floor, shaking the sheets. I saw
nothing was burning. I awoke, I saw
I was holding two lighted cigarettes. . . .
They come this path, old friends, old buffs of death.
Tonight it's Randall, his spark still fire though humble,

his gnawed wrist cradled like *Kitten*. "What kept you
so long,
racing the cooling grindstone of your ambition?
You didn't write, you *rewrote*.... But tell me,
Cal, why did we live? Why do we die?"
(2003)

CHILD'S SONG

My heap toy lamp
gives little light
all night, all night,
when my muscles cramp.

Sometimes I touch your hand
across my cot,
and our fingers knot,
but there's no hand

to take me home–
no Carribean
island, where even
the shark is at home.

It must be heaven
There on that island,
she white sand shines
like a birchwood fire.

Help, saw me in two,
put me on the shelf!
Sometimes the little muddler
can't stand itself!

53

GWENDOLYN BROOKS (1917-2000)

Gwendolyn Brooks was born on 7th June,1917 in Topeka, Kansas United States of America. She was an American poet, author and teacher. Her work often dealt with the personal celebration and struggles of the ordinary people in her community. Her parents were David Brooks, a janitor and Keziah (Wims) Brooks, a teacher. She studied in Kennedy King College. She got married to Henry Blakely. Her collections of poems are – *Annie Allen* (1949), *A Street in Brozville* (1945) and *The Bean Eaters* (1960). For her work *Annie Allen* she won the Pulitzer Prize for Poetry in 1950. At the age of 83, she died on 3rd, December, 2000 in South Side, Chicago.

THE BEAN EATERS

They eat beans mostly, this old yellow pair.
Dinner is a casual affair.
Plain chipware on a plain and creaking wood,
Tin flatware.

Two who are Mostly Good.
Two who have lived their day,
But keep on putting on their clothes
And putting things away.

And remembering ...
Remembering, with twinklings and twinges,
As they lean over the beans in their rented back room
that is full of beads and receipts and
dolls and cloths, tobacco crumbs, vases and fringes.
(1963)

THE CHILDREN OF THE POOR

Launch Audio in a New Window
People who have no children can be hard:
Attain a mail of ice and insolence:
Need not pause in the fire, and in no sense
Hesitate in the hurricane to guard.
And when wide world is bitten and bewarred
They perish purely, waving their spirits hence
Without a trace of grace or of offense
To laugh or fail, diffident, wonder-starred.
While through a throttling dark we others hear
The little lifting helplessness, the queer
Whimper-whine; whose unridiculous
Lost softness softly makes a trap for us.

And makes a curse. And makes a sugar of
The malocclusions, in the conditions of love.

2

What shall I give my children? who are poor,
Who are adjudged the leastwise of the land,
Who are my sweetest lepers, who demand
No velvet and no velvety velour;
But who have begged me for a brisk contour,
Crying that they are quasi, contraband
Because unfinished, graven by a hand
Less than angelic, admirable or sure.
My hand is stuffed with mode, design, device.
But I lack access to my proper stone.
And plenitude of plan shall not suffice
Nor grief nor love shall be enough alone
To ratify my little halves who bear
Across an autumn freezing everywhere.

3

And shall I prime my children, pray, to pray?
Mites, come invade most frugal vestibules
Spectered with crusts of penitents' renewals
And all hysterics arrogant for a day.
Instruct yourselves here is no devil to pay.
Children, confine your lights in jellied rules;
graves; be metaphysical mules.
Learn Lord will not distort nor leave the fray.
Behind the scurryings of your neat motif
I shall wait, if you wish: revise the psalm
If that should frighten you: sew up belief
If that should tear: turn, singularly calm
At forehead and at fingers rather wise,
Holding the bandage ready for your eyes.

AN ASPECT OF LOVE, ALIVE IN THE ICE AND FIRE

La Bohem Brown
In a package of minutes there is this We.
How beautiful.
Merry foreigners in our morning,
we laugh, we touch each other,
are responsible props and posts.

A physical light is in the room.

Because the world is at the window
we cannot wonder very long.

You rise. Although
genial, you are in yourself again.
I observe
your direct and respectable stride.
You are direct and self-accepting as a lion
in Afrikan velvet. You are level, lean,
remote.

There is a moment in Camaraderie
when interruption is not to be understood.
I cannot bear an interruption.
This is the shining joy;
the time of not-to-end.

On the street we smile.
We go
in different directions
down the imperturbable street.

54

JAMES KIRKUP (1918-2009)

James Harold Kirkup FRSL, was an English poet, translator and travel writer. He was born on 23rd April, 1918 in England. His parents were Robert Darnley Kirkup and Eleanor Kirkup. He studied in Grey College, and later in Durham University. He wrote over 45 books, including autobiographies, novels and plays under many pen-names. His collections of poems are – *The Drowned Sailor* (1947), *The Submerged Village and Other Poems* (1951) and *The Prodigal Son, Poems 1952-1953* (1954). and *No Men are Foreign* (1966). He died on 10th May, 2009 in Andorra.

NO MORE HIROSHIMAS

At the station exit, my bundle in my hand,
Early the winter afternoon's wet snow
Falls thinly round me, out of a crudded sun.
I had forgotten to remember where I was
Looking about, I see it might be anywhere –
A station, a town like any other in Japan,
Ramshackle, muddy, noisy, drab; a cheerfully
Shallow permanence: peeling concrete, litter, 'Atomic
Lotion, for hair fall-out,' a flimsy department-store;
Racks and towers of neon, flashy over tiled and tilted
waves
Of little roofs, shacks cascading lemons and persimmons,
Oranges and dark-red apples, shanties awash with
rainbows
Of squid and octopus, shellfish, slabs or tuna, oysters,
ice,
Ablaze with fans of soiled nude-picture books
Thumbed abstractedly by schoolboys, with second-
hand looks.

The river remains unchanged, sad, refusing
rehabilitation
In this long, wide, empty, official boulevard
The new trees are still small, the office blocks
Barely functional, the bridge a slick abstraction.
But the river remains unchanged, sad, refusing
rehabilitation.

In the city centre, far from the station's lively squalor,
A kind of life goes on, in cinemas and hi-fi coffee bars,
In the shuffling racket of pin-table palaces and parlous,
The souvenir-shops piled with junk, kimonoed kewpie-
dolls,

Models of the bombed Industry Promotion Hall, memorial ruin
Tricked out with glitter-frost and artificial pearls.

Set in an awful emptiness, the modern tourist hotel is trimmed
With jaded Christmas frippery, flatulent balloons; in the hall,
A giant dingy iced cake in the shape of a Cinderella coach.
Deserted, my room an overheated morgue, the bar in darkness.
Punctually, the electric chimes ring out across the tidy waste
Their doleful public hymn – the tune unrecognisable, evangelist
Here atomic peace is geared to meet the tourist trade.
Let it remain like this, for all the world to see,
Without nobility or loveliness, and dogged with shame
That is beyond all hope of indignation. Anger, too, is dead.
And why should memorials of what was far
From pleasant have the grace that helps us to forget?

In the dying afternoon, I wander dying round the Park of Peace.
It is right, this squat, dead place, with its left-over air
Of an abandoned International Trade and Tourist Fair.
The stunted trees are wrapped in straw against the cold.
The gardeners are old, old women in blue bloomers, white aprons,
Survivors weeding the dead brown lawns around the Children's Monument.

A hideous pile, the Atomic Bomb Explosion Centre, freezing cold,

'Includes the Peace Tower, a museum containing
Atomic-melted slates and bricks, photos showing
What the Atomic Desert looked like, and other
Relics of the catastrophe.'

The other relics:
The ones that made me weep;
The bits of burnt clothing,
The stopped watches, the torn shirts.
The twisted buttons,
The stained and tattered vests and drawers,
The ripped kimonos and charred boots,
The white blouse polka-dotted with atomic rain, indelible,
The cotton summer pants the blasted boys crawled home in, to bleed
And slowly to die.

Remember only these.
They are the memorials we need.

55

ROBERT DUNCUN (1919-1988)

Robert Duncun was born on 7th January, 1919 in Oakland, California. He was an American poet and a devotee of Hilda Doolittle and the Western esoteric tradition who spent most of his time in and around San Francisco. His parents Edward Howard Duncun and Marguerite Pearl Duncun died early. He first studied in Black Mountain College and later in Philadelphia and University of California. His collections of poems are – *The Opening of the Filed* (1960), *Roots and Branches* (1968), and *Bending the Bow* (1968). He died on 3rd February, 1988 in San Francisco, USA.

AN AFRICAN ELEGY

In the groves of Africa from their natural wonder
the wildebeest, zebra, the okapi, the elephant,
have entered the marvelous. No greater marvelous
know I than the mind's
natural jungle. The wives of the Congo
distil there their red and the husbands
hunt lion with spear and paint Death-spore
on their shields, wear his teeth, claws and hair
on ordinary occasions. There the Swahili
open his doors, let loose thru the trees
the tides of Death's sound and distil
from their leaves the terrible red. He
is the consort of dreams I have seen, heard
in the orchestral dark
like the barking of dogs.

Death is the dog-headed man zebra striped
and surrounded by silence who walks like a lion,
who is black. It was his voice crying come back,
that Virginia Woolf heard, turned
her fine skull, hounded and haunted, stopt,
pointed into the scent where
I see her in willows, in fog, at the river of sound
in the trees. I see her prepare there
to enter Death's mountains
like a white Afghan hound pass into the forest,
closed after, let loose in the leaves
with more grace than a hound and more wonder there
even with flowers wound in her hair, allowing herself
like Ophelia a last
pastoral gesture of love toward the world.
And I see
all our tortures absolved in the fog,
dispersed in Death's forests, forgotten. I see

all this gentleness like a hound in the water
float upward and outward beyond my dark hand.

I am waiting this winter for the more complete black-
out,
for the negro armies in the eucalyptus, for the cities
laid open and the cold in the love-light, for hounds
women and birds to go back to their forests and leave us
our solitude.

. . .

Negroes, negroes, all those princes,
holding cups of rhinoceros bone, make
magic with my blood. Where beautiful Marijuana
towers taller than the eucalyptus, turns
within the lips of night and falls,
falls downward, where as giant Kings we gathered
and devour'd her burning hands and feet, O Moonbar
thee and Clarinet! those talismans
that quickened in their sheltering leaves like thieves,
those Negroes, all those princes
holding to their mouths like Death
the cups of rhino bone,
were there to burn my hands and feet,
divine the limit of the bone and with their magic
tie and twist me like a rope. I know
no other continent of Africa more dark than this
dark continent of my breast.

And when we are deserted there,
when the rustling electric has passt thru the air,
once more we begin in the blind and blood throat
the African catches; and Desdemona, Desdemona
like a demon wails within our bodies, warns
against this towering Moor of self and then
laments her passing from him.

And I cry, Hear!
Hear in the coil'd and secretive ear
the drums that I hear beat. The Negroes, all those princes
holding cups of bone and horn, are there in halls
of blood that I call forests, in the dark
and shining caverns where
beats heart and pulses brain, in
jungles of my body, there
Othello moves, striped black and white,
the dog-faced fear. Moves I, I, I,
whom I have seen as black as Orpheus,
pursued deliriously his sound and drownd
in hunger's tone, the deepest wilderness.

Then it was I, Death singing,
who bewildered the forest. I thot him
my lover like a hound of great purity
disturbing the shadow and flesh of the jungle.
This was the beginning of the ending year.
From all of the empty the tortured appear,
and the bird-faced children crawl out of their fathers
and into that never fill'd pocket,
the no longer asking but silent, seeing nowhere
the final sleep.

The halls of Africa we seek in dreams
as barriers of dream against the deep, and seas
disturb'd turn back upon their tides
into the rooms deserted at the roots of love.
There is no end. And how sad then
is even the Congo. How the tired sirens
come up from the water, not to be toucht
but to lie on the rocks of the thunder.
How sad then is even the marvelous!

A LITTLE LANGUAGE

I know a little language of my cat, though Dante says
that animals have no need of speech and Nature
abhors the superfluous. My cat is fluent. He
converses when he wants with me. To speak

is natural. And whales and wolves I've heard
in choral soundings of the sea and air
know harmony and have an eloquence that stirs
my mind and heart—they touch the soul. Here

Dante's religion that would set Man apart
damns the effluence of our life from us
to build therein its powerhouse.

It's in his animal communication Man is
true, immediate, and
in immediacy, Man is all animal.

His senses quicken in the thick of the symphony,
old circuits of animal rapture and alarm,
attentions and arousals in which an identity rearrives.
He hears
particular voices among
the concert, the slightest
rustle in the undertones,
rehearsing a nervous aptitude
yet to prove *his*. He sees the flick
of significant red within the rushing mass
of ruddy wilderness and catches the glow
of a green shirt
to delight him in a glowing field of green
—it *speaks* to him—
and in the arc of the spectrum color
speaks to color.

The rainbow articulates
a promise he remembers
he but imitates
in noises that he makes,

this speech in every sense
the world surrounding him.
He picks up on the fugitive tang of mace
amidst the savory mass,
and taste in evolution is an everlasting key.
There is a pun of scents in what makes sense.

Myrrh it may have been,
the odor of the announcement that fill'd the house.
He wakes from deepest sleep
upon a distant signal and waits
as if crouching, springs
to life.

POETRY, A NATURAL THING

Neither our vices nor our virtues
further the poem. "They came up
and died
just like they do every year
on the rocks."

The poem
feeds upon thought, feeling, impulse,
to breed itself,
a spiritual urgency at the dark ladders leaping.

This beauty is an inner persistence
toward the source
striving against (within) down-russet of the river,

a call we heard and answer
in the lateness of the world
primordial bellowings
from which the youngest world might spring,

salmon not in the well where the
hazelnut falls
but at the falls battling, inarticulate,
blindly making it.
This is one picture apt for the mind.

A second: a moose painted by Stubbs,
where last year's extravagant antlers
lie on the ground.
The forlorn mousey-faced poem wears
new antler-buds,
the same,

"a little heavy, a little contrived",

his only beauty to be
all moose.

56

RICHARD WILBUR (1921-2017)

Richard Wilbur was born on 1st March, 1921 in New York. He was an American poet and literary translator. Wilbur's work, often employing rhyme, was composed primarily in the traditional forms. He was appointed as the second Poet Laureate Consultant in Poetry to the Library of Congress. He studied B.A., in Amherst College, and M.A., in Harvard University. His collections of poems are – *The Beautiful Changes and Other Poems* (1947), *A Bestiary* (1955), *The Mind reader: New Poems* (1976), and *Collected Poems, 1943-2004* (2004). He married Mary Heyes Ward in 1942 and lived up to 2017. Twice, he won the Pulitzer Prize for poetry in 1957 and 1989. He died on 14th October, 2017, at Belmont, Massachusetts, USA.

THE DEATH OF A TOAD

A toad the power mower caught,
Chewed and clipped of a leg, with a hobbling hop has
got
To a garden verge, and sancturied him
Under the cineraria leaves, in the shade
of the ashen heart shaped leaves, in a dim,
Low, and a final glade.

The rare original heart blood goes,
Spends on the earthen hide, in the folds and wizenings,
flows
In the gutters of the banked and staring eyes. He lies
As still as if he would return to stone,
And soundlessly attending, dies
Toward some deep monotone,

Toward misted and ebullient seas
And cooling shores, toward lost Amphibia's emperies
Day dwindles, drowning, and at length is gone
In the wide and antique eyes, which still appear
To watch, across the castrate lawn,
The haggard daylight steer.

CEREMONY

A stripped blouse in a clearing by Bazille
is, you may say, a patroness of boughs
Too queenly kind toward nature to be kin.
But ceremony never did conceal,
Save to the silly eye, which all allows,
How much we are in woods we wander in.

Let her be some Sabrina fresh from stream
Lucent as shallows slowed by wading sun,
Bedded on fern, the flowers cynosure:
Then nymph and wood must nod and strive to dream
That she is airy earth, the trees, undone,
Must ape her languor natural and pure.

Ho-hum. I am for wit and wakefulness,
And love this feigning lady by Bazille.
What's lightly hid is deepest understood,
And when with social smile and formal dress
She teaches leaves to curtsey and quadrille,
I think there are most tigers in the wood.

ADVICE TO A PROPHET

Launch Audio in a New Window
When you come, as you soon must, to the streets of our
city,
Mad-eyed from stating the obvious,
Not proclaiming our fall but begging us
In God's name to have self-pity,

Spare us all word of the weapons, their force and range,
The long numbers that rocket the mind;
Our slow, unreckoning hearts will be left behind,
Unable to fear what is too strange.

Nor shall you scare us with talk of the death of the race.
How should we dream of this place without us? —
The sun mere fire, the leaves untroubled about us,
A stone look on the stone's face?

Speak of the world's own change. Though we cannot
conceive

Of an undreamt thing, we know to our cost
How the dreamt cloud crumbles, the vines are blackened
by frost,
How the view alters. We could believe,

If you told us so, that the white-tailed deer will slip
Into perfect shade, grown perfectly shy,
The lark avoid the reaches of our eye,
The jack-pine lose its knuckled grip

On the cold ledge, and every torrent burn
As Xanthus once, its gliding trout
Stunned in a twinkling. What should we be without
The dolphin's arc, the dove's return,

These things in which we have seen ourselves and
spoken?
Ask us, prophet, how we shall call
Our natures forth when that live tongue is all
Dispelled, that glass obscured or broken

In which we have said the rose of our love and the clean
Horse of our courage, in which beheld
The singing locust of the soul unshelled,
And all we mean or wish to mean.

Ask us, ask us whether with the worldless rose
Our hearts shall fail us; come demanding
Whether there shall be lofty or long standing
When the bronze annals of the oak-tree close.

57

JACK KEROUAC (1922-1969)

Jack Kerouac was born in a French speaking farming family on 12th March, 1922 in Lowell, Massachusetts, USA. He was an American novelist and poet who was a pioneer of the Beat Generation. His parents were Canadian Leo – Alcide Kerouac and Grabrielle Ange-Levesque. He studied in local school and learnt English. As a young man he also wrote poetry in French. He married Eddie Parker in 1944 and Joan Havetry in 1950. His collections of poems are – *On the Road* (1957), *The Dharma Bums* (1958), and *Big Sur* (1962). *Mexico City Blues* is a great religious poem. He died on 21st October, 1969 in St Petersburg, Florida US.

FROM BOOK OF HAIKUS

Snap yr finger,
stop the world!
–Rain falls harder

Nightfall–too dark
to read a page
Too cold

In my medicine cabinet
the winter fly
Has died of old age

Following each other,
my cats stop
When it thunders

Spring evening–
the two
Eighteen year old sisters

The postman is late
–The toilet window
Is shining

Wash hung out
by moonlight
–Friday night

Empty baseball field
–a robin,
Hops along the bench

Blackbrid– no!
bluebird–pear
Branch still jumping

My rumpled couch
–The lady's voice
Next door

The bottoms of my shoes
are clean
From walking in the rain

Bee, why are you
staring at me?
I'm not a flower!

The barn, swimming
in a sea
Of windblown leaves

Glow worm sleeping
on this flower,
Your light's on!
Spring night–
a leaf falling
From my chimney

114TH CHORUS FROM *MEXICO CITY BLUES*

Everything is perfect, dear friend.
When you wrote the letter
I was writing you one,
I checked on the dates,
Just about right, and One.

You don't have to worry
about colics & fits
From me anymore
or evermore either

You don't have to worry about death.
Everything you do, is like your hero
The Sweetest angelic tenor of man
Wailing sweet bop
On a front afternoon
When not leading the band
And note Call for Loss
of out Love and Mastery–
just so, eternalized–

You are a great man
I've gone inside myself
And there to find you
And little ants too

58

SIDNEY KEYES (1922-1943)

Sidney Keyes was born on 27th May,1922 in Dartford, in Kent, United Kingdom. His mother died of peritonitis a few weeks after he was born. He was one of the war poets during the World War II. He studied in Ton bridge School. He began to write poetry in early age. In October 1940, he went to Queen's College, Oxford. He was, like John Keats, a young poet of infinite promises and the winner of Hawthorndon Prize. He was killed at the age of twenty on the Tunisia Front in the war. His collections of poems are – *Eight Oxford Poets*, and *The Collected Poems* (2002) He died on 29th April, 1943 in Tunisia.

WAR POET

I am the man who looked for peace and found
My own eyes barbed
I am the man who groped for words and found
An arrow in my hand.
I am the builder whose firm walls surround
A slipping land.
When I grow sick or mad
Mock me not nor chain me;
When I reach the wind
Cast me not down:

Though my face is a burnt book
And a wasted town.

EUROPE'S PRISONERS

Never a day, never a day passes
But I remember them, their stone-blind faces
Beaten by arc lights, their eyes turned inward
Seeking an answer and their passage
homeward.

For being citizens of time, they never
Would learn the body's nationality.
Tortured for years now, they refuse to sever
Spirit from flesh or accept our callow century.

Not without hope, but lacking present solace
The preacher knows the feel of nails and grace
The singer snores; the orator's facile hands
Are fixed in a gesture no one understands.

Others escaped, yet paid for their betrayal:
Even the politicians with their stale
Visions and cheap flirtation with the past
Will not die any easier at the last.

The ones who took to garrets and consumption
In foreign cities, found a deeper dungeon
Than any Dachau. Free but still confined
The human lack of pity split their mind.

Whatever days, whatever seasons pass,
The prisoners must stare in pain's white face:
Until at last the courage they have learned
Shall burst the walls and overturn the world.

TIME WILL NOT GRANT

May 1941

Time will not grant the unlined page
Completion or the hand respite:
The Magi stray, the heavens rage,
The careful pilgrim stumbles in the night.

Take pen, take eye and etch
Your vision on this unpropitious time;
Faces are fluid, actions never reach
Perfection but in reflex or in rhyme.

Take now, not soon; your lost
Minutes roost home like curses.
Nicolo, Martin, every unhoused ghost
Proclaims time's strange reverses.

Fear was Donne's peace; to him
Charted between the minstrel cherubium,
Terror was decent. Rilke tenderly
Accepted autumn like a rooted tree.
But I am frightened after every good day
That all my life must change and fall away.

POEM FOR MAY THE FIRST

In May brought down and blinkered
When summer calls the tune and fondles
Fond wish not will, as the magnolia's candles
But white to greet the courteous evening light
I have my strength, yet lack ability.

Having desire, yet without energy
My fingers trance the soft – faced season's features
Too easily, forgetting all the strictures
They learn in picking sharper strings and hardly
Stray to May's chord, nor seek the blackthorn's secret.
Others have made the May since Juliet
Held in her face four centuries of summer
Creating a pedantic myth. We later
Must root in print our young endeavour
Without the promise of an August saviour.

having no increase but the willing labour
As tulips gulp the sun, of procreation,
I praise this unheroic generation
Anchored to earth and confident and hopeless
Of bloom this May as nay wry-limbed cypress.

59

PHILLIP LARKIN (1922-1985)

Phillip Larkin was born on 9th August, 1922 in Coventry, United Kingdom. His parents were Sydney Larkin and Eva Emily Day. He was a poet, teacher, novelist and librarian. He studied in St. John College, Oxford. His early years were "unspent' and "bring". He grew up as the son of the City Treasurer. His collections of poems are – *The North Ship* (1945), *The Less Deceived* (1955), *Whitsun Weddings* (1964), *This Be Verse* (1971), *High Windows* (1974) and died on 2nd December, 1985 in Kingston Upon Hull, United Kingdom. For his lifetime contribution he was awarded with FRSL by the Queen of England.

NEXT, PLEASE

Always too eager for the future, we
Pick up bad habits of expectancy.
Something is always approaching; every day
Till then we say,

Watching from a bluff the tiny, clear
Sparkling armada of promises draw near.
How slow they are! And how much time they waste,
Refusing to make haste!

Yet still they leave us holding wretched stalks
Of disappointment, for, though nothing balks
Each big approach, leaning with brasswork prinked,
Each rope distinct,

Flagged, and the figurehead wit golden tits
Arching our way, it never anchors; it's
No sooner present than it turns to past.
Right to the last

We think each one will have to and unload
All good into our lives, all we are owed
For waiting so devoutly and so long.
But we are wrong:

Only one ship is seeking us, a black-
Sailed unfamiliar, towing at her back
A huge and birdless silence. In her wake
No waters breed or break.

TOADS

Why should I let the toad *work*
Squat on my life?
Can't I use my wit as a pitchfork
And drive the brute off?

Six days of the week it soils
With its sickening poison –
Just for paying a few bills!
That's out of proportion.

Lots of folk live on their wits:
Lecturers, lispers,
Losers, loblolly-men, louts-
They don't end as paupers.

Lots of folk live up lanes
With fires in a bucket,
Eat windfalls and tinned sardines.
They seem to like it.

Their nippers have got bare feet,
Their unspeakable wives
Are skinny as whippets – and yet
No one actually *starves*.

Ah, were I courageous enough
To shout, *Stuff your pension*!
But I know, all too well, that's the stuff
That dreams are made on:

For something sufficiently toad-like
Squats in me, too;
Its hunkers are heavy as hard luck,
And cold as snow,

And will never allow me to blarney
My way of getting
The fame and the girl and the money
All at one sitting.

I don't say, one bodies the other
One's spiritual truth;
But I do say it's hard to lose either,
When you have both.

AMBULANCES

Closed like confessionals, they thread
Loud noons of cities, giving back
None of the glances they absorb.
Light glossy grey, arms on a plaque,
They come to rest at any kerb:
All streets in time are visited.

Then children strewn on steps or road,
Or women coming from the shops
Past smells of different dinners, see
A wild white face that overtops
Red stretcher-blankets momently
As it is carried in and stowed,

And sense the solving emptiness
That lies just under all we do,
And for a second get it whole,
So permanent and blank and true.
The fastened doors recede. Poor soul,
They whisper at their own distress;

For borne away in deadened air
May go the sudden shut of loss
Round something nearly at an end,
And what cohered in it across
The years, the unique random blend
Of families and fashions, there

At last begin to loosen. Far
From the exchange of love to lie
Unreachable inside a room
The traffic parts to let go by
Brings closer what is left to come,
And dulls to distance all we are.

POETRY OF DEPARTURES

Sometimes you hear, fifth-hand,
As epitaph:
He chucked up everything
And just cleared off,
And always the voice will sound
Certain you approve
This audacious, purifying,
Elemental move.

And they are right, I think.
We all hate home
And having to be there:
I detest my room,
It's specially-chosen junk,
The good books, the good bed,
And my life, in perfect order:
So to hear it said

He walked out on the whole crowd
Leaves me flushed and stirred,
Like Then she undid her dress
Or Take that you bastard;
Surely I can, if he did?
And that helps me to stay
Sober and industrious.
But I'd go today,

Yes, swagger the nut-strewn roads,
Crouch in the fo'c'sle
Stubbly with goodness, if
It weren't so artificial,
Such a deliberate step backwards
To create an object:
Books; china; a life
Reprehensibly perfect.

60

RICHARD HUGO (1923-1997)

Richard Hugo was born n 21ˢᵗ December, 1923 in White Center, Washington, a suburb of Seattle. His father Franklin Hogan left the family shortly the birth of his son. He was bred up by his grandparents. Critics regarded him as primarily regionalist and his work resonates broadly across the places. He did his B.A., and M.A., from the University Washington and he married Barbara Williams in 1952. *A Run of Jacks* (1961) was his first collection of poems. His other collections of poems are – *Good Luck in Cracked Italian* (1969), *Selected Poems* (1979), *White Center* (1980), and *Sea Lanes Out* (1983). He died of Leukemia on 22ⁿᵈ October, 1982.

PLANS FOR ALTERING THE RIVER

Those who favor our plan to alter the river
raise your hand. Thank you for your vote.
Last week, you'll recall, I spoke about how water
never complains. How it runs where you tell it,
seemingly at home, flooding grain or pinched
by geometric banks like those in this graphic
depiction of our plan. We ask for power:
a river boils or falls to turn our turbines.
The river approves our plans to alter the river.

Due to a shipwreck downstream, I'm sad to report
our project is not on schedule. The boat
was carrying cement for our concrete rip rap
balustrade that will force the river to run
east of the factory site through the state-owned
grove of cedar. Then, the uncooperative
carpenters union went on strike. When we get
that settled, and the concrete, given good weather
we can go ahead with our plan to alter the river.

We have the injunction. We silenced the opposition.
The workers are back. The materials arrived
and everything's humming. I thank you
for this award, this handsome plaque I'll keep
forever above my mantle, and I'll read
the inscription often aloud to remind me
how with your courageous backing I fought
our battle and won. I'll always remember
this banquet this day we started to alter the river.

Flowers on the bank? A park on Forgotten Island?
Return of cedar and salmon? Who are these men?
These Johnnys-come-lately with plans to alter the river?
What's this wild festival in May

celebrating the runoff, display floats on fire
at night and a forest dance under the stars?
Children sing through my locked door, 'Old stranger,
we're going to alter, to alter, alter the river.'
Just when the water was settled and at home.
(1984)

BIRTHDAY

For Paul Levitt
with equal shares in December, 21
Wind deserted the pond this morning. The day
aged badly under a single cloud, and birds
abandoned this air where lilies stop waving
and microscum moors to the base of reeds.
Cattails doze under the light's warm weight
Remember salmon, how they once climbed
over each other frantic to die? Even rivers fade.
Under wings, sudden, out of a birdless north
cats are out of gear and my life runs
empty roads like a sick hand on a map.

Regions beyond worn needs to clown, a man
waits by the road for out-of-date wagons.
The wagons won't come. His children grew weary
calling clouds candy, fraying mud on a rock.
They ran from the calendar south. He grows
the same sick corn every year. He tries reading
the girls better ways. Miss August is best,
the least stained by the wine he throws at the wall.

If wind would return, south to north, some
old comforting motion, opening, closing the skies,
letting man peek at the stars and his grave,
I could face those years I lived ashamed

of the demented grocer and his run down store,
dust on jars, meat dark in the case, the tab
he ran for the poor. I could use the wind
like others use religion, to tell myself
it's ok to be out of rivers and weak.

DEGREES OF GRAY IN PHILIPSBURG

You might come here Sunday on a whim.
Say your life broke down. The last good kiss
you had was years ago. You walk these streets
laid out by the insane, past hotels
that didn't last, bars that did, the tortured try
of local drivers to accelerate their lives.
Only churches are kept up. The jail
turned 70 this year. The only prisoner
is always in, not knowing what he's done.

The principal supporting business now
is rage. Hatred of the various grays
the mountain sends, hatred of the mill,
The Silver Bill repeal, the best liked girls
who leave each year for Butte. One good
restaurant and bars can't wipe the boredom out.
The 1907 boom, eight going silver mines,
a dance floor built on springs—
all memory resolves itself in gaze,
in panoramic green you know the cattle eat
or two stacks high above the town,
two dead kilns, the huge mill in collapse
for fifty years that won't fall finally down.

Isn't this your life? That ancient kiss
still burning out your eyes? Isn't this defeat
so accurate, the church bell simply seems

a pure announcement: ring and no one comes?
Don't empty houses ring? Are magnesium
and scorn sufficient to support a town,
not just Philipsburg, but towns
of towering blondes, good jazz and booze
the world will never let you have
until the town you came from dies inside?

Say no to yourself. The old man, twenty
when the jail was built, still laughs
although his lips collapse. Someday soon,
he says, I'll go to sleep and not wake up.
You tell him no. You're talking to yourself.
The car that brought you here still runs.
The money you buy lunch with,
no matter where it's mined, is silver
and the girl who serves your food
is slender and her red hair lights the wall.
(1984)

61

DENISE LEVERTOV (1923-1997)

Denise Levertov was born on 24th October, 1923 in the town of Ilford, Essex, England. Her Welsh mother descended a line of the mystics and her father was raised as a Hasidic Jew. She grew up in a book-loving, book-filled household. She married Mitchell Goodman, an American writer and left England and moved on to America. Her collections of poems are – *Breathing the Water* (1987), *A Door in the Hive* (1989), *Evening Train* (1992), *The Sands of the Well* (1996) and posthumously published *This Great Unknowing: Last Poems* (1999). She died on 20th December, 1997 in Seattle, Washington from Lymphoma.

THE ACHE OF MARRIAGE

The ache of marriage:
thigh and tongue, beloved,
are heavy with it,
it throbs in the teeth

We look for communion
and are turned away, beloved,
each and each

It is leviathan and we in its belly
looking for joy, some joy
not to be known outside it

two by two in the ark of
the ache of it.

ANOTHER SPRING

In the gold mouth of a flower
the black smell of spring earth.
No more skulls on our desks.

but the pervasive
testing of death- - as if we had need
of new ways of dying? No,

we have no need
of new ways of dying.
Death in us goes on

testing the wild
chance of living
as Adam chanced it.

Golden-mouth, the tilted smile
of the moon westering
is at the black window,

Calavea of Spring.
Do you mistake me?
I am speaking of living

of moving from one moment into
the next, and into the
one after, breathing

death in the spring air, knowing
air also means
music to sing to.

A WOMAN ALONE

When she cannot be sure
which of two lovers it was with whom she felt
this or that moment of pleasure, of something fiery
streaking from head to heels, the way the white
flame of a cascade streaks a mountainside
seen from a car across a valley, the car
changing gear, skirting a precipice,
climbing.....
When she can sit or walk for hours after a movie
talking earnestly and with bursts of laughter
with friends, without worrying
that it's late, dinner at midnight, her time
spent without counting her change...
When half her bed is covered with books
and no one is kept awake by the reading light
and she disconnects the phone, to sleep till noon...
Then

self-pity dries up, a joy
untainted by guilt lifts her,
She has fears, but not about loneliness;
ears about how to deal with the aging
of her body–how to deal
with photographs and the mirror. She feels
so much younger and more beautiful
than she looks. At her happiest
–or even in the midst of
some less than joyful hour, sweating
patiently through a heat-wave in the city
or hearing the sparrows at day-brake, dully gray,
toneless, the sound of fatigue–
a kind of sober euphoria makes her believe
in her future as an old woman, a wanderer,
seamed and brown,
little luxuries of the middle, of life all gone,
watching, cities and rivers, people and mountains,
without being watched; not grim nor sad,
an old wine-drinking woman, who knows
the old roads, grass-grown, and laughs to herself...
She knows it can't be:
that's Mrs. Doasyouwouldbe done by from
The Water-Babies,
no one can walk the world any more,
a world of fumes and decibels.
But she thinks maybe
she could get to be tough and wise, some way,
anyway. Now at least
she is past the time of mourning,
now she can say without shame or deceit,
blessed Solitude.

62

JAMES DICKEY (1923-1997)

James Dickey was born on 2ne February, 1923 in Atlanta, Georgia, USA. He was an American poet and novelist. He was appointed as the eighteenth Poet Laureate in 1966. For his poetry, he also received the Order of the South. He married twice – once to Maxine Syerson in 1948 and next, to Deborah Dodson. His children are Kevin Dickey, Christopher Dickey, and Bronwen Dickey. He published more twenty-five collections of which some are notable – *Deliverance* (1970) rpt., *Poems 1957-1967* (1967) *Falling, May Day Sermon and Other Poems* (1981), *The Whole Motion* (1992) and *Summons* (1988). He died on 19th January, 1997 in Columbia, South Carolina.

IN THE TREE HOUSE AT NIGHT

And now the green household is dark.
The half-moon completely is shining
On the earth-lighted tops of the trees.
To be dead, a house must be still.
The floor and the walls wave me slowly;
I am deep in them over my head.
The needles and pine cones about me

Are full of small birds at their roundest,
Their fists without mercy gripping
Hard down through the tree to the roots
To sing back at light when they feel it.
We live here like angels in bodies,
My brothers and I, one dead,
The other asleep from much living,

In mid-air huddled beside me.
Dark climbed to us here as we climbed
Up the nails I have hammered all day
Through the sprained, comic rungs of the ladder
Of broom handles, crate slats, and laths
Foot by foot up the trunk to the branches
Where we came out at last over lakes

Of leaves, of fields disencumbered of earth
That move with the moves of the spirit.
Each nail that sustains us I set here;
Each nail in the house is now steadied
By my dead brother's huge, freckled hand.
Through the years, he has pointed his hammer
Up into these limbs, and told us

That we must ascend, and all lie here.
Step after step he has brought me,

Embracing the trunk as his body,
Shaking its limbs with my heartbeat,
Till the pine cones danced without wind
And fell from the branches like apples.
In the arm-slender forks of our dwelling

I breathe my live brother's light hair.
The blanket around us becomes
As solid as stone, and it sways.
With all my heart, I close
The blue, timeless eye of my mind.
Wind springs, as my dead brother smiles
And touches the tree at the root;

A shudder of joy runs up
The trunk; the needles tingle;
One bird uncontrollably cries.
The wind changes round, and I stir
Within another's life. Whose life?
Who is dead? Whose presence is living?
When may I fall strangely to earth,

Who am nailed to this branch by a spirit?
Can two bodies make up a third?
To sing, must I feel the world's light?
My green, graceful bones fill the air
With sleeping birds. Alone, alone
And with them I move gently.
I move at the heart of the world.
(1992)

OF HOLY WAR

O sire, I dreamed
You danced with greaves

Afire (it seemed)
At Acre, or leaves
In Caen gave on
A peregrine
Coal under plume
Penumbrally seen.

That phoenix watched
Rood and gate
Embered and percht
His spreaded weight.
Sire, flee this shadow.
I grass his meadow.
And with them I move gently.
I move at the heart of the world.

THE ANNIVERSARY

She is who,
Aligned to joy,
A candle's blue
And quiet alloy,
Took me as wonder
Far into summer
Allayed the ear
Come down through fear,
Broke clear as hazard
And perisht hard
Against the breast
The sun not help
Nor moon destroy,
Left whole the beast
And bled the boy.

By lights and signs
Beneath the arch
And breach of loins
We lay from other
And coined a stitch
To lace the river
An inch from sight
And soaring brother
From that odd night.
Warm in such braces,
Mentioning grasses,
Grinning disgraces
And opulent faces,
We led each other
Two golds together,
That else would've been
No hue of the scene.

Now this is a stranger,
And letting the strings
Out over the river,
The slow grass ring
The hell of the ear,
I splay the guitar,
Bleeding my faces
Out of disaster
And into disgraces,
And kneel in time
Deep as a look
Where none may shine,
Shaping the book
The heart deceives,
Folding a tongue
In five dead leaves.

63

ROBERT CREELEY (1926-2005)

Robert Creeley was born on 21st May, 1926 in Arlington, USA. He grew up with his elder sister and lost one eye at an early age. He studied in Black Mountain College, and Harvard University. His collections of poems are – *The Door: Selected Poems* (1975), *Selected Poems* (1976), *The Collected Poems of Robert Creeley 1945-1975* (1982). He was an American poet and author of more than sixty books. He usually associated with the Black Mountain Poets, though he was verse aesthetic diverged from that school of poetry. He died on 30th March, 2005 in Odessa, Texas.

THE END

When I know what people think of me
I am plunged into my loneliness. The grey
hat bought earlier sickens.
I have no purpose no longer distinguishable.
A feeling like being choked
enters my throat.
(1966)

FOR LOVE

for Bobbie
Yesterday I wanted to
speak of it, that sense above
the others to me
important because all

that I know derives
from what it teaches me.
Today, what is it that
is finally so helpless,

different, despairs of its own
statement, wants to
turn away, endlessly
to turn away.

If the moon did not ...
no, if you did not
I wouldn't either, but
what would I not

do, what prevention, what
thing so quickly stopped.
That is love yesterday
or tomorrow, not

now. Can I eat
what you give me. I
have not earned it. Must
I think of everything

as earned. Now love also
becomes a reward so
remote from me I have
only made it with my mind.

Here is tedium,
despair, a painful
sense of isolation and
whimsical if pompous

self-regard. But that image
is only of the mind's
vague structure, vague to me
because it is my own.

Love, what do I think
to say. I cannot say it.
What have you become to ask,
what have I made you into,

companion, good company,
crossed legs with skirt, or
soft body under
the bones of the bed.

Nothing says anything
but that which it wishes
would come true, fears
what else might happen in

some other place, some
other time not this one.
A voice in my place, an
echo of that only in yours.

Let me stumble into
not the confession but
the obsession I begin with
now. For you

also (also)
some time beyond place, or
place beyond time, no
mind left to

say anything at all,
that face gone, now.
Into the company of love
it all returns.
(1991)

AMERICA

America, you ode for reality!
Give back the people you took.

Let the sun shine again
on the four corners of the world

you thought of first but do not
own, or keep like a convenience.

People are your own word, you
invented that locus and term.

Here, you said and say, is
where we are. Give back

what we are, these people you made,
us, and nowhere but you to be.
(1969)

AIR: "THE LOVE OF A WOMAN"

The love of a woman
is the possibility which
surrounds her as hair
her head, as the love of her

follows and describes
her. But what if
they die, then there is
still the aura

left, left sadly, but
hovers in the air, surely,
where this had taken place?
Then sing, of her, of whom

it will be said, he
sand of her it was the
song he made which made her
happy, so she lived.

64

ALLEN GINSBERG (1926-1997)

Allen Ginsberg was born on 3rd June, 1926 in Newark, New Jersey, USA. He was an American poet and writer. As a student at Columbia University in the 1940s, he began friendships with Lucien Carr, William S. Burroughs and Jack Kerouac, forming the core of the Beat Generation of Poets. He was rather influenced by his friend-poets. e wasHe HdeHis parents were Louis Ginsberg and Naomi Ginsberg. He became a Buddhist and lived the monk's simplest life. He married Harlene Susan Rosen and later, he had relationship with Peter Anton Orlovsky for a long time. His collections of poems are – *Howl* (1957), *Howl and Other Poems* (1956) *Kaddish and Other Poems* (1961), and *Planet News 1961-1967* (1968) and *The Fall of America: Poems of These States 1965-71* (1973). He died on 5th April, 1997 in New York.

AMERICA

America I've given you all and now I'm nothing.
America two dollars and twenty seven cents January 17, 1956.
I can't stand my own mind.
America when will we end the human war?
Go fuck yourself with your atom bomb.
I don't feel good don't bother me.
I won't write my poem till I'm in my right mind.
America when will you be angelic?
When will you take off your clothes?
When will you look at yourself through the grave?
When will you be worthy of your million Trotskyites?
America why are your libraries full of tears?
America when will you send your eggs to India?
I'm sick of your insane demands.
When can I go into the supermarket and buy what I need with my good looks?
America after all it is you and I who are perfect not the next world.
Your machinery is too much for me.
You made me want to be a saint.
There must be some other way to settle this argument.
Burroughs is in Tangiers I don't think he'll come back it's sinister.
Are you being sinister or is this some form of practical joke?
I'm trying to come to the point.
I refuse to give up my obsession.
America stop pushing I know what I'm doing.
America the plum blossoms are falling.
I haven't read the newspapers for months, everyday somebody goes ontrial for murder.
America I feel sentimental about the Wobblies.

America I used to be a communist when I was a kid I'm
not sorry.
I smoke marijuana every chance I get.
I sit in my house for days on end and stare at the roses
in the closet.
When I go to Chinatown I get drunk and never get laid.
My mind is made up there's going to be trouble.
You should have seen me reading Marx.
My psychoanalyst thinks I'm perfectly right.
I won't say the Lord's Prayer.
I have mystical visions and cosmic vibrations.
America I still haven't told you what you did to Uncle
Max after he came over from Russia.
I'm addressing you.
Are you going to let your emotional life be run by Time
Magazine?
I'm obsessed by Time Magazine.
I read it every week.
Its cover stares at me every time I slink past the corner
candystore.
I read it in the basement of the Berkeley Public Library.
It's always telling me about responsibility. Businessmen
are serious. Movie producers are serious. Everybody's
serious but me.
It occurs to me that I am America.
I am talking to myself again.

Asia is rising against me.
I haven't got Chinaman's chance.
I'd better consider my national resources.
My national resources consist of two joints of marijuana
millions of genitals an unpublishable private literature
that jet planes 1400 miles an hour and twenty five-
thousand mental institutions.
I say nothing about my prisons nor the millions of

underprivileged who live in my flowerpots under the light of five hundred suns.
I have abolished the whorehouses of France, Tangiers is the next to go.
My ambition is to be President despite the fact that I'm a Catholic.

America how can I write a holy litany in your silly mood?
I will continue like Henry Ford my strophes are as individual as his automobiles more so they're all different sexes.
America I will sell you strophes $2500 apiece $500 down on your old strophe
America free Tom Mooney
America save the Spanish Loyalists
America Sacco & Vanzetti must not die
America I am the Scottsboro boys.
America when I was seven momma took me to Communist Cell meetings they sold us garbanzos a handful per ticket a ticket costs a nickel and the speeches were free everybody was angelic and sentimental about the workers it was all so sincere you have no idea what a good thing the party was in 1835 Scott Nearing
was a grand old man a real mensch Mother Bloor the Silk-strikers' Ewig- Weibliche made me cry I once saw the Yiddish orator Israel Amter plain. Everybody must have been a spy.
America you don't really want to go to war.
America its them bad Russians.
Them Russians them Russians and them Chinamen. And them Russians.
The Russia wants to eat us alive. The Russia's power mad. She wants to take our cars from out our garages.

Her wants to grab Chicago. Her needs a Red *Reader's Digest*. Her wants our auto plants in Siberia. Him big bureaucracy running our fillingstations.
That no good. Ugh. Him make Indians learn read. Him need big black niggers. Hah. Her make us all work sixteen hours a day. Help.
America this is quite serious.
America this is the impression I get from looking in the television set.
America is this correct?
I'd better get right down to the job.
It's true I don't want to join the Army or turn lathes in precision parts factories, I'm nearsighted and psychopathic anyway.
America I'm putting my queer shoulder to the wheel.
(Berkeley, January 17, 1956)

65

FRANK O'HARA (1926-1966)

Frank O'Hara was born on 27th March,1926 in Baltimore, Maryland, USA. He was a poet, critic, writer, and art-critic. His parents were-Russell Joseph O'Hara and Katherine (nee Broderick). He studied B.A., in Harvard University and did his M.A., University of Michigan. From 1941-44, he served in U.S., Navy during the World War II. He was the curator of Museum of Modern Art in New York. For writing poetry, he drew inspiration from Jazz, Surrealism, Abstract Expressionism and Action Painting and contemporary *avant-grade* movement. His main collection of poems is *The Collected Poems of Frank O'Hara* (1971). He died on 25th July,1966 in Mastic Beach, New York.

TO YOU

What is more beautiful than night
and someone in your arms
that's what we love about art
it seems to prefer us and stays

if the moon or a gasping candle
shed a little light or even dark
you become a landscape in a landscape
with rocks and craggy mountains

and valleys full of sweety ferns
breathing and lifting into the clouds
which have actually come low
as a blanket of aspirations' blue

for once not a melancholy color
because it is looking back at us
there's no need for vistas we are one
in the complicated foreground of space

the architects are most courageous
because it stands for all to see
and for a long long time just as
the words "I 'll always love you"

impulsively appear in the dark sky
and we are happy and stick by them
like a couple of painters in neon allowing
the light to glow there over the river

THE DAY LADY DIED

It is 12.20 in New York a Friday
three days after Bastille day, yes
it is 1959 and I go get a shoeshine
because I will get off the 4.19 in Easthampton
at 7:15 and then go straight to dinner
and I don't know the people who will feed me.

I walk up the muggy street beginning to sun
and have a hamburger and a malted and buy
an ugly NEW WRLD WRITING to see what the poets
in Ghana are doing these days
I go on to the
bank
and Miss Stillwagon (first name Linda I once heard)
doesn't even look up my balance for oence in her life
and in the GOLDEN GRIFFIN I get a little
Verlaine
for Party with drawings by Bonnard although I do
think of Hesiod, trans. Richmond Lattimore or
Brendan Behan's new play or *Le Balcon* or *Les Negres*
of Genet, but I don't, I stick with Verlaine
after practically going to sleep with quadariness

and for Mike I just stroll into the PARK LANE
Liquor Store and ask for a bottle of Strega and
then I go back where I came from to 6th Avenue
of Picayunes, and a NEW YORK POST with her face
on it.

and I am sweating a lot by now and thinking of
leaning on the join door in the 5 SPOT
while she whispered a song along the keyboard
to Mal Waldron and everyone and I stopped breathing

WHY I AM NOT A PAINTER

I am not a painter, I am a poet
Why? I think I would rather be
a painter, but I am not. Well,

for instances, Mike Goldberg
is starting a painting. I drop in.
"Sit down and have a drink" he
says. I drink; we drink. I look
up. "You have SARDINES in it."
"Yes, it needed something there."
"Oh." I go and the days go by
and I drop in again. The painting
is going on, and I go, and the days
go by. I drop in. The painting is
finished. "Where's SARDINES?"
All that's left is just
letters, " It was too much," Mike says.

But me? One day I am thinking of
a color: orange. I write a line
about orange. Pretty soon it is a
whole of page of words, not lines.
Then another page. There should be
so much more, not of orange, of
words, of how terrible orange is
and life. Days go by. It is even in
prose, I am a real poet. My poem
is finished and I haven't mentioned
orange yet. It's twelve poems, I call
it ORANGES. And one day in a gallery
I see Mike's painting, called SARDINES.
(2008)

66

PHILIP LEVINE (1928-2015)

Philip Levine was born on 10th June, 1928 in Detroit, Michigan, USA. His parents were Harry Levine and Esther Priscol Levine. He studied in Central High School, and later in Wayne State University and University of Iowa. He married twice – first with Patty Kanterman in 1951 and next with Frances J Artley in 1954. He became famous for his poetry about the working class of Detroit. His collections of poems are-*On the Edge* (1963), *Red Dust* (1971), *They Feed They Lion* (1972), *One of the Rose* (1981) and *Unselected Poems* (1997). He died on 14th February, 2015 in Fresno, California.

THE SECOND GOING

Again the
day begins, only
no one wants its sanity
or its blinding clarity. Daylight is
not what we came all this way for. A
pinch of salt, a drop of schnapps in our cup
of tears, the ticket to the life to come, a short life of
long nights & absent dawns & a little mercy in the tea.

INHERITANCE

A rectangular Bulova, my Zadie
called a dress watch, I wore it for years,
and though it gave the wrong time
I treasured the sense of community
it offered, the beauty of certain numerals —
the seven especially, the way it leaned
into its subtle work and never changed,
and signified exactly what it was
and no more. In dreams I learned
that only the watch and the circle
of ash trees surrounding me, and the grass
prodding my bare feet, and of course
my nakedness were necessary, though
common. Just surrendering my youth,
I still believed everything in dreams
meant something I could parse to discover
who we were.

As I write these words

in sepia across a lined page I have
no idea why they've taken the shape

I've given them, some cursive, some not,
some elegantly articulated, others plain,
many of no use at all. They go on working
as best they can, like the Parker 51
that spent its coming of age stumbling
backwards into Yiddish or the Bulova
that finally threw up its twin baroque arms
in surrender to the infinite and quit
without a word. The Parker still works
and is never to blame. On good days
it works better than I, and when it leaks
it leaks only ink, never a word best
left unsaid.
As a boy I would steal

into Zadie's bedroom, find the watch
in a velvet box, wind it, hold it
to each ear — back then both worked —
to hear its music, the jeweled wheels
and axles that kept time alive.
There is still such joy in these tokens
from back of beyond: the watch,
the Parker pen, the tiny pocket knife
he used to separate truth from lies,
the ivory cigarette holder —
a gift, he claimed, from FDR
who mistook him for a famous
Russian violinist. I could call them
"Infinite riches in a little room"
or go cosmic and regard them
as fragments of a great mystery
instead of what they are,
amulets against nothing.
(2015)

CALL IT MUSIC

Some days I catch a rhythm, almost a song
in my own breath. I'm alone here
in Brooklyn Heights, late morning, the sky
above the St. George Hotel clear, clear
for New York, that is. The radio playing
"Bird Flight," Parker in his California
tragic voice fifty years ago, his faltering
"Lover Man" just before he crashed into chaos.
I would guess that outside the recording studio
in Burbank the sun was high above the jacarandas,
it was late March, the worst of yesterday's rain
had come and gone, the sky washed blue. Bird
could have seen for miles if he'd looked, but what
he saw was so foreign he clenched his eyes,
shook his head, and barked like a dog—just once—
and then Howard McGhee took his arm and assured him
he'd be OK. I know this because Howard told me
years later that he thought Bird could
lie down in the hotel room they shared, sleep
for an hour or more, and waken as himself.
The perfect sunlight angles into my little room
above Willow Street. I listen to my breath
come and go and try to catch its curious taste,
part milk, part iron, part blood, as it passes
from me into the world. This is not me,
this is automatic, this entering and exiting,
my body's essential occupation without which
I am a thing. The whole process has a name,
a word I don't know, an elegant word not
in English or Yiddish or Spanish, a word
that means nothing to me. Howard truly believed
what he said that day when he steered
Parker into a cab and drove the silent miles
beside him while the bright world

unfurled around them: filling stations, stands
of fruits and vegetables, a kiosk selling trinkets
from Mexico and the Philippines. It was all
so actual and Western, it was a new creation
coming into being, like the music of Charlie Parker
someone later called "glad," though that day
I would have said silent, "the silent music
of Charlie Parker." Howard said nothing.
He paid the driver and helped Bird up two flights
to their room, got his boots off, and went out
to let him sleep as the afternoon entered
the history of darkness. I'm not judging
Howard, he did better than I could have
now or then. Then I was 19, working
on the loading docks at Railway Express,
coming day by day into the damaged body
of a man while I sang into the filthy air
the Yiddish drinking songs my Zadie taught me
before his breath failed. Now Howard is gone,
eleven long years gone, the sweet voice silenced.
"The subtle bridge between Eldridge and Navarro,"
they later wrote, all that rising passion
a footnote to others. I remember in '85
walking the halls of Cass Tech, the high school
where he taught after his performing days,
when suddenly he took my left hand in his
two hands to tell me it all worked out
for the best. Maybe he'd gotten religion,
may be he knew how little time was left,
may be that day he was just worn down
by my questions about Parker. To him Bird
was truly Charlie Parker, a man, a silent note
going out forever on the breath of genius
which now I hear soaring above my own breath
as this bright morning fades into afternoon.

Music, I'll call it music. It's what we need
as the sun staggers behind the low gray clouds
blowing relentlessly in from that nameless ocean,
the calm and endless one I've still to cross.
(2000)

ANNE SEXTON (1928-1974)

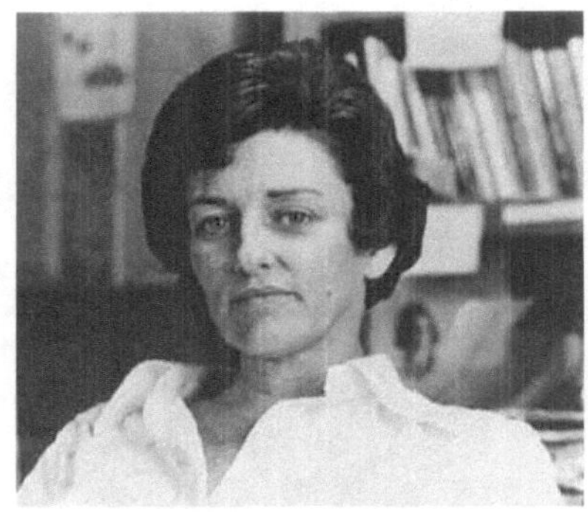

Anne Sexton was born 9th November, 1928 in Newton, Massachusetts, USA. She was known for her highly personal 'confessional' verse. Her parents were Ralph Churchill Harvey and Mary Gray Staples. She studied Rogers Hall Boarding School, in Lowell, Massachusetts and Garland School, and later in Boston University. She married Alfred Muller Sexton II (1948-1973). She killed herself by poisoning carbon monoxide emitted by her car in the shut garage. Her collections of poems – *Live or Die* (1966), *Love Poems* (1969), *Transformations* (1971), *Complete Poems* (1981) and *Selected Poems* (1988). She won the Pulitzer Prize for poetry in 1967 for her book *Live or Die* (1966). She died on 4th October, 1974 in Weston, Massachusetts.

HER KIND

I have gone out, a possessed witch,
haunting the black air, braver at night;
dreaming evil, I have done my hitch
over the plain houses, light by light:
lonely thing, twelve-fingered, out of mind.
A woman like that is not a woman, quite.
I have been her kind.

I have found the warm caves in the woods,
filled them with skillets, carvings, shelves,
closets, silks, innumerable goods;
fixed the suppers for the worms and the elves:
whining, rearranging the disaligned.
A woman like that is misunderstood.
I have been her kind.

I have ridden in your cart, driver,
waved my nude arms at villages going by,
learning the last bright routes, survivor
where your flames still bite my thigh
and my ribs crack where your wheels wind.
A woman like that is not ashamed to die.
I have been her kind.

BUYING THE WHORE

You are the beef I have purchased
and I stuff you with my very own onion.

You are a boat I have rented by the hour
and I steer you with my rage until you run aground

You are a glass that I have paid to shatter
and I swallow the pieces down with my spit.

You are the grate I warm my trembling hands on,
searing the flesh until it's nice and juicy

You stink like my Mama under your bra
and I vomit into your hand like a jackpot
its cold hard quarters.

SYLVIA'S DEATH

For Sylvia Plath
Sylvia, Silvia
with a dead box of stones and spoons,

with two children, two meteors
wandering loose in the tiny playroom,

(O Sylvia, Sylvia,
where did you go
after you wrote me
from Devonshire
about raising potatoes
and keeping bees?)

what did you stand by,
just now did you lie down into?

Thief!–
how did you crawl into,

crawl down alone
into the death I wanted so badly and for so long

the death we said we both outgrew,
the one we wore on our skinny breasts.

MAYA ANGELOU (1928-2014)

Maya Angelou was born on 4th April, 1928 in St Louis, Missouri, USA. She was a famous memoirist, poet and civil rights activist. She published seven autobiographies and three books of essays in addition to considerable amount of poetry. She married twice – first to Tosh Angelos in 1951 and next to Paul de Feu in 1974. Her collections are – *I Know Why the Caged Bird sings* (1969), *The Heart of a Woman* (1981), *A Song Flung up to Heaven* (2002) and *Morn, Me & Mom*. She died on 28th May, 2014 in Winston, Salem, North Carolina.

STILL I RISE

You may write me down in history
With your bitter, twisted lies,
You may trod me in the very dirt
But still, like dust, I'll rise.

Does my sassiness upset you?
Why are you beset with gloom?
'Cause I walk like I've got oil wells
Pumping in my living room.

Just like moons and like suns,
With the certainty of tides,
Just like hopes springing high,
Still I'll rise.

Did you want to see me broken?
Bowed head and lowered eyes?
Shoulders falling down like teardrops,
Weakened by my soulful cries?

Does my haughtiness offend you?
Don't you take it awful hard
'Cause I laugh like I've got gold mines
Diggin' in my own backyard.

You may shoot me with your words,
You may cut me with your eyes,
You may kill me with your hatefulness,
But still, like air, I'll rise.

Does my sexiness upset you?
Does it come as a surprise
That I dance like I've got diamonds
At the meeting of my thighs?

Out of the huts of history's shame
I rise
Up from a past that's rooted in pain
I rise
I'm a black ocean, leaping and wide,
Welling and swelling I bear in the tide.

Leaving behind nights of terror and fear
I rise
Into a daybreak that's wondrously clear
I rise
Bringing the gifts that my ancestors gave,
I am the dream and the hope of the slave.
I rise
I rise
I rise.

ON THE PULSE OF MORNING

A Rock, A River, A Tree
Hosts to species long since departed,
Marked the mastodon,
The dinosaur, who left dried tokens
Of their sojourn here
On our planet floor,
Any broad alarm of their hastening doom
Is lost in the gloom of dust and ages.

But today, the Rock cries out to us, clearly, forcefully,
Come, you may stand upon my
Back and face your distant destiny,
But seek no haven in my shadow,
I will give you no hiding place down here.

You, created only a little lower than
The angels, have crouched too long in
The bruising darkness
Have lain too long
Facedown in ignorance,
Your mouths spilling words
Armed for slaughter.

The Rock cries out to us today,
You may stand upon me,
But do not hide your face.

MOTHER, A CRADLE TO HOLD ME

"It is true
I was created in you.
It is also true
That you were created for me.
I owned your voice.
It was shaped and tuned to soothe me.
Your arms were molded
Into a cradle to hold me, to rock me.
The scent of your body was the air
Perfumed for me to breathe. Mother,
During those early, dearest days
I did not dream that you had
A large life which included me,
For I had a life
Which was only you.
Time passed steadily and drew us apart.
I was unwilling.
I feared if I let you go
You would leave me eternally.
You smiled at my fears, saying
I could not stay in your lap forever.

That one day you would have to stand
And where would I be?
You smiled again.
I did not.
Without warning you left me,
But you returned immediately.
You left again and returned,
I admit, quickly,
But relief did not rest with me easily.
You left again, but again returned.
You left again, but again returned.
Each time you reentered my world
You brought assurance.
Slowly I gained confidence.
You thought you know me,
But I did know you,
You thought you were watching me,
But I did hold you securely in my sight,
Recording every moment,
Memorizing your smiles, tracing your frowns.
In your absence
I rehearsed you,
The way you had of singing
On a breeze,
While a sob lay
At the root of your song.
The way you posed your head
So that the light could caress your face
When you put your fingers on my hand
And your hand on my arm,
I was blessed with a sense of health,
Of strength and very good fortune.
You were always
the heart of happiness to me,
Bringing nougats of glee,
Sweets of open laughter.

I loved you even during the years
When you knew nothing
And I knew everything, I loved you still.
Condescendingly of course,
From my high perch
Of teenage wisdom.
I spoke sharply of you, often
Because you were slow to understand.
I grew older and
Was stunned to find
How much knowledge you had gleaned.
And so quickly.
Mother, I have learned enough now
To know I have learned nearly nothing.
On this day
When mothers are being honored,
Let me thank you
That my selfishness, ignorance, and mockery
Did not bring you to
Discard me like a broken doll
Which had lost its favor.
I thank you that
You still find something in me
To cherish, to admire and to love.
I thank you, Mother.
I love you."

69

DONALD HALL (1928-2018)

Donald Hall was a famous American poet, editor, critic and prose writer. He was born on 28th September, 1928 in Hamden, Connecticut. His parents were Lucy Wells and Donald Andrew Hall. He studied in Harvard University and Christ Church, Oxford. He married Kirby Thompson in 1952 and next, Jane Kenyon in 1972. He was the author of 50 books across several genres from children literature, biography, memoir, essays etc. His collections of poems – *Exile* (1952), *The Alligator Bride* (1969) *Ox-Cart Man* (1979), *Here at Eagle Pond* (1990) and *The Selected Poems of Donald Hall* (2015). He died on 23rd June 2018 in Wilmot, New Hampshire, USA.

HER GARDEN

I let her garden go.
How can I watch the hummingbird
Hover to sip
With its beak's tip
The purple bee balm—whirring as we heard
It years ago?

The weeds rise rank and thick
let it go let it go
Where annuals grew and burdock grows,
Where standing she
At once could see
The peony, the lily, and the rose
Rise over brick
She'd laid in patterns. Moss
let it go let it go

Turns the bricks green, softening them
By the gray rocks
Where hollyhocks
That lofted while she lived, stem by tall stem,
Blossom with loss.

WHITE APPLES

when my father had been dead a week
I woke
with his voice in my ear
I sat up in bed
and held my breath
and stared at the pale closed door

white apples and the taste of stone

if he called again
I would put on my coat and galoshes.

AFFIRMATION

To grow old is to lose everything.
Aging, everybody knows it.
Even when we are young,
we glimpse it sometimes, and nod our heads
when a grandfather dies.
Then we row for years on the midsummer
pond, ignorant and content. But a marriage,
that began without harm, scatters
into debris on the shore,
and a friend from school drops
cold on a rocky strand.
If a new love carries us
past middle age, our wife will die
at her strongest and most beautiful.
New women come and go. All go.
The pretty lover who announces
that she is temporary
is temporary. The bold woman,
middle-aged against our old age,
sinks under an anxiety she cannot withstand.
Another friend of decades estranges himself
in words that pollute thirty years.
Let us stifle under mud at the pond's edge
and affirm that it is fitting
and delicious to lose everything.

70

THOMAS GUNN (1929-2004)

He was born on 29th August, 1929 in Gravesend, Kent, in United Kingdom. His parents were divorced when he was a small boy. Being frustrated, his mother committed suicide. It was his mother who sparked him to read English literature seriously. He was an English poet who was praised for his early verse in England where he was closely associated Phillip Larkin and Donald Davie of the contemporary movement and his later poetry in America. He studied Trinity College, Cambridge and did his B.A. in 1953. He was first in Part I of the Tripos. His collections of poems are – *Touch* (1967), *Jack Straw's Castle* (1976), and *The Man with Night Sweets* (1992). He died on 25th April, 2004 in Haight-Ashbury, California, USA.

CONSIDERING THE SNAIL

The snail pushes through a green
night, for the grass is heavy
with water and meets over
the bright path he makes, where rain
has darkened the earth's dark. He
moves in a wood of desire,

pale antlers barely stirring
as he hunts. I cannot tell
what power is at work, drenched there
with purpose, knowing nothing.
What is a snail's fury? All
I think is that if later

I parted the blades above
the tunnel and saw the thin
trail of broken white across
litter, I would never have
imagined the slow passion
to that deliberate progress.

THE ANNIHILATION OF NOTHING

Nothing remained: Nothing, the wanton name
That nightly I rehearsed till led away
To a dark sleep, or sleep that held one dream.

In this a huge contagious absence lay,
More space than space, over the cloud and slime,
Defined but by the encroachments of its sway.

Stripped to indifference at the turns of time,
Whose end I knew, I woke without desire,
And welcomed zero as a paradigm.

But now it breaks — images burst with fire
Into the quiet sphere where I have bided,
Showing the landscape holding yet entire:

The power that I envisaged, that presided
Ultimate in its abstract devastations,
Is merely change, the atoms it divided

Complete, in ignorance, new combinations.
Only an infinite finitude I see
In those peculiar lovely variations.

It is despair that nothing cannot be
Flares in the mind and leaves a smoky mark
Of dread.
Look upward. Neither firm nor free,
Purposeless matter hovers in the dark.

71

ADRIENNE RICH (1929-2012)

Adrienne Rich was born on 16th May, 1929 in Baltimore, Maryland, USA. She was an American poet, teacher, critic, essayist and feminist. She studied her B.A., Harvard University. She married Alfred Haskell Conrad in 1953 and Michelle Cliff was her partner from 1976-2012. Her father Arnold Rice Rich was a pathologist and Mother, Helen Elizabeth (Jones) was a consort pianist and composer. *A Change of World* (1951), *Necessities of Life: Poems* (1962-1965) (1966), *Selected Poems* (1967), *Collected Early Poems* (1993) and *Collected Poems* (2016) are her main collections of poems. She died on 27th March, 2012, in Santa Cruz, California.

SISTERS

Can I easily say,
I know you of course now,
no longer the fellow-victim,
reader of my diaries, heir
to my outgrown dresses,
ear for my poems and invectives?
Do I know you better
than that blue-eyed stranger
self-absorbed as myself
raptly knitting or sleeping
through a third-class winter journey?
Face to face all night
her dreams and whimpers
tangled with mine,
sleeping but not asleep
behind the engine drilling
into dark Germany,
her eyes, mouth, head
reconstructed by dawn
as we nodded farewell.
Her I should recognize
years later, anywhere.

PEACE

Lashes of white light
binding another hailcloud–
the whole onset all over
bursting against our faces,
sputtering like dead holly
fired in a grate:
And the birds go mad
potted by grapeshot

while the sun shines
in one quarter of heaven
and the rainbow
breaks out its enormous flag–
oily, unnegotiable–
over the sack-draped backs
of the cattle in their kingdom.

PEELING ONIONS

Only to have a grief
equal to all these tears!

There's not a sob in my chest.
Dry-hearted as Peer Gynt
I pare away, no hero,
merely a cook.

Crying was labor, once
when I'd good cause.
Walking, I felt my eyes like wounds
raw in my head,
so postal-clerks, I thought, must stare.
A dog's look, a cat's, burnt to my brain–
yet all that stayed
stuffed in my lungs like smog.

These old tears in the chopping-bowl.

72

ED DORN (1929-1999)

Ed Dorn was born on 2nd April, 1929 in Villa Grove, Illiois, USA. He was an American poet and teacher often associated with the Black Mountain poets. His most famous poetic work *Gunslinger*, an epic. He was educated in Black Mountain College and University of Illinois, Urbana Campaign. He married Helene Jennifer Dunbar. His main works are – *Gunslinger* (1969), *Collected Poems* (1975), and *Collected Poems* (2012). He died on 10th December, 1999 in Denver, Colorado, USA.

IF IT SHOULD EVER COME

And we are all there together
time will wave as willows do
and adios will be truly, yes,
laughing at what is forgotten
and talking of what's new
admiring the roses you brought.
How sad.

You didn't know you were at the end
thought it was your bright pear
the earth, yes

another affair to have been kept
and gazed back on
when you had slept
to have been stored
as a squirrel will a nut, and half
forgotten,
there were so many, many
from the newly fallen.

DEFFOLDIL SONG

The horns of yellow
On this plan resound
and the twist on the air
of their brilliance
Say where
say where I will find
a love.
or an arabesque
of such rash fortune.

THIS MARCH AFTERNOON

Pride kept me sway.
Her eyes indelicate
as they were,
were there nonetheless
and her yes guided
me into recesses of my own
untrackable
world, oh, goddesses
did I like Harpagus crave a future rule
of this world as over the years I grow older?
A bitter clot of time rides in my throat
and Nay once again the Graces say.

73

GREGORY CORSO (1930-2001)

He was born on 26th March 1930 in New York, New York, USA. He was an American poet and key member of the Beat Movement. He was one of the youngest of the inner circle writers. His parents were Michelina Corso and Sam Corso. He studied in local school and college. He married Belle Carpenter and lived up to her with 2001. He his main collections of poems are – *The Vestal Lady and Other Poems* (1955), *Bomb* (1958), *Long Live Man* (1962), *Mind Field* (1989) and *Mind Field: New and Selected Poems* (1989). He died on 17th January, 2001 in Robbins dale, Minnesota.

THE AMERICAN WAY

I am a great American
I am almost nationalistic about it!
I love America like a madness!
But I am afraid to return to America
I'm even afraid to go into the American Express—

2

They are frankensteining Christ in America
in their Sunday campaigns
They are putting the fear of Christ in America
under their tents in their Sunday campaigns
They are driving old ladies mad with Christ in America
They are televising the gift of healing and the fear of
hell
in America under their tents in their Sunday
campaigns
They are leaving their tents and are bringing their Christ
to the stadiums of America in their Sunday
campaigns
They are asking for a full house an all get out
for their Christ in the stadiums of America
They are getting them in their Sunday and Saturday
campaigns
They are asking them to come forward and fall on their
knees
because they are all guilty and they are coming
forward
in guilt and are falling on their knees weeping their
guilt
begging to be saved O Lord O Lord in their Monday
Tuesday Wednesday Thursday Friday Saturday
and Sunday campaigns

3

It is a time in which no man is extremely wondrous
It is a time in which rock stupidity
outsteps the 5th Column as the sole enemy in America
It is a time in which ignorance is a good Ameri-cun
ignorance is excused only where it is so
it is not so in America
Man is not guilty Christ is not to be feared
I am telling you the American Way is a hideous monster
eating Christ making Him into Oreos and Dr. Pepper
the sacrament of its foul mouth
I am telling you the devil is impersonating Christ in
America
America's educators & preachers are the mental-
dictators
of false intelligence they will not allow America
to be smart
they will only allow death to make America smart
Educators & communicators are the lackeys of the
American Way
They enslave the minds of the young
and the young are willing slaves (but not for long)
because who is to doubt the American Way
is not the way?
The duty of these educators is no different
than the duty of a factory foreman
Replica production make all the young think alike
dress alike believe alike do alike
Togetherness this is the American Way
The few great educators in America are weak & helpless
They abide and so uphold the American Way
Wars have seen such men they who despised things about
them
but did nothing and they are the most dangerous
Dangerous because their intelligence is not denied

and so give faith to the young
who rightfully believe in their intelligence
Smoke this cigarette doctors smoke this cigarette
and doctors know

Educators know but they dare not speak their know
The victory that is man is made sad in this fix
Youth can only know the victory of being born
all else is stemmed until death be the final victory
and a merciful one at that
If America falls it will be the blame of its educators
preachers communicators alike
America today is America's greatest threat
We are old when we are young
America is always knew the world is always new
The meaning of the world is birth not death
Growth gone in the wrong direction
The true direction grows ever young
In this direction what grows grows old
A strange mistake a strange and sad mistake
for it has grown into an old thing
while all else around it is new
Rockets will not make it any younger —
And what made America decide to grow?
I do not know I can only hold it to the strangeness in man
And America has grown into the American Way —
To be young is to be ever purposeful limitless
To grow is to know limit purposelessness
Each age is a new age
How outrageous it is that something old and sad
from the pre-age incorporates each new age —
Do I say the Declaration of Independence is old?
Yes I say what was good for 1789, is not good for 1960
It was right and new to say all men were created equal
because it was a light then

But today it is tragic to say it
today it should be fact—
Man has been on earth a long time
One would think with his mania for growth
he would, by now, have outgrown such things as
constitutions manifestos codes commandments
that he could well live in the world without them
and know instinctively how to live and be
—for what is being but the facility to love?
Was not that the true goal of growth, love?
Was not that Christ?
But man is strange and grows where he will
and chalks it all up to Fate whatever be—
America rings with such strangeness
It has grown into something strange and
the American is good example of this mad growth
The boy man big baby meat
as though the womb were turned backwards
giving birth to an old man
The victory that is man does not allow man
to top off his empirical achievement with death
The Aztecs did it by yanking out young hearts
at the height of their power
The Americans are doing it by feeding their young to
the Way
For it was not the Spaniard who killed the Aztec
but the Aztec who killed the Aztec
Rome is proof Greece is proof all history is proof
Victory does not allow degeneracy
It will not be the Communists will kill America
no but America itself—
The American Way that sad mad process
is not run by any one man or organization
It is a monster born of itself existing of its self
The men who are employed by this monster

are employed unknowingly
They reside in the higher echelons of intelligence
They are the educators the psychiatrists the ministers
the writers the politicians the communicators
the rich the entertainment world
And some follow and sing the Way because they
sincerely
believe it to be good
And some believe it holy and become minutemen in it
Some are in it simply to be in
And most are in it for gold
They do not see the Way as monster
They see it as the "Good Life"
What is the Way?
The Way was born out of the American Dream
a nightmare —
The state of Americans today compared to the
Americans
of the 18th century proves the nightmare —
Not Franklin not Jefferson who speaks for America
today
but strange red-necked men of industry
and the goofs of show business
Bizarre! Frightening! The Mickey Mouse sits on the
throne
and Hollywood has a vast supply —
Could grammar school youth seriously look upon
a picture of George Washington and "Herman Borst"
the famous night club comedian together at Valley
Forge?
Old old and decadent gone the dignity
the American sun seems headed for the grave
O that youth might raise it anew!
The future depends solely on the young
The future is the property of the young

What the young know the future will know
What they are and do the future will be and do
What has been done must not be done again
Will the American Way allow this?
No.
I see in every American Express
and in every army center in Europe
I see the same face the same sound of voice
the same clothes the same walk
I see mothers & fathers
no difference among them
Replicas
They not only speak and walk and think alike
they have the same face!
What did this monstrous thing?
What regiments a people so?
How strange is nature's play on America
Surely were Lincoln alive today
he could never be voted President not with his
looks —
Indeed Americans are babies all in the embrace
of Mama Way
Did not Ike, when he visited the American Embassy in
Paris a year ago, say to the staff — "Everything is fine,
just drink Coca Cola, and everything will be all right."
This is true, and is on record
Did not American advertising call for TOGETHERNESS?
not orgiasticly like today's call
nor as means to stem violence
This is true, and is on record.
Are not the army centers in Europe ghettos?
They are, and O how sad how lost!
The PX newsstands are filled with comic books
The army movies are always Doris Day
What makes a people huddle so?

Why can't they be universal?
Who has smalled them so?
This is serious! I do not mock or hate this
I can only sense some mad vast conspiracy!
Helplessness is all it is!
They are caught caught in the Way —
And those who seek to get out of the Way
can not
The Beats are good example of this
They forsake the Way's habits
and acquire for themselves their own habits
And they become as distinct and regimented and lost
as the main flow
because the Way has many outlets
like a snake of many tentacles —
There is no getting out of the Way
The only way out is the death of the Way
And what will kill the Way but a new consciousness
Something great and new and wonderful must happen
to free man from this beast
It is a beast we cannot see or even understand
For it be the condition of our minds
God how close to science fiction it all seems!
As if some power from another planet
incorporated itself in the minds of us all
It could well be!
For as I live I swear America does not seem like America
to me

Americans are a great people
I ask for some great and wondrous event
that will free them from the Way
and make them a glorious purposeful people once
again
I do not know if that event is due deserved
or even possible

I can only hold that man is the victory of life
And I hold firm to American man

I see standing on the skin of the Way
America to be as proud and victorious as St.
Michael on the neck of the fallen Lucifer —
(1970)

74

TED HUGHES (1930-1998)

He was born on 17th August, 1930 in Mytholmroyd, United Kingdom. He was a poet, translator and children writer. William Henry and Edith Hughes were his parents. He studied in Pembroke College, Cambridge. He married Carol Orchard (m.1970-1998) and Sylvia Plath (m.1956-1963). He did many odd jobs, even after attending the university. His poetical works are – *Hawk in the Rain* (1957), *Lupercal* (1960), *Selected Poems 1957-1967)* (1972), *Cave Birds* (1975), and *New Selected Poems – 1957-1994*. For his great contribution to the modern poetry, he was made a Poet Laureate. He died at the age of 68 on 28th October, 1998 in London 1998.

HER HUSBAND

Comes home dull with coal-dust deliberately
To grime the sink and foul towels and let her
Learn with scrubbing brush and scrubbing board
The stubborn character of money.
And let her learn through what kind of dust
He has earned his thirst and the right to quench it
And what sweat he has exchanged for his money
And the blood-weight of money. He'll humble her
With new light on her obligations.
The fried, woody, chips, kept warm two hours in the oven,
Are only part of her answer.
Hearing the rest, he slams them to the fire back
And is away round the house-end singing
'Come back to Sorrento' in a voice
Of resounding corrugated iron.
Her back has bunched into a hump as an insult.
For they will have their rights.
Their jurors are to be assembled
From the little crumbs of soot. Their brief
Goes straight up to heaven and nothing more is heard of it.

THE RIVER IN MARCH

Now the river is rich, but her voice is low.
It is her Mighty Majesty the sea
Travelling among the villages incognito.

Now the river is poor. No song, just a thin mad whisper.
The winter floods have ruined her.
She squats between draggled banks, fingering her rags and rubbish.

And now the river is rich. A deep choir.
It is the lofty clouds, that work in heaven,
Going on their holiday to the sea.

The river is poor again. All her bones are showing.
Through a dry wig of bleached flotsam she peers up
ashamed
From her slum of sticks.

Now the river is rich, collecting shawls and minerals.
Rain brought fatness, but she takes ninety-nine percent
Leaving the fields just one percent to survive on.

And now she is poor. Now she is East wind sick.
She huddles in holes and corners. The brassy sun gives
her a headache.
She has lost all her fish. And she shivers.

But now once more she is rich. She is viewing her lands.
A hoard of king-cups spills from her folds, it blazes. it
cannot be hidden.
A salmon, a sow of solid silver.
Bulges to glimpse it.

HAWK ROOSTING

I sit in the top of the wood, my eyes closed.
Inaction, no falsifying dream
Between my hooked head and hooked feet:
Or in sleep rehearse perfect kills and eat.
The convenience of the high trees!
The air's buoyancy and the sub's ray
Are of advantage to me;
And the earth's face upward for my inspection.
My feet are locked upon the rough bark.

It took the whole of Creation
To produce my foot, my each feather:
Now I hold Creation in my foot.
Or fly up, and revolve it all slowly —
I kill where I please because it is all mine.
There is no sophistry in my body:
My manners are tearing off heads.
The allotment of death.
For the one path of my flight is direct
Through the bones of the living.
No arguments assert my right.
The sun is behind me.
Nothing has changed since I began,
My eye has permitted no change.
I am going to keep things like this.

75

GARY SNYDER (1930-)

Gary Snyder was born on 8th May 1930 in San Francisco, California, USA. His parents were Harold Snyder and Lois Hennessy Snyder. He was educated in Reed College (950-1953) and University of California, and Berkeley (1953-56). He was an American poet, essayist and lecturer and environmentalist activist. He was influenced by Ezra Pound and Robin Jeffers. His early poetry has been associated with the Beat Generation and San Francisco Renaissance. His collections of poems are – *Turtle Island* (1974), *The Real Work* (1980), *A Place in Space* (1995), and *Mountains and Rivers Without End* (1996).

OLD WOMAN NATURE

Old Woman Nature
naturally has a bag of bones
tucked away somewhere.
whole room full of bones!

A scattering of hair and cartilage
bits in the woods.

A fox scat with hair and a tooth in it.
a shellmound
a bone flake in a streambank.
A purring cat, crunching
the mouse head first,
eating on down toward the tail–

The sweet old woman
calmly gathering firewood in the
moon . . .
Don't be shocked,
She's heating
(1983)

WAITING FOR A RIDE

Standing at the baggage passing time:
Austin Texas airport—my ride hasn't come yet.
My former wife is making websites from her home,
one son's seldom seen,
the other one and his wife have a boy and girl of their
own.
My wife and stepdaughter are spending weekdays in
town
so she can get to high school.

My mother ninety-six still lives alone and she's in town too,
always gets her sanity back just barely in time.
My former former wife has become a unique poet;
most of my work,

such as it is.... is done.
Full moon was October second this year,
I ate a mooncake, slept out on the deck
white light beaming through the black boughs of the pine
owl hoots and rattling antlers,
Castor and Pollux rising strong

— it's good to know that the Pole Star drifts!
that even our present night sky slips away,
not that I'll see it.
Or maybe I will, much later,
some far time walking the spirit path in the sky,
that long walk of spirits — where you fall right back into the
"narrow painful passageway of the Bardo"
squeeze your little skull
and there you are again
waiting for your ride

(2001)

76

ETHERIDGE KNIGHT (1931-1991)

Etheridge Knight was born on 19th April, 1931 in Corinth Mississippi, USA. He was an Afro-American poet, who made his name in 1968 with his debut volume *Poems from Prison*. His father was failed farmer, worked as a labourer on the Kentucky Dam Construction site. He was a school dropout and joined army in 1947. In 1960, he was with his friends were arrested in case of robbery. His collections of poems are – *A Poem for a Brother Man* (1972.) *Belly Song and Other Poems* (1973), *The Essential Etheridge* (1986). He won Guggenheim Fellowship in 1974. He died on 10th March,1991 in Indiana Polis, Indiana State, USA.

APOLOGY FOR APOSTASY?

Soft songs, like birds, die in poison air
So my song cannot now be candy.
Anger rots the oak and elm; roses are rare,
Seldom seen through blind despair.

And my murmur cannot be heard
Above the din and damn. The night is full
Of buggers and bastards; no moon or stars
Light the sky. And my candy is deferred

Till peacetime, when my voice shall be light,
Like down, lilting in the air; then shall I
Sing of beaches, white in the magic sun,
And of moons and maidens at midnight.
(1986)

THE BONES OF MY FATHER

1

There are no dry bones
here in this valley. The skull
of my father grins
at the Mississippi moon
from the bottom
of the Tallahatchie,
the bones of my father
are buried in the mud
of these creeks and brooks that twist
and flow their secrets to the sea.
but the wind sings to me
here the sun speaks to me
of the dry bones of my father.

2

There are no dry bones
in the northern valleys, in the Harlem alleys
young / black / men with knees bent
nod on the stoops of the tenements
and dream
of the dry bones of my father.

And young white longhairs who flee
their homes, and bend their minds
and sing their songs of brotherhood
and no more wars are searching for
my father's bones.

3

There are no dry bones here.
We hide from the sun.
No more do we take the long straight strides.
Our steps have been shaped by the cages
that kept us. We glide sideways
like crabs across the sand.
We perch on green lilies, we search
beneath white rocks...
THERE ARE NO DRY BONES HERE

The skull of my father
grins at the Mississippi moon
from the bottom
of the Tallahatchie.
(1971)

HAIKU

1

Eastern guard tower
glints in sunset; convicts rest
like lizards on rocks.

2

The piano man
is stingy, at 3 A.M.
his songs drop like plum.

3

Morning sun slants cell.
Drunks stagger like cripple flies
On jailhouse floor.

4

To write a blues song
is to regiment riots
and pluck gems from graves.

5

A bare pecan tree
slips a pencil shadow down
a moonlit snow slope.

6

The falling snow flakes
Cannot blunt the hard aches nor
Match the steel stillness.

7

Under moon shadows
A tall boy flashes knife and
Slices star bright ice.

8

In the August grass
Struck by the last rays of sun
The cracked teacup screams.

9

Making jazz swing in
Seventeen syllables AIN'T
No square poet's job
(1986)

77

MICHAEL MCCLURE (1932-2020)

Michael McClure was born on 20th October, 1932 in Marysville, Kansas, USA. His parents were – Thomas McClure and Marian Dixie Johnston McClure. He was a poet, playwright, song writer and novelist. He did his B.A., in San Francisco State College. He was educated at Municipal University of Wichita (1951-1953) and University of Arizona. He published innumerable collections of poems. His main collections of poems are – *Of Indigo and Saffron* (2011), *Mephistos and Other Poems* (2016) and *Persian Pony* (2017). At the age of 68, he died on 4th May, 2020 in Oakland, California, USA.

THE CHAMBER

for Jack Kerouac
IN LIGHT ROOM IN DARK HELL IN UMBER IN
CHROME,
I sit feeling the swell of the cloud made about by
movement

of arm leg and tongue. In reflections of gold
light. Tints and flashes of gold and amber spearing
and glinting. Blur glass…blue Glass,

black telephone. Match flame of violet and flesh
seen in the clear bright light. It is not night

and night too. In Hell, there are stars outside.
And long sounds of cars. Brown shadows on walls
in the light
of the room. I sit or stand

wanting the huge reality of touch and love.
In the turned room. Remember the long-ago dream

of stuffed animals (owl, fox) in a dark shop. Wanting
only the purity of clean colors and new shapes
and feelings.

I WOULD CRY FOR THEM USELESSLY

I have ten years left to worship my youth
Billy the Kid, Rimbaud, Jean Harlow
IN DARK HELL IN LIGHT ROOM IN UMBER AND
CHROME I
feel the swell of

smoke the drain and flow of motion of exhaustion, the
long sounds of cars
the brown shadows
on the wall. I sit or stand. Caught in the net of glints
from corner table to
dull plane
from knob to floor, angles of flat light, daggers of beams.
Staring at love's face.
The telephone in cataleptic light. March flames of blue
and red seen in the
clear grain.
I see myself—ourselves—in Hell without radiance.
Reflections that we are.

The long cars make sounds and brown shadows over
the wall.

I am real as you are real whom I speak to.
I raise my head, see over the edge of my nose. Look up

and see that nothing is changed. There is no flash
to my eyes. No change to the room.

Vita Nuova—No! The dead, dead world.
The strain of desire is only a heroic gesture.
An agony to be so in pain without release

when love is a word or kiss.

THE MYSTERY OF THE HUNT

It's the mystery of the hunt that intrigues me,
That drives us like lemmings, but cautiously—
The search for a bright square cloud—the scent of
lemon verbena—

Or to learn rules for the game the sea otters
Play in the surf.

It is these small things — and the secret behind them
That fill the heart.
The pattern, the spirit, the fiery demon
That link them together
And pull their freedom into our senses,

The smell of a shrub, a cloud, the action of animals

— The rising, the exuberance, when the mystery is
unveiled.
It is these small things

That when brought into vision become an inferno.

MEXICO SEEN FROM THE
MOVING CAR

THERE ARE HILLS LIKE SHARKFINS
and clods of mud.
The mind drifts through
in the shape of a museum,
in the guise of a museum
dreaming dead friends:
Jim, Tom, Emmet, Bill.
— Like billboards their huge faces droop
and stretch on the walls,
on the walls of the cliffs out there,
where trees with white trunks
makes plumes on rock ridges.

My mind is fingers holding a pen.

Trees with white trunks
make plumes on rock ridges.
Rivers of sand are memories.
Memories make movies
on the dust of the desert.
Hawks with pale bellies
perch on the cactus,
their bodies are portholes
to other dimensions.

This might go on forever.

I am a snake and a tiptoe feather
at opposite ends of the scales
as they balance themselves
against each other.
This might go on forever.

78

GEOFFREY HILL (1932-2016)

He was an English poet, professor emeritus of English Literature and religion and former Co-Director of the Editorial Institute of Boston University. He was born on 18th June, 1932 in Bromsgrove, United Kingdom. He was the son of a police constable. He studied in Keble College, Oxford in 1950 and Oxford University and he became professor in the same university. He married Alice Goodman in 1987 and Nancy Whittaker in 1956. His collections of poems are – *For the Unfallen:Poems1952-1958* (1959), *Collected Poems* (1958), *New and Collected Poems1952-1992* (1994). He died on 30th June, 2016 in Cambridge.

FROM "ODI BARBARE"

XXIV

What is far hence led to the den of making:
Moves unlike wildfire | not so simple-happy
Ploughman hammers ploughshare his *durum dentem*
Digging the *Georgics*

Vision loads landscape | lauds *Idoto Mater*
Bearing up sacrally so graced with bodies
Voids the challenge how far from Igboland *great-*
Stallioned Argos

Vehemencies minus the ripe arraignment
Clapper this art taken to heart the fiction
What are those harsh cryings astrew the marshes
Weep not to hear them

Accolades Muses' dithyrambics far-fraught
Borrowed labour ashen with sullen harrow
Cruel past that | Sidney and vesperal Tom
Campion courted

Put to claim not otherwise vowed the era
What else here goes | I am no Igbo wit well
Versed in Virgil Pindar Euripides child-
Hallowed I do to

Revelation blessed in its unforthcoming
Closed with *tempus aedificandi tempus*
Destruendi bringing discharge of measure
Blasting the home-straight

XXV

Lovelace there come difficult times between us
Though in your place I cannot well imagine
Why I should not follow her chequered steps in-
Out of the sunlight

Candlelight here given the invocation
Starlit even ' whatever else is silence
Gratiana somewhere still ' she is dancing
Dancing and singing

Singing not her heart out beyond the fable
Grand carotid arteries self-fulfilling
How the blood's tempered in its modulation
Balanced impulsive

So are our storms trackered from solemn orbit
Turbulence granted our sequestered sphere now
Buffetted now spun on an awl now baffled
Wreathed in cloud-garlands

Masques do so challenge and compose to labour
Hers the masque-like venture the scenes mechanic
Stars have held being since creation's fourth day
Turned to their music

Noble her frame troubling the fame we yield her
All rites well done short of a consummation
Treading down nothingness to ever-dealing
Maker unmonstrant

XXVI

Łodz I've been there done that the vanished children
Klezmer makes glad music at Lazarus gate
If as straggling voices the dead return now
They have our number

Breathing hard we wrestled asbestos brake-pads
Luminously radioactive watches
Fizzled green plaque riding elastic wrist-bands
Glue smelt of pear drops

Someone those taut days was predicting biros
Not my blubbered Jewish pal bright a bully
That we knew klezmer I much doubt the *Wedding
Dance for the Old Men*

Time released me from him as I could not have
Many then had foresight but I was not one
Vital spinners counting there's no subtraction
Ever can oust them

Odds are for pittance where redemption strands us
Debts of those long-dead sparks of phantom brain cells:
Who's to dance *broyges tants* the dance of anger's
Conciliation?

There is no known voice but a clarinet sounds
Almost human touting a melt to die for
Hurl of things fast bound the last-known survivors'
Wailed diminution

XXVII

Breathe on my nesh eyes as upon a glass ⌡ this
Something so exquisite I scarce can bear it
I do not think I ever could have borne it
If not for real

Make estrangement all our desires that age so
Perfect empowerment the imperfection
How indemnify a degraded legend
Lost to computing

Contumacious that I am and that now like
Poggio I ⌡ too much enjoy invective —
This for our good — so what you saw me *turned on*
Mind if I stress this

Breathe on my nose, eyes I am tired of sleeping
Largo ma non troppo affettuoso
Well becomes fierce *Didone trionfante*
Lyric oblation

As fantastic here as in those odd films we
Watched albeit singly *The Tales of Hoffmann*
What we must be not to be worked with mirrors
Hives of perspective

Could I have found you in a film by Ophüls
Silent resonances of glass configured
Had I but struck us off *The Masque of Blackness*
As it was playing

FUNERAL MUSIC

William de la Pole, Duke of Suffolk: beheaded 1450
John Tiptoft, Earl of Worcester: beheaded 1470
Anthony Woodville, Earl Rivers: beheaded 1483

1

Processionals in the exemplary cave,
Benediction of shadows. Pomfret. London.
The voice fragrant with mannered humility,
With an equable contempt for this world,
'In honorem Trinitatis'. Crash. The head
Struck down into a meaty conduit of blood.
So these dispose themselves to receive each
Pentecostal blow from axe or seraph,
Spattering block-straw with mortal residue.
Psalteries whine through the empyrean. Fire
Flares in the pit, ghosting upon stone
Creatures of such rampant state, vacuous
Ceremony of possession, restless
Habitation, no man's dwelling-place.

2

For whom do we scrape our tribute of pain —
For none but the ritual king? We meditate
A rueful mystery; we are dying
To satisfy fat Caritas, those
Wiped jaws of stone. (Suppose all reconciled
By silent music; imagine the future
Flashed back at us, like steel against sun,
Ultimate recompense.) Recall the cold
Of Towton on Palm Sunday before dawn,
Wakefield, Tewkesbury: fastidious trumpets
Shrilling into the ruck; some trampled
Acres, parched, sodden or blanched by sleet,

Stuck with strange-postured dead. Recall the wind's
Flurrying, darkness over the human mire.

3

They bespoke doomsday and they meant it by
God, their curved metal rimming the low ridge.
But few appearances are like this. Once
Every five hundred years a comet's
Over-riding stillness might reveal men
In such array, livid and featureless,
With England crouched beastwise beneath it all.
'Oh, that old northern business …' A field
After battle utters its own sound
Which is like nothing on earth, but is earth.
Blindly the questing snail, vulnerable
Mole emerge, blindly we lie down, blindly
Among carnage the most delicate souls
Tup in their marriage-blood, gasping 'Jesus'.

4

Let mind be more precious than soul; it will not
Endure. Soul grasps its price, begs its own peace,
Settles with tears and sweat, is possibly
Indestructible. That I can believe.
Though I would scorn the mere instinct of faith,
Expediency of assent, if I dared,
What I dare not is a waste history
Or void rule. Averroes, old heathen,
If only you had been right, if Intellect
Itself were absolute law, sufficient grace,
Our lives could be a myth of captivity
Which we might enter: an unpeopled region
Of ever new-fallen snow, a palace blazing
With perpetual silence as with torches.

5

As with torches we go, at wild Christmas,
When we revel in our atonement
Through thirty feasts of unction and slaughter,
What is that but the soul's winter sleep?
So many things rest under consummate
Justice as though trumpets purified law,
Spikenard were the real essence of remorse.
The sky gathers up darkness. When we chant
'Ora, ora pro nobis' it is not
Seraphs who descend to pity but ourselves.
Those righteously-accused those vengeful
Racked on articulate looms indulge us
With lingering shows of pain, a flagrant
Tenderness of the damned for their own flesh:

6

My little son, when you could command marvels
Without mercy, outstare the wearisome
Dragon of sleep, I rejoiced above all —
A stranger well-received in your kingdom.
On those pristine fields I saw humankind
As it was named by the Father; fabulous
Beasts rearing in stillness to be blessed.
The world's real cries reached there, turbulence
From remote storms, rumour of solitudes,
A composed mystery. And so it ends.
Some parch for what they were; others are made
Blind to all but one vision, their necessity
To be reconciled. I believe in my
Abandonment, since it is what I have.

7

'Prowess, vanity, mutual regard,
It seemed I stared at them, they at me.
That was the gorgon's true and mortal gaze:
Averted conscience turned against itself.'
A hawk and a hawk-shadow. 'At noon,
As the armies met, each mirrored the other;
Neither was outshone. So they flashed and vanished
And all that survived them was the stark ground
Of this pain. I made no sound, but once
I stiffened as though a remote cry
Had heralded my name. It was nothing ...'
Reddish ice tinged the reeds; dislodged, a few
Feathers drifted across; carrion birds
Strutted upon the armour of the dead.

8

Not as we are but as we must appear,
Contractual ghosts of pity; not as we
Desire life but as they would have us live,
Set apart in timeless colloquy.
So it is required; so we bear witness,
Despite ourselves, to what is beyond us,
Each distant sphere of harmony forever
Poised, unanswerable. If it is without
Consequence when we vaunt and suffer, or
If it is not, all echoes are the same
In such eternity. Then tell me, love,
How that should comfort us — or anyone
Dragged half-unnerved out of this worldly place,
Crying to the end 'I have not finished'.
(1994)

79

SYLVIA PLATH (1932-1960)

Sylvia Plath was born on 27th October, 1932 in Jamaica, Boston, Massachusetts, USA. She was a poet, novelist, and short story writer. She is credited with the advancing the genre of 'confessional' poetry. Her parents were-Otto Plath and Aurelia Plath. She was educated in the Boston University. On a scholarship, she went to England, studied in Cambridge, befriended and married Ted Hughes, the famous English poet. Her main poetical works are – *The Colossus and Other Poems* (1960), *The Bell Jar* (1966), *The Lady Lazarus* (1965), *Journals of Sylvia Plath* (1982) and *Sylvia Plath: Poems* (1985). She died on 11th February, 1963 in Primrose Hill, London, United Kingdom and buried at St Thomas A Beckett Churchyard, Heptonstall.

LADY LAZARUS

I have done it again.
One year in every ten
I manage it—
A sort of walking miracle, my skin
Bright as a Nazi lampshade,
My right foot
A paperweight,
My face a featureless, fine
Jew linen.
Peel off the napkin
O my enemy.
Do I terrify?—
The nose, the eye pits, the full set of teeth?
The sour breath
Will vanish in a day.
Soon, soon the flesh
The grave cave ate will be
At home on me
And I a smiling woman.
I am only thirty.
And like the cat I have nine times to die.
This is Number Three.
What a trash
To annihilate each decade.
What a million filaments.
The peanut-crunching crowd
Shoves in to see
Them unwrap me hand and foot—
The big strip tease.
Gentlemen, ladies
These are my hands
My knees.
I may be skin and bone,
Nevertheless, I am the same, identical woman.

The first time it happened I was ten.
It was an accident.
The second time I meant
To last it out and not come back at all.
I rocked shut
As a seashell.
They had to call and call
And pick the worms off me like sticky pearls.
Dying
Is an art, like everything else.
I do it exceptionally well.
I do it so it feels like hell.
I do it so it feels real.
I guess you could say I've a call.
It's easy enough to do it in a cell.
It's easy enough to do it and stay put.
It's the theatrical
Comeback in broad day
To the same place, the same face, the same brute
Amused shout:
'A miracle!'
That knocks me out.
There is a charge
For the eyeing of my scars, there is a charge
For the hearing of my heart—
It really goes.
And there is a charge, a very large charge
For a word or a touch
Or a bit of blood
Or a piece of my hair or my clothes.
So, so, Herr Doktor.
So, Herr Enemy.
I am your opus,
I am your valuable,
The pure gold baby
That melts to a shriek.

I turn and burn.
Do not think I underestimate your great concern.
Ash, ash —
You poke and stir.
Flesh, bone, there is nothing there-
A cake of soap,
A wedding ring,
A gold filling.
Herr God, Herr Lucifer
Beware
Beware.
Out of the ash
I rise with my red hair
And I eat men like air.
(23-29 October 1962)

80

ADRIAN HENRI (1932-2000)

Henri Adrian (1932 –)is the poet Laureate of contemporary English. He was wall-painter and performer in the theatre. He was born on 10th April, 1932, in Birkenhead, in United Kingdom. He studied in at Newcastle and taught at the Preston Catholic College. For ten years, he was with Carol Ann Duffy. He was the founder of Poetry-rock group the Liverpool Scene and one of the three poets in the best-selling anthology. *The Liverpool Scene* and *The Mersey Sound* (1967) and *Collected Poems 1967-1985* (1986) are the main collections of poems. He died on 20th December, 2000 in Liverpool, England.

WITHOUT YOU

Without you every morning would feel going back to
work after a holiday,
Without you I could n't stand the smell of the East Lancs
Road,
Without you ghost ferries would cross the Mersey
manned by skelton crews,
Without you I'd probably feel happy and have more
money and time and nothing to do with it.
Without you I'd have t leave my still born poems on
other people's doorsteps,
wrapped in brown paper.
Without you there' d never be sauce to put on sausage
buttes,
Without you plastic flowers in shop windows would
just be plastic in shop windows,
Without you Id spend my summers picking morosely
over the remains of train crashes,
Without you white birds would wrench themselves free
from my paintings and fly off dripping blood into the
night.
Without you green apples wouldn't taste greener,
Without you Mothers would n't let their children play
out after tea,
Without you every musician in the world would forget
how to play the blues,
Without you Public houses would be public again,
Without you Sunday Times colour supplement would
come out in black and white,
Without you indifferent colonels would shrug their
shoulders and press the button,
Without you they's stop changing the flowers in
Piccadilly Gardens,
Without you Clark Kent would forget how to become
Superman,

Without you Sunshine breakfast would only consist of Cornflakes,
Without you there 'd no colour in Magic colouring books,
Without you Mahler's 8th would only be performed by street musicians in derelict houses.
Without you they'd forget to put the salt in every packet of crisps,
Without you it would an offence punishable by a fine of up to 200 or
two months imprisonment to be found in possession of curry powder,
Without you not police are massing in quiet side streets,

LOVE IS.....

Love is...
Love is feeling cold in the back of vans
Love is a fan club with only two fans
Love is walking holding paint stained hands
Love is.

Love is fish and chips on winter nights
Love is blankets full of strange delights
Love is when you don't put out the light
Love is

Love is the presents in Christmas shops
Love is when you're feeling Top of the Pops
Love is what happens when the music stops
Love is

Love is white panties lying all forlorn
Love is pink nightdresses still slightly warm
Love is when you have to leave at dawn

Love is
Love is you and love is me
Love is prison and love is free
Love's what's there when you are away from me
Love is...

ANY PRINCE TO ANY PRINCESS

August is coming
and the goose, I'm afraid,
is getting fat.
There have been
no golden eggs for some months now.
Straw has fallen well below market price
despite my frantic spinning
and the sedge is,
as you rightly point out,
withered.

I can't imagine how the pea
got under your mattress. I apologize
humbly. The chambermaid has, of course,
been sacked. As has the frog footman.
I understand that, during my recent fact-finding tour of
the Golden River,
despite your nightly unavailing efforts,
he remained obstinately
froggish.

I hope that the Three Wishes granted by the General
Assembly
will go some way towards redressing
this unfortunate recent sequence of events.
The fall in output from the shoe-factory, for example:

no one could have foreseen the work-to-rule
by the National Union of Elves. Not to mention the fact
that the court has been fast asleep
for the last six and a half years.

The matter of the poisoned apple has been taken up
by the Board of Trade: I think I can assure you
the incident will not be
repeated.

I can quite understand, in the circumstances,
your reluctance to let down
your golden tresses. However
I feel I must point out
that the weather isn't getting any better
and I already have a nasty chill
from waiting at the base
of the White Tower. You must see
the absurdity of the
situation.
Some of the courtiers are beginning to talk,
not to mention the humble villagers.
It's been three weeks now, and not even
a word.

Princess,
a cold, black wind
howls through our empty palace.
Dead leaves litter the bedchamber;
the mirror on the wall hasn't said a thing
since you left. I can only ask,
bearing all this in mind,
that you think again,
let down your hair,
reconsider

81

PHILLIP WHALEN (1932-2002)

Phillip Whalen was born on 20th October, 1923 in Portland Oregon, USA. He studied B.A., in the Reed College and served in the US Army Air Forces during World War II. His collections of poems are – *The Calendar, a Book of Poems* (1951), *Scenes of Life at the Capital* (1970), *Overtime: Selected Poems by Phillip Whalen* ((1999). *The Collected Poems of Phillip Whalen* (2007). In 1973, he became Buddhist monk. He was an American poet and Zen Buddhist by religiosity and key figure in the San Francisco Renaissance and close to the Beat Generation. He died on 26th June, 2002 in San Francisco.

A VISION OF THE BODHISATTVAS

They pass before me one by one riding on animals
"What are you waiting for," they want to know

Z—, young as he is (& mad into the bargain) tells me
"Someday you'll drop everything & become a *rishi*, you
know."

I know
The forest is there, I've lived in it
More certainly than this town? Irrelevant—

What am I waiting for?
A change in customs that will take 1000 years to come
about?
Who's to make the change but me?

"Returning again and again," Amida says

Why's that dream so necessary? walking out of
whatever house alone
Nothing but the clothes on my back, money or no
Down the road to the next place the highway leading
to the
mountains
From which I absolutely must come back

What business have I to do that?
I know the world and I love it too much and it
Is not the one I'd find outside this door.

HISTORICAL DISQUISITIONS

Hello, hello, what to tell you was
The world's invisible

You see only yourself, that's not the world
although you are of it
Are you there

hello
why do you have your head in a sack?
a roomy-bomb dream tank?
Why you got a banana in your ear?
You where?
Brown eyes they see blue sky

The world imagines you
Figure it's a planet
You hear?
an obscure star in the middle
Once you were pleasure-milk and egg
Were you there

Now you are eggs of milk between your legs
Are you there

"I am situated somewhere near the rim of a fairly large
galaxy
which is one of a group of same & outside of which a
considerable number take their way at incredible
speeds &
apparently in the opposite direction..."

You are a wish to squirt pleasantly
You want a lot of things & they are nice & you imagine
They are you and therefore you are nice
You are a wish to be here
Wishing yourself
elsewhere

"Hello. Try to talk some sense even if you
don't think any
It is history
(your mistake: "History WAS")
now
*

History an explanation of why I deserve what I take
*

History an explanation of why I get what I deserve
*

(Through more or less clenched teeth):
"How can you sit there & look at the faces
you see in Montgomery Street wiped blank
from selling whatever brains they got faces
in 3rd Street blank from facing a lathe all day
& TV all night African tromped-on faces Asiatic
hunger faces Washington war-masks & smile at me
about how after all this is a Moral Universe
gives me the screaming jumping enemies I thought
you were bright enough had enough work-experience
yourself to have some faint idea of..."
*

hello.

"The wind rattles the window i can't
Sleep friday night is very large in san
Francisco the lower classes get paid on
Friday & get on their way to spend it in
Upper-middle-class clip joints they claim
Aren't tourist traps the upper classes are
Lushed out of their heads down in pebble

Beach sucking each other's & will skip the
Shrinker monday he's gay himself the
Silly son of a bitch as long as i'm not out
Hustling sailors on market street & only
When i'm lushed out on my own premises
(for which i pay excessively high taxes)

I DON'T CARE"

"The middle classes the middle class is mainly from
out of town (that's what I like about San Francisco
everybody's either up or down) they come & look at us
they go away puzzled where they remain,
outclassed...
(they will fight the Rooshuns &c.
they will fight the gooks & wogs & chinks &
japs & niggers & commies & catholics & wall
street & any man that tries to tell them
different...)"

"The upper class don't bother me a bit except
why do they let themselves be buffaloed into
hiring the creepy managers they do? Faceless men to
represent a legal fiction? The upper
well, the..."

"UPPER CLASSES ARE HARMLESSLY IMBE-
CILE THE CLASSES PRETEND NOT TO EXIST (&
VERY NEARLY CAN'T, OUTSIDE OF JAIL) THE
MIDDLE
CLASS   MANAGER   MERCHANT   BANKER
PROFESSIONAL
PROFESSIONAL THE SOLID (IT'S THE CHEESE
THAT

MAKES IT BINDING) CALVINISTFREUDIAN
DEMOC-
RACY SWELLS

&BLOSSOMS!"

TERMINAL LUES ACROSS THE SHOULDERS
OF THE WORLD

"The Roman Empire went to hell when the Romans
bought them-
selves a goon-squad; bankrupted themselves trying to
enforce moral
and sumptuary laws..."

IF YOU'RE SO SMART, WHY AIN'T
YOU RICH?

I need everything else
Anything else
Desperately
But I have nothing
Shall have nothing
but this
Immediate, inescapable
and invaluable
No one can afford
THIS
Being made here and now

(Seattle, Washington
7 May, 1955)

MARIGOLDS

Concise (wooden)
Orange.
Behind them, the garage door
Pink
(Paint sold under a fatuous name:
"Old Rose"
which brings a war to mind)

And the mind slides over the fence again
Orange against pink and green
Uncontrollable!

Returned of its own accord
It can explain nothing
Give no account

What good? What worth?

Dying!

You have less than a second
To live
To try to explain:
Say that light
in particular wave-lengths
or bundles wobbling at a given speed
Produces the experience
Orange against pink
Better than a sirloin steak?
A screen by Korin?

The effect of this, taken internally
The effect

of beauty
on the mind

There is no equivalent, least of all
These objects
Which ought to manifest
A surface disorientation, pitting
Or stride
Admitting *some* plausible interpretation

But the cost
Can't be expressed in numbers
dodging between
a vagrancy rap
and the newest electrical brain-curette
Eating what the rich are bullied into giving
Or the poor willingly share
Depriving themselves

More expensive than ambergris
Although the stink
isn't as loud. (A few
Wise men have said,
"Produced the same way . . .
Vomited out by sick whales.")
Valuable for the same qualities
Staying-power and penetration
I've squandered every crying dime.

82

LEROI JONES (IMAMU AMIRI BARAKA-1934-2014)

Leroi Jones (Imamu Amiri Baraka) is a famous jazz trumpeter. Born 20th February,1958 in New York. Jones began playing trumpet at the age of ten. His collections of poems are – *Welcome Says the Angel* (2003) and *The Girl with the Hungry Eyes* (1995). He did his Ph.D. in Organic Chemistry from the University of South Carolina at Columbia. His early poetry has the influence of Ezra Pound and William Carlos Williams. Closely associated with Harlem Renaissance, he pleaded for a separate Black Cultural Nationalism. He died on 9th January, 2014 in Newark, Beth Israel medical center, Newark, New Jersey, USA.

AN AGONY AS NOW

I am inside someone
who hates me. I look
out from his eyes. Smell
what fouled tunes come in
to his breath. Love his
wretched women.

Slits in the metal, for sun. Where
my eyes sit turning, at the cool air
the glance of light, or hard flesh
rubbed against me, a woman, a man,
without shadow, or voice, or meaning.

This is the enclosure (flesh,
where innocence is a weapon. An
abstraction. Touch. (Not mine.
Or yours, if you are the soul I had
and abandoned when I was blind and had
my enemies carry me as a dead man
(if he is beautiful, or pitied.

It can be pain. (As now, as all his
flesh hurts me.) It can be that. Or
pain. As when she ran from me into
that forest.
Or pain, the mind
silver spiraled whirled against the
sun, higher than even old men thought
God would be. Or pain. And the other. The
yes. (Inside his books, his fingers. They
are withered yellow flowers and were never
beautiful.) The yes. You will, lost soul, say
'beauty.' Beauty, practiced, as the tree. The
slow river. A white sun in its wet sentences.

Or, the cold men in their gale. Ecstasy. Flesh
or soul. The yes. (Their robes blown. Their bowls
empty. They chant at my heels, not at yours.) Flesh
or soul, as corrupt. Where the answer moves too quickly.
Where the God is a self, after all.)

Cold air blown through narrow blind eyes. Flesh,
white hot metal. Glows as the day with its sun.
It is a human love, I live inside. A bony skeleton
you recognize as words or simple feeling.

But it has no feeling. As the metal, is hot, it is not,
given to love.

It burns the thing
inside it. And that thing
screams.

BABYLON REVISITED

The gaunt thing
with no organs
creeps along the streets
of Europe, she will
commute, in her feathered bat stomach-gown
with no organs
with sores on her insides
even her head
a vast puschamber
of pus(sy) memories
with no organs
nothing to make babies
she will be the great witch of euro-american legend
who sucked the life
from some unknown nigger

whose name will be known
but whose substance will not ever
not even by him
who is dead in a pile of dopeskin

This bitch killed a friend of mine named Bob Thompson
a black painter, a giant, once, she reduced
to a pitiful imitation faggot
full of American holes and a monkey on his back
slapped airplanes
from the empire state building

May this bitch and her sisters, all of them,
receive my words
in all their orifices like lye mixed with
co cola and alaga syrup

feel this shit, bitches, feel it, now laugh your
hysteretic laughs
while your flesh burns
and your eyes peel to red mud.

LEGACY

(For Blues People)
In the south, sleeping against
the drugstore, growling under
the trucks and stoves, stumbling
through and over the cluttered eyes
of early mysterious night. Frowning
drunk waving moving a hand or lash.
Dancing kneeling reaching out, letting
a hand rest in shadows. Squatting
to drink or pee. Stretching to climb
pulling themselves onto horses near

where there was sea (the old songs
lead you to believe). Riding out
from this town, to another, where
it is also black. Down a road
where people are asleep. Towards
the moon or the shadows of houses.
Towards the songs' pretended sea.
(1969)

83

DIANE DE PRIMA (1934-2020)

Diane de Prima was born on 6th August, 1934 in Brooklyn New York. She was an American poet known for association with the Beat Movement school of poetry. Her father was Francis, a lawyer and Emma, a teacher. She was also an artist, prose writer and teacher. She attended Swarthmore College. She married thrice – Ian Marlowe in 1962, Grant Fisher in 1972, and also Sheppard Powell. Her collections of poems are – *Revolutionary Letters* (1968), *Memoirs of Beatnik*, *The Poetry Deal* (2014) and *Pieces of a Song* (1990). She died on 25th October, 2020 in San Francisco, California.

AN EXERCISE IN LOVE

for Jackson Allen

My friend wears my scarf at his waist
I give him moonstones
He gives me shell & seaweeds
He comes from a distant city & I meet him
We will plant eggplants & celery together
He weaves me cloth

Many have brought the gifts
I use for his pleasure
silk, & green hills
& heron the color of dawn

My friend walks soft as a weaving on the wind
He backlights my dreams
He has built altars beside my bed
I awake in the smell of his hair & cannot remember
his name, or my own.

THE WINDOW

you are my bread
and the hairline
noise
of my bones
you are almost
the sea

you are not stone
or molten sound
I think
you have no hands

this kind of bird flies backward
and this love
breaks on a windowpane
where no light talks

this is not time
for crossing tongues
(the sand here
never shifts)

I think
tomorrow
turned you with his toe
and you will
shine
and shine
unspent and underground

FIRST SNOW, KERHONKSON

for Alan
This, then, is the gift the world has given me
(you have given me)
softly the snow
cupped in hollows
lying on the surface of the pond
matching my long white candles
which stand at the window
which will burn at dusk while the snow
fills up our valley
this hollow
no friend will wander down
no one arriving brown from Mexico
from the sunfields of California, bearing pot
they are scattered now, dead or silent

or blasted to madness
by the howling brightness of our once common vision
and this gift of yours —
white silence filling the contours of my life.
(1990)

84

MARY OLIVER (1938-2019)

Mary Oliver was born on 10th Sept, 1938 in Mapis Heights, Ohio, USA. Her parents were Helen M.V.Oliver, Edward William. She studied in Vassar College, Ohio State University. Her partner was Molly Malone Cook. Her collections were – *Wild Geese* (2004), *Devotions: The Selected Poems* (2017), *Dog Songs* (2013) and *A Thousand Mornings* (2012). She found inspiration for her work in future and had a lifelong habit of solitary walks in the wild. She was an American poet who won the National book award and the Pulitzer Prize. She died on 17th January, 2019 in Hobe Sound, Florida.

FALL

the black oaks
fling their bronze fruit
into all the pockets of the earth
pock pock

they knock against the thresholds
the roof the sidewalk
fill the eaves
the bottom line

of the old gold song
of the almost finished year
what is spring all that tender
green stuff

compared to this
falling of tiny oak trees
out of the oak trees
then the clouds

gathering thick along the west
then advancing
then closing over
breaking open

the silence
then the rain
dashing its silver seeds
against the house

HUMMING BIRDS

The female, and the two chicks,
each no bigger than my thumb,
scattered,
shimmering

in their pale-green dresses;
	then they rose, tiny fireworks,
	into the leaves
	and hovered;
	then they sat down,
	each one with dainty, charcoal feet–
	each one on a slender branch-
	looked at me

	I had meant no harm,
	I had simply
	climbed the tree
	for something to do

	on a summer day,
	not knowing they were there,
	ready to burst the ledges
	of their mossy nest
	and to fly, for the first time,
	in their sea-green helmets,
	with brisk, metallic tails–
	each tulled wing.

	with every dollop of light,
	drawing a perfect wheel
	across the air.
	Then, with a series of jerks,

they paused in front of me
and, dark-eyed, stared–
as though I were a flower–
and then,

like three tosses of silvery water
they were gone.
Alone,
in the crown of the tree.

I went to China,
I went to Prague;
I died, and was born in the spring;
I found you, and loved you, again.

Later the darkness fell
and the solid moon
like a white pond rose.
But I wasn't in any hurry.

Likely I visited all
the shimmering, heart-stabbing
questions without answers
before I climbed down.

85

SEAMUS HEANEY (B.1939)

Seamus Heaney, a poet, playwright and translator, was born on 13th April, 1939 in Castle Dawson, United Kingdom. He was educated at Bates College, and later in the Queen's University, Belfast. His parents were Patrick Heaney and mother, Sarah Heaney. He married Marie Devlin. His collections of poems – *The Death of a Naturalist* (1966), *Bog Poems* (1975), *Clearances* (1989), *Poems* (1996), and *Human Chain* (2010). He died on 30th August, 2013 in Blackrock, Health Blackrock Clinic in Dublin, Ireland. He was influenced by W.B.Yeats, Robert Frost, William Words worth and T.S. Eliot. For Literature, he won the Nobel Prize for Literature in 1995.

DIGGING

Between my finger and my thumb
The squat pen rests; snug as a gun.

Under my window, a clean rasping sound
When the spade sinks into gravelly ground:
My father, digging. I look down

Till his straining rump among the flowerbeds
Bends low, comes up twenty years away
Stooping in rhythm through potato drills
Where he was digging.

The coarse boot nestled on the lug, the shaft
Against the inside knee was levered firmly.
He rooted out tall tops, buried the bright edge deep
To scatter new potatoes that we picked,
Loving their cool hardness in our hands.

By God, the old man could handle a spade.
Just like his old man.

My grandfather cut more turf in a day
Than any other man on Toner's bog.
Once I carried him milk in a bottle
Corked sloppily with paper. He straightened up
To drink it, then fell to right away
Nicking and slicing neatly, heaving sods
Over his shoulder, going down and down
For the good turf. Digging.

The cold smell of potato mould, the squelch and slap
Of soggy peat, the curt cuts of an edge
Through living roots awaken in my head.
But I've no spade to follow men like them.

Between my finger and my thumb
The squat pen rests.
I'll dig with it.

CHURNING DAY

A thick crust, coarse-grained as limestone rough-cast,
hardened gradually on top of the four crocks
that stood, large pottery bombs, in the small pantry.
After the hot brewery of gland, cud and udder,
cool porous earthenware fermented the buttermilk
for churning day, when the hooped churn was scoured
with plumping kettles and the busy scrubber
echoed daintily on the seasoned wood.
It stood then, purified, on the flagged kitchen floor.

Out came the four crocks, spilled their heavy lip
of cream, their white insides, into the sterile churn.
The staff, like a great whisky meddler fashioned
in dead wood, was plunged in, the lid fitted.
My mother took first turn, set up rhythms
that slugged and thumped for hours. Arms ached.
Hands blistered. Cheeks and clothes were spattered

with flabby milk.
Where finally gold flecks
began to dance. They poured hot water then,
sterilized a birch wood-bowl
and little corrugated butter-spades.
Their short stroke quickened, suddenly
a yellow curd was weighting the churned up white,
heavy and rich, coagulated sunlight
that they fished, dripping, in a wide tin strainer,
heaped up like gilded gravel in the bowl.

The house would stink long after churning day,
acrid as a sulphor mine. The empty crocks
were ranged along the wall again, the butter
in soft printed slabs was piled on pantry shelves.
And in the house we moved with gravid ease,
our brains turned crystals full of clean deal churns,
the plash and gurgle of the sour-breathed milk,
the pat and slap of small spades on wet lumps.

RITE OF SPRING

So winter closed its fist
And got it stuck in the pump.
The plunger froze up a lump

In its throat, ice founding itself
Upon iron. The handle
Paralyzed at an angle.

Then the twisting of wheat straw
into ropes, lapping them tight
Round stem and snout, then a light

That sent the pump up in a flame
It cooled, we lifted her latch,
Her entrance was wet, and she came.

86

LINDA MARSHALL (1941-)

She was born on 6th January,1941 in Dallas, Texas, United States. She was an American actress and a poetess. She started her television career in 1963 situation comedy, *My Three Sons* and in 1965 appeared in her first movie, *Tammy and the Millionaire* (1967). She was married to Sohrab Youseffian in 1968.

SHE PAINTS HER

she paints her
in a green sea of
feathery fronds,
as a goddess
of maidenhair fern
in gentle poise
and soft natural grace

her skin rich,
deep mahogany
echoing the hues
of sepia dreams
arcing upward
into the light
as if born to seek
sunny rays

the water
playing in a giggle
of soft ripples
weaving around her
in flowing threads
dappled peach and orange
by the hot African sun

amid browns as varied
as sand dunes at dawn,
as intricately shaded
as the lightest of wood
carried ashore
upon windswept waves

each colored
brushstroke
strong and true,
bold and gentle,
telling us of the day
that passes in
a world beyond

Christ is risen! Praise be to God!
Our Lord gave everything to humankind,
And we should love Him for the love He gave,
And we, so selfish and so blind,
Were saved by His victory over the grave.

Christ is our all in all, the one who cares
So much for us poor sinners, that He died
Upon a cross in a field sown with tears
Yet triumphed over all man's foolish pride.

Even the Cross of shame became a sign
That God is far above our mortal ken.
And through Christ's rising He showed His design
That through His grace we too might live again.

87

LOUSIE GLUCK (1943-2023)

She was born on 22nd April, 1943 in New York USA, and grew in the Long Island. She was a brilliant poet and essayist. She married John Dranow in 1977. She attended Sarah Lawrence College, Later she studied in the School of the Arts in Columbia University 1967-1968. In her poetry, she explored the trauma. She won the Nobel Prize for literature in 2020. She died on 13th October, 2013 in Cambridge, Massachusetts, USA..

AFTERWORD

LAUNCH AUDIO IN A NEW WINDOW

Reading what I have just written, I now believe
I stopped precipitously, so that my story seems to have been
slightly distorted, ending, as it did, not abruptly
but in a kind of artificial mist of the sort
sprayed onto stages to allow for difficult set changes.

Why did I stop? Did some instinct
discern a shape, the artist in me
intervening to stop traffic, as it were?

A shape. Or fate, as the poets say,
intuited in those few long ago hours —

I must have thought so once.
And yet I dislike the term
which seems to me a crutch, a phase,
the adolescence of the mind, perhaps —

Still, it was a term I used myself,
frequently to explain my failures.
Fate, destiny, whose designs and warnings
now seem to me simply
local symmetries, metonymic
baubles within immense confusion —

Chaos was what I saw.
My brush froze — I could not paint it.

Darkness, silence: that was the feeling.

What did we call it then?

A "crisis of vision" corresponding, I believed,
to the tree that confronted my parents,

but whereas they were forced
forward into the obstacle,
I retreated or fled—

Mist covered the stage (my life).
Characters came and went, costumes were
changed,
my brush hand moved side to side
far from the canvas,
side to side, like a windshield wiper.

Surely this was the desert, the dark night.
(In reality, a crowded street in London,
the tourists waving their colored maps.)

One speaks a word: *I.*
Out of this stream
the great forms—

I took a deep breath. And it came to me
the person who drew that breath
was not the person in my story, his childish hand
confidently wielding the crayon—

Had I been that person? A child but also
an explorer to whom the path is suddenly clear,
for whom
the vegetation parts—

And beyond, no longer screened from view, that exalted
solitude Kant perhaps experienced
on his way to the bridges —
(We share a birthday.)

Outside, the festive streets
were strung, in late January, with exhausted
Christmas lights.
A woman leaned against her lover's shoulder
singing Jacques Brel in her thin soprano —

Bravo! the door is shut.
Now nothing escapes, nothing enters —

I hadn't moved. I felt the desert
stretching ahead, stretching (it now seems)
on all sides, shifting as I speak,

so that I was constantly
face to face with blankness, that
stepchild of the sublime,

which, it turns out,
has been both my subject and my medium.

What would my twin have said, had my thoughts
reached him?

Perhaps he would have said
in my case there was no obstacle (for the sake of
argument)
after which I would have been
referred to religion, the cemetery where
questions of faith are answered.

The mist had cleared. The empty canvases
were turned inward against the wall.

The little cat is dead (so the song went).

Shall I be raised from death, the spirit asks.
And the sun says yes.
And the desert answers
your voice is sand scattered in wid.
(2012)

88

DAVID NASH (1945-)

David Nash was born in County Cork and lives between Ireland and Chile. He completed his M.,A, in Writing in Goldsmiths, University to London in 2010 where he won Kavanagh Award for his Best Portfolio, the first poet to do so. His collections of poems are – *The Islands of Chile* (2022). and *No Man's Land* (2023).

SYNECDOCHE

The man from O'Mahoney's
Tree Services Ltd. says that the only
difference between himself and an arborist
is softer hands and clout.
He recommends felling, to no one's surprise.
For all we know he's right, filling
his boots with Mom's brown bread, though
I find his further grounds
overkill: *comes a storm*, says he,
this Cúil Aodha Cassandra,
comes a storm and it's through
your windshield you'll find it.
Or through your eye, God forbid.
And the masterstroke: *Or through some young thing.*
That settles it for Mom.
June that same year and the grasshoppers
are all saying *heat.* I emerge
from the dead-still lake in a film
of scum and water striders to the far-off wasping
of a chainsaw, and march home towards it.
I am in time for the fall,
the tree genuflecting to its own expiry
and the leading-lady swoon of the leaves on the ground
like all its life's breath had arrived at once.
We stand over what's left, a halo
of sawdust around what looks, from above,
like a map of a city – old town
in the centre; high-rise splinters
to the side where it was tipped; monochrome,
but only if you squint and from this far up.
Zoom out further, and in a time
before cities there was real fatalism
and risk was an afterthought, quotidian.
If something killed you, it killed you –
there would be other lives.

NETTLE

I'd like to bring my grandfather back to life just to get him stoned,
the good kind, the thirst and laughter kind. He had, I think, kind laughter.
My plan is this: I'd tell him the weed was nettle seeds I'd honed
to be smoke able, we'd use his pipe. *I hope tw on't kill me,* he'd say, *and me just after*
dying. But I am his. People of his don't do him harm, we're reliable as clothing.
I'd watch him reinhabit his trout-skin, retake stock of his own mouth,
suck his false tooth like he used, laugh about this. I need to know some things.
Did being called Gaga put in or put out on him? Is it true that in this part of the south
they used to make known their love by whipping the object of it with a nettle?
True, Gaga would tell me, *the grasping of the stinger was the pain that proved it.*
Here he'd open his big bready hands and stroke out the lines where the leaves should settle.
Gentleness won't work. It should be in your hand before it knows you've moved it.
He'd fix his bloodshot eyes on Granny's masscard, curling on the shelf.
He'd tell me all of this. I wouldn't have to find out for myself.

IMAGINARY FARMER

You don't know shit, says my imaginary farmer
when we have debates about reducing the national
herd.
Literally, like. You don't know the first thing
about it. Not the gleaming cakes the cows leave
in their wake, not the ripe road-apples of the coach horse,
not the rat-slick, not the castings of the worms, earth's
afterbirth, not the stuff people are happy as pigs in,
not bunny bullets, not spirant, not frats, not scat, not fumets.
Not squat. You wouldn't know the dropping from the bird
that drops it.
(He is something of a poet himself, of course,
and uses lists as shock-and-awe.)
I do though, I protest. *Couldn't I tell you your future*
from the pattern of the cracks in week-old locum,
which, by the way, is bespoke Nash family vocal for cow-pats?
And don't I know my own? And am I not an alchemist myself,
like every other beast? Do you think you're above or apart
from it?
And we go on like this, knowing things at each other
while gravity draws every step closer in to land
and all our eyes roll heavenwards.

89

BARRY MACSWEENNEY (1948-2000)

Barry Mac Sweeny was born on 17th July,1948 in Newcastle upon Tyne, England. He was an English poet and journalist. Through his organizing work he contributed a lot to the English poetry. *Elegy for January* (1970), *Blackbird: Elegy for William Gordon Calvert* (1980), *The Book of Demons* (1997), *Far Cliff Babylon* (1978), *Hellhound Memos* (1993) are his main collections of poems. He died on 9th May, 2000. in Denton, Bum, Newcastle upon Tyne, United Kingdom.

DAFT PATTER

If anyone knows about sullen loneliness, you do
Yet there's a grin in the wind, heartless and cold
There's dark in the darkness, beauty of streams
I low m beams to you, from tunnel o tunnel

as if the frozen air had a distinct personality
Standing in the lonnen head, holding leeks, you
sawed my glance in half with yours. What keen eyes!
Such strange, out-dated clothes. What's inside counts.

Leaning into the tall grass grandness of your alert stance
towards the west and the brilliant beauties of Ireland.
I know now why you took sickle hook
backing the beasts into their shutdown shed

You chopped the gate for want of sound
but you had sound, all sound, my purr mistress
my fantastic slavver merchant, when we peeled te sky

together we had water and silence and fire and
togetherness
the lights of all you didn't say knots of life and all
dreams.

90

ANDREW MOTION (1952-)

Andrew Motion (1952 –) is, being 72 years old, the poet Laureate of contemporary England. He is the poet, biographer and novelist. He was born on 26th October, 1952 in London. He was educated in Radley College. and University College, Oxford. He is a FRSL English poet. He married Joanna Powell in 1983, Jan Dalley in 1985 and Kyeong Soo Kim in 2010. His main collections of poems are – *Goodstone: A Sequence* (1972), *Inland* (1976), *The Pleasure Streamers* (1978), *Natural Causes* (1987), *Salt Water* (1997) and *Randomly Moving Particles* (2020). He was the poet Laureate from 1999 to 2009; during that period he founded Poetry Archive.

A DYING RACE

The less I visit, the more
I think myself back to your house
I grew up in. The lane uncurled
through candle-lit chestnuts
discovers it standing four-square,
whitewashed unnaturally clear,
as if it were shown me by lightning.

It's always the place I see,
not you You've somewhere outside.
waving goodbye were I left you
a decade ago. I've even lost sight
of losing you now; all I can find
are the mossy steps you stood on
a visible loneliness.

I' m living four centuries away, and still
I think of you driving south each night
to the ward where your wife is living.
How long will it last?

You've made that journey six years
Already, taking each broken-off day
as a present, to please her.

I can remember the fields you pass,
the derelict pill-boxes squatting
in shining plough. If I was still there,
watching your hand push back
the hair from her desperate face,
I might have discovered by now
the way love looks, its harrowing clarity.

LOOK

I pull back the curtain
and what I do I see
but my wife on a sheet
and the screen beside her
showing her twins
put of their capsule
in mooning blue,
their dawdlers' legs
kicking through silence
enormously slowly,
while blotches beneath them
revolve like the earth
which will bring them to grief
or into their own.

I pull back the curtain
and what do I see
but my mother asleep,
or at least not awake,
and the sheet folded down
to show me her throat
with its wrinkled hole
and the tube inside
which leads to oxygen
stashed round her bed,
as though any day now
she might lift into space
and never return
to breathe our air.

91

CAROL ANN DUFFY (1955-)

Carl Ann Duffy is the poet Laureate of contemporary England. She was born on 23rd December, 1955 in Glasgow, United Kingdom. She studied B.A., with Philosophy in the University of Liverpool. She, being a Professor of Contemporary Poetry at Manchester Metropolitan University, Manchester, England, is honored with FRSL by the Queen Elizabeth II of England. She is a famous Scottish poet and playwright. Her collections of poems are – *Standing Female Nude* (1985), *Selling Manhattan* (1987), *The World's Wife* (1999) and *Rapture* (2005).

ANN HAWTHAWAY

The bed we loved in was a spinning world
of forests, castles, torchlight, clifftops, seas
where we could dive for peals. My lover's words
were shooting stars which fell to earth as kisses
on these lips; my body now a softer rhyme
to his, now echo, assonance; his touch
a verb dancing in the centre of a noun.
Some nights, I dreamed he'd written me, the bed
a page beneath his writer's hands. Romance
and drama played by touch, by scent, by taste.
In the other bed, the best, our guests dozed on,
dribbling their prose. My living laughing love-
I told him in the casket of my widow's head
as he held me upon that next best bed.

EDUCATION FOR LEISURE

Today I am going to kill something. Anything.
I have had enough of being ignored and today
I am going to play God. It is an ordinary day,
a sort of grey with boredom stirring in the streets.

I squash a fly against the window with my thumb.
We did that in school. Shakespeare. It was in
another language and now the fly is in another language.
I breathe out talent on the glass to write my name.

I am a genius. I could be anything at all, with half
the chance. But today I am going to change the world.
Something's world. The cat avoids me. The cat
knows I am a genius and has hidden itself.

I pour the goldfish down the bog. I pull the chain.
I see that it is good. The budgie is panicking.
Once a fortnight, I walk the two miles into town
for signing on. They don't appreciate my autograph.

There is nothing left to kill. I dial the radio
and tell the man he's talking to a superstar
He cuts me off. I get out bread knife and go out
The pavements glitter suddenly. I touch your arm.

LAST POST (2009)

In all my dreams, before my helpless sight,
He plunges at me, guttering, choking, drowning.

If poetry could tell it backwards, true, begin
that moment shrapnel you to the stinking mud…
but you get up, amazed, watch bled bad blood
run upwards from the slime into its wounds;
see lines and lines of British boys rewind
back to their trenches, kiss the photographs from home –
mothers, sweethearts, sisters, younger brothers
not entering the story now
to die and die and die.
Dulce – No – Decorum – No – Pro patria mori.
You walk away.

You walk away; drop your gun (fixed bayonet)
like all your mates do too –
Harry, Tommy, Wilfred, Edward, Bert –
and light a cigarette.
There's coffee in the square,
warm French bread

and all those thousands dead
are shaking dried mud from their hair
and queuing up for home. Freshly alive,
a lad plays Tipperary to the crowd, released
from History; the glistening, healthy horses fit for
heroes, kings.

You lean against a wall,
your several million lives still possible
and crammed with love, work, children, talent, English
beer, good food.
You see the poet tuck away his pocket-book and smile.
If poetry could truly tell it backwards,
then it would.

HAVISHAM

Beloved Sweet heart bastard.
Not a day since then
I haven't wished him dead. Prayed for it
so hard I've dark green pebbles for eyes
ropes on the back of my hands I could I could strangle
with.
Spinster. I stink and remember. Whole days
in bed cawing Nooooo at the wall; the dress
yellowing, trembling if I open the wardrobe ;
the slewed mirror, full-length, her, myself, who did this
to me? Puce curses that are sounds not words
Some nights better, the lost body over me,
my fluent tongue in its mouth in its ear
then down till suddenly bite awake. Love's
hate behind a white veil; a red balloon bursting
in my face. Bang. I stabbed at a wedding – cake.
Give me a male corpse for a long slow honeymoon
Don't think it's only the heart that b-b-b – breaks.

92

CARL PHILLIPS (1959-)

Carl Phillips was born on 23rd July, 1959 in Everett, Washington, USA. He studied for his BA in Harvard University and M.A, in Boston University. He married twice – once to Doug Macomber and then Reston Allen in 2013. Being is a professor of English in at Washington University in St Louis, he was an American writer and a poet. *In the Blood* and *The Rest of Love* were his early collections of poems. In 2023, he was awarded a Pulitzer prize for his poetry for his then the war: and selected poems 2007-2020.

STOP SHAKING

Not the bell, I said—one of us did;
Not the bell, but the smaller sounds, barely noticeable,
trapped inside it. It seemed the kind of thing I might say
to remind myself, when I've forgotten again, what I
want
to believe, even now, matters most—precision; though
it's hard,
these days, to know for sure what's true. Isn't every
season,
no matter what we call it, shadow season? Didn't
timothy
use to mean a meadow—a common name, back then
at least,

for the sweetest grass? I keep making the same avoidable
few mistakes that I've always made, and then regretting
them,
and then regretting them less. Think of all the suffering
happening everywhere, all the time, for nothing.
What if memory's just the dead, flourishing differently
from how they flourished alive?

THEN THE WAR

They planted flowers because the house had many
rooms
and because they'd imagined a life in which
cut flowers punctuate each room, as if each were a
sentence

not just to be decorated but to be given some discipline,
what the most memorable sentences — like people —
always
slightly resist…Spit of land; rags

of cloud-rack. Meanwhile,
hawk's-nest, winter-nest, stamina as a form of faith,
little
cove that a life equals, what they meant, I think, by

what they called the soul, twilight taking hold
deep in the marshweed, in the pachysandra, where the
wind
can't reach.

Then the war.
Then the field, and the mounted police
parading their proud-looking horses across it.

Then the next morning's fog, the groundsmen barely
visible
inside it, shadow-like, shade-like,
grooming the field back to immaculateness.

Then the curtains billowing out from the lightless room
toward the sea.
Then the one without hair

stroked the one who had some. They closed their eyes.
If gently, hard to say *how* gently.
Then the war was nothing that still bewildered them, if
it ever had.

JACKIE KAY (1961-)

Jacqueline Margaret Kay CBE, FRSE, FRSL, was born in Edinburg, on 9th November 1961 in Edinburg, Scotland. Her adopted parents were Helen Kay and John Kay, Scottish mother and Nigerian father. She is a Scottish poet, playwright and novelist. She studied in the university of Stirling. She was a professor of Creative Writing in at New Castle University. known for her works *Other Lovers* (1993), *Trumpet* (1998), and *Red Dust Road* (2011) etc.,

MARGARET'S MOON

After she died, I swear the sky
Had the most beautiful of all sunsets,
A blush of pink, then red, a glass of red,
Sudden dark and a hammock moon,
Then its faint silhouette, almost secret.
Life half-written, half unsaid.
I had kissed your head in the strange room.
Then later, I blew a kiss to the stars, to regret.
Margaret,
I imagined you lifting your head, your arms,
Loosening them, shedding skin and cells and bone
Till you became all spirit, released
Into the cairns, hills, the braes, barley,
The sea lochs and the sea and at last,
At least it seemed to me, you were free.

OLD TONGUE

When I was eight, I was forced south.
Not long after, when I opened
my mouth, a strange thing happened.
I lost my Scottish accent.
Words fell off my tongue:
eedyit, dreich, wabbit, crabbit
stummer, teuchter, heidbanger,
so you are, so am ur, see you, see ma ma,
shut yer geggie or I'll gie you the malkie!
My own vowels started to stretch like my bones
and I turned my back on Scotland.
Words disappeared in the dead of night,
new words marched in: ghastly, awful,
quite dreadful, *scones* said like *stones.*
Pokey hats into ice cream cones.
Oh where did all my words go –

my old words, my lost words?
Did you ever feel sad when you lost a word,
did you ever try and call it back
like calling in the sea?
If I could have found my words wandering,
I swear I would have taken them in,
swallowed them whole, knocked them back.
Out in the English soil, my old words
buried themselves. It made my mother's blood boil.
I cried one day with the wrong sound in my mouth.
I wanted them back; I wanted my old accent back,
my old tongue. My dour soor Scottish tongue.
Sing-songy. I wanted to *gie it laldie*.

LATE LOVE

How they strut about, people in love,
how tall they grow, pleased with themselves,
their hair, glossy, their skin shining.
They don't remember who they have been.
How filmic they are just for this time.
How important they've become – secret, above
the order of things, the dreary mundane.
Every church bell ringing, a fresh sign.
How dull the lot that are not in love.
Their clothes shabby, their skin lustreless;
how clueless they are, hair a mess; how they trudge
up and down streets in the rain,
remembering one kiss in a dark alley,
a touch in a changing-room, if lucky, a lovely wait
for the phone to ring, maybe, baby.
The past with its rush of velvet, its secret hush
already miles away, dimming now, in the late day.
(2006)

94

SIMON ARMITAGE (1963-)

Simon Armitage CBE, FRSL was born on 26th May, 1963 in Marsden, a village in West Yorkshire. Huddersfield, U.K. He studied in Colane Valley High School and later B.A., from University Portsmouth, and Victoria University of Manchester. He belongs to the West Yorkshire and became a Professor of Poetry in the University of Leeds. His collections of poems – *Out of the Blue* (2008), *The Not Dead* (2008), *Kid* (1992), Stanza Stones (2012), *Sir Gawain and the Green* (2000), *Book of Matches* (1993) etc., received various prizes and awards.

I SAY, I SAY, I SAY

Anyone here had a go at themselves
for a laugh? Anyone opened their wrists
with a blade in the bath? Those in the dark
at the back, listen hard. Those at the front
in the know, those of us who have, hands up,
let's show that inch of lacerated skin
between the forearm and the fist. Let's tell it
like it is: strong drink, a crimson tidemark
round the tub, a yard of lint, white towels
washed a dozen times, still pink. Tough luck.
A passion then for watches, bangles, cuffs.
A likely story: you were lashed by brambles
picking berries from the woods. Come clean, come good,
repeat with me the punch line 'Just like blood'
when those at the back rush forward to say
how a little love goes a long long long way

POEM

And if it snowed and snow covered the drive
he took a spade and tossed it to one side.
And always tucked his daughter up at night
And slippered her the one time that she lied.
And every week he tipped up half his wage.
And what he didn't spend each week he saved.
And praised his wife for every meal she made.
And once, for laughing, punched her in the face.

And for his mum he hired a private nurse.
And every Sunday taxied her to church.

And he blubbed when she went from bad to worse.
And twice he lifted ten quid from her purse.

Here's how they rated him when they looked back:
sometimes he did this, sometimes he did that.

95

DAVID WHEATLEY (1970-)

David Wheatley was an Irish poet and critic. He was born in 1970 in Dublin and studied at Trinity College, Dublin where he edited magazine *Icarus*. He is the author of four volumes of poetry as well as several chapbooks. He teaches in the University of Aberdeen, having previously taught in the University of Hull. His collections of poems are – *Thirst* (1067), *The Misery Hill* (2000), *Three Legged Dog* (2003) and *Drift* (2008). He was awarded The Vincent Buckley Poetry Prize in 2008.

THE OEDIPUS RIDDLE

To a cat with swollen paw

Left-hook at the air in big-eyed fury,
on your belly, on your back,
jump and jump again and fail to snag
the foe that is your own sweet paw:

swell foot, Oedipus, your fury
doom to swallow your pride, swallow my pills
and give me thanks, a two-leg, that you still
can walk on one, two, three legs, four.

STAN

Stan: the bouquets in the window
spell his name. He is cunning
the corner out of view

as I press for the traffic to stop
four black cars slinking
behind him. The hearse pulls up.

Stan, though he has an appointment, has time.
I signal discreetly, *wouldn't you rather...*
sure of what feels like a rule of thumb

until the driver uncurls his fist
and extends a finger politely
demanding *you go first.*